WEAPONS WITHOUT A CAUSE

Weapons without a Cause

The Politics of Weapons Acquisition in the United States

Theo Farrell
Lecturer in Security Studies
Department of Politics
University of Exeter

First published in Great Britain 1997 by
MACMILLAN PRESS LTD
Houndmills, Basingstoke, Hampshire RG21 6XS and London
Companies and representatives throughout the world

A catalogue record for this book is available from the British Library.

ISBN 0–333–65412–9

First published in the United States of America 1997 by
ST. MARTIN'S PRESS, INC.,
Scholarly and Reference Division,
175 Fifth Avenue, New York, N.Y. 10010

ISBN 0–312–16103–4

Library of Congress Cataloging-in-Publication Data
Farrell, Theo, 1967–
Weapons without a cause : the politics of weapons acquisition in
the United States / Theo Farrell.
p.   cm.
Includes bibliographical references and index.
ISBN 0–312–16103–4
1. United States—Armed Forces—Procurement.   2. United States-
-Armed Forces—Weapons systems.   3. United States—Politics and
government.   I. Title.
UC263.F37   1996
355.8'2'0973—dc20   96–22369
                                          CIP

This book is printed on paper suitable for recycling and made from fully managed and
sustained forest sources.

10   9   8   7   6   5   4   3   2   1
06   05   04   03   02   01   00   99   98   97

Printed in Great Britain by
The Ipswich Book Company Ltd
Ipswich, Suffolk

To Hélène

Contents

List of Tables

Acknowledgements

I had plenty of assistance in first producing my Ph.D. thesis and then turning it into a book. I owe my largest intellectual debt to my Ph.D. supervisor, friend and colleague, Eric Herring. Whenever I lost sight of my work, Eric was there to provoke new ideas, structure thoughts, check details, and map out the big picture. I also owe special thanks to Thomas H. Hammond. Tom volunteered to read my entire manuscript (some parts twice!), which he returned with suggestions and corrections literally scribbled on every page along with fifteen pages of single-spaced feedback; much of the revision was shaped by Tom's incisive comments.

I am also grateful for the support and assistance of several other people. Nick Rengger, who was my co-supervisor for a time, constantly reminded me that there is more to the study of international relations than bombs and bullets. The Head of Politics at Bristol University, (where I took my Ph.D.), Richard Hodder-Williams, was generous in his support and encouragement; as my internal Ph.D. examiner, he also made helpful suggestions for revising the thesis, as did my external examiner, Colin McInnis. David H. Dunn, Lynn Eden and Malcolm Shaw read and commented on sections on the MX, US nuclear strategy and the presidency respectively; naturally, any errors or shortcomings that may exist in these sections are solely mine. David also kindly let me photocopy his private files on the MX. My thanks to Matthew Evangelista and Graham Spinardi for sending me useful documents that I could not have otherwise obtained. I am particularly grateful to my parents, Brian and Marie-Therese Farrell, who gave me the inspiration to embark on a career in academia; their loving support made such a career choice possible. I should also like to thank my commissioning editor at Macmillan, Annabelle Buckley, for enthusiastically responding to my book proposal, and for being accommodating as I reworked my Ph.D. I also owe much to my former mentors at University College Dublin, Ronan Fanning and Richard Sinnott, for fostering my interest in US national security policy in my undergraduate and Masters studies.

I am indebted to several institutions for their financial support. The Foreign and Commonwealth Office gave me a generous scholarship for the first couple of years of my Ph.D. studies. The Economic and Social Research Council also gave me a scholarship which enabled me to complete my third year of studies at Bristol. In addition, I received financial assistance from Bristol University and the Politics Department at Bristol.

Lastly, I wish to thank my partner, Hélène Lambert; her unwavering support, sound advice, gentle nudges, and boundless confidence in me, made the tough job of producing this book a lot easier.

Portions of this book have appeared in earlier forms as 'Weapons Without A Cause: Buying Stealth Bombers the American Way', *Arms Control*, 14/2 (1993) and 'Waste in Weapons Acquisition: How the Americans Do It All Wrong', *Contemporary Security Policy*, 16/2 (1995). I am grateful to these journals for their permission to reuse this material.

Abbreviations and Acronyms

ACDA	Arms Control and Disarmament Agency
ACM	advanced cruise missile
AD	air defence
AFSC	Air Force Systems Command
ALCM	air-launched cruise missile
ASD, R&E	Assistant Secretary of Defence for Research and Engineering
ASW	anti-submarine warfare
ATF	auto-terrain following radar; also Advanced Tactical Fighter
ATGM	anti-tank guided missile
AWACS	airborne warning and control system
BA	budget authority
BEA	Budget Enforcement Act
C3I	command, control and communications and intelligence
CAW	Carrier Air Wing
CBF	Carrier Battle Force
CBO	Congressional Budget Office
CG	Consolidated Guidance
CINC	commander-in-chief
CINCSAC	Commander-in-Chief of Strategic Air Command
CJCS	Chairman of the Joint Chiefs of Staff
CNO	Chief of Naval Operations
CRS	Congressional Research Service
CVBG	Carrier Battle Group
DAB	Defence Acquisition Board
D, DT&E	Director of Developmental Testing and Evaluation
DIVAD	Divisional Air Defence System
DMR	Defence Management Review
DoD	Department of Defence
D, OT&E	Director, Operational Testing and Evaluation
DPRB	Defence Planning and Resources Board
DRB	Defence Resources Board
DSARC	Defence Systems Acquisition Review Council
DSB	Defence Science Board
DT&E	development, testing and evaluation

ECM	electronic counter measures
EOP	Executive Office of the President
FAADS	Forward Area Air Defence System
FEBA	forward edge of the battlefield area
FLIR	forward looking infra-red
FLOT	front line of troops
FM	Field Manual
FOC	full operational capability
FYDP	Five Year Defence Plan; also Future Years Defense Plan
GAO	General Accounting Office
GOC	Government Operations Committee
GPO	General Printing Office
GRH	Gramm-Rudman-Hollings
HASC	House Armed Services Committee
HDAS	House Defence Appropriations Subcommittee
ICBM	intercontinental ballistic missile
IFV	infantry fighting vehicle
IOC	initial operational capability
IUM	inertial measurements units
JCS	Joint Chiefs of Staff
JSTPS	Joint Strategic Target Planning Staff
LHX	Light Helicopter Experimental
LNO	Limited Nuclear Option
LO	low observability
LOW	Launch On Warning
MAD	Mutually Assured Destruction
MARV	manoeuvrable re-entry vehicle
MBT	main battle tank
MGCS	missile guidance and control sets
MIC	military-industrial complex
MIRV	multiple independently targeted re-entry vehicle
MPS	multiple point system
MX	Missile Experimental
NATO	North Atlantic Treaty Organisation
NCA	National Command Authorities
NSA	National Security Advisor
NSC	National Security Council
NSDD	National Security Decision Document
NSDM	National Security Decision Memorandum
NSTDB	Nuclear Strategic Targeting Data Base

NTPR	Nuclear Targeting Policy Review
NUWEP	Nuclear Weapons Employment Plan
O&M	operations and maintenance
OMB	Office of the Management of the Budget
OMG	Operational Manoeuvre Group
O&S	operations and support
OSA	Office of Systems Analysis
OSD	Office of the Secretary of Defence
OT&E	operational testing and evaluation
PA&E	programme analysis and evaluation
PEO	Programme Executive Officer
PD	Presidential Directive
PMNSS	Procurement and Military Nuclear Systems Subcommittee
PPBS	Planning, Programming and Budgeting System
R&D	research and development
RCS	radar cross-section
RDS	Research and Development Subcommittee
RD,T&E	research, development, test and evaluation
RT	relocatable target
SAC	Strategic Air Command
SAE	Service Acquisition Executive
SALT	Strategic Arms Limitation Talks
SAR	Selected Acquisition Report
SASC	Senate Armed Services Committee
SBC	Senate Budget Committee
SDAS	Senate Defence Appropriations Subcommittee
SFRC	Senate Foreign Relations Subcommittee
SGAC	Senate Governmental Affairs Committee
SHORAD	short-range air defence
SICBM	small intercontinental ballistic missile
SIOP	Single Integrated Operational Plan
SLBM	submarine-launched ballistic missile
SLOC	sea lanes of communication
SRAM	Short Range Attack Missile
SSBN	ballistic missile submarine
SSCMS	Seapower and Strategic and Critical Materials Subcommittee
SSN	nuclear-powered attack submarine
START	Strategic Arms Reduction Talks
TACAIR	Tactical Air Forces

T&E	test and evaluation
TOA	total obligational authority
TOW	tube-launched, optically guided, wire-tracked (missile)
TRADOC	Training and Doctrine Command
TWS	Tactical Warfare Subcommittee
TY	Then Year
US	United States
USD(A)	Under Secretary of Defence for Acquisition
USD(P)	Under Secretary of Defence for Policy
USD(R&E)	Under Secretary of Defence for Research and Engineering
USN	United States Navy
VCJCS	Vice Chairman of the Joint Chiefs of Staff
VHTs	very hard targets
WTO	Warsaw Treaty Organisation, also called Warsaw Pact

1 Explaining Weapons Acquisition

Why does the United States acquire certain weapons and not others? There are really two questions here: why are weapons acquired in the United States, and how are they acquired? Both need to be addressed in order to explain, say, why the US Air Force acquires its new stealth bomber but the Navy fails to get its one. This book is unique in addressing this issue. Studies abound on how the United States goes about acquiring weapons and how it could do so better (Gansler, 1989; McNaugher, 1989). There are also some studies on the preferences of military services – what kinds of weapons they like – and how this influences weapons acquisition (Builder, 1989; Brown, 1992). As discussed below, there is also a wealth of literature addressing either why states arm *or* how they do so. Few studies have attempted to answer both questions and none have applied them to US weapons acquisition in general.

This book will use the terms 'weapon' and 'weapon programme' interchangeably to mean a major weapon programme. This is defined by the US Department of Defence (DoD) as a weapon costing more than $200 million to develop or $1 billion to procure.[1] Naturally, this is just the tip of the iceberg. In the case of one weapon examined in this book, $1 billion would not even buy you one B-2 stealth bomber. The mere fact that they cost so much means that they are important to public policy if not national security; it is worthwhile alone to explain why and how such money is being spent. These weapon programmes can demand such huge amounts of money because they are supposedly so vital to national security.

Weapons acquisition, then, refers to the research, development, production and procurement of a weapon. This definition is generally accepted and used in the relevant literature. This book will look at the whole weapons acquisition process as it is interested in the origins and development as well as the outcomes of weapon programmes. It is necessary to understand where weapons are coming from in order to explain where they end up. This way crucial questions are not overlooked. Can an ill-conceived weapon be acquired? This book shows it can. Does a weapon have to prove itself in development before it is bought? Not according to this book. Does the expected cost of a weapon affect its chances of survival? This book shows when it does and when it does not.

PREVIOUS EXPLANATIONS

The metaphor most likely to spring to mind when one is discussing weapons acquisition is that of the 'arms race'. This is when two (or more) states are engaged in a direct competition to increase the quantity and/or quality of their weapons. Do states really race when acquiring arms? On occasion it would appear that they do. Britain and Germany engaged in a naval arms race in the lead up to World War One. The superpowers were commonly assumed to have been engaged in an arms race during the Cold War. From this perspective the Soviets raced to catch up with the United States which, in turn, raced to stay ahead of the Soviet Union. But states do not always race to acquire arms. Barry Buzan maintains that a more useful term for expressing the full set of pressures that makes states arm is the arms dynamic'; for Buzan '[t]he term arms racing is reserved for the most extreme manifestation of the arms dynamic, when the pressures are such as to lead states into major competitive expansions of military capability'. Buzan distinguishes arms racing from 'maintenance of the military status quo' which for him is the 'the normal operation of the arms dynamic' (1987, p. 73). Were the superpowers arms racing or trying to maintain the military status quo? Buzan maintains that they were doing both: the armament patterns of the superpowers 'falls into the grey area between maintenance of the military status quo and arms racing' (1987, p. 119). The whole notion of an arms race is based on a particular assumption of what drives states to arm, namely that rival states react to each others' patterns of armament. Alternative explanations for state armament may be found in the domestic pressures which are exerted on this process and the very nature of technological development itself.

Action-Reaction Model

Robert McNamara, Secretary of Defence under the Kennedy administration, argued that the superpower arms race was fuelled by the 'action-reaction phenomenon'. He maintained that:

> the Soviet Union and the United States mutually influence one another's strategic plans. Whatever their intentions or our intentions,

actions – or even realistically potential actions – on either side relating to the build up of nuclear forces necessarily trigger reactions on the other side (McNamara, 1968, pp. 58–9).

The action-reaction model is based on the notion of the state as being a rational actor. According to this model, the manner in which a state arms itself is determined by its perception of the nature of the military threat that it faces.

The superpowers may not have been racing against each other but rather engaging in separate armament patterns. Thus Colin Gray argues that both the Soviet Union, because of its centrally planned economy, and the United States, because of the 'technical, budgetary and political hazards' facing a weapon over 'its very long gestation period', would have been unable to develop timely and specific counter measures to each others actions (1986, pp. 216–17). This raises the question of how agile did each side have to be in their responses in order to support the action-reaction model. Certainly for our purposes, if one is trying to determine why particular weapons are acquired in the United States, the longer the time-lag between actions and reactions, the harder it is to identify a causal relationship between specific threats and specific responses. It is not at all clear that any examination of a superpower arms race along these lines would be able to untangle actions from reactions. Indeed, in order to be able to respond in a timely fashion to Soviet actions, the United States would have had to anticipate those actions. This is what McNamara meant by 'potentially realistic actions'. This process of anticipating Soviet actions needs to be explained, and the action-reaction model is unable to do this. If it is unable to reveal how threats are determined then it cannot reveal how states react to these threats. As Graham Allison and Frederic Morris argue, when one examines case histories of weapon programmes one finds that 'the factors emphasized by the [action-reaction model] are not sufficient to explain why one weapon emerged rather than another' (1989 [1972], p. 105).

Domestic Process Model

The domestic process model is based on approaches which seek to explain state behaviour by examining internal pressures. From this perspective, the actions of other states may provide impetus for a state to arm, but the scale and manner in which the state arms will be determined by domestic forces. These forces include bureaucratic determinism, economic interests, national politics and military-industrial networks.

Bureaucratic determinism refers to the notion that programmes are started to serve bureaucratic interests, and once these programmes gather momentum and support, the weapons will be acquired regardless of whether they are needed or not. This perspective holds that research centres will back the weapons they design and the military services will support weapons which serve their organisational needs. Given their near monopoly on expertise in the area, these bureaucratic actors are able to exert tremendous influence on weapons acquisition (Kossiakoff, 1980).

Another variant on the domestic model holds that economic interests drive weapons acquisition. Mary Kaldor and James Kurth both argue that the military industries' dependency on government contracts create 'follow-on imperatives' for continuous armament. Governments target contract awards to support specific key military industries. Kurth analyses the awarding of government contracts to the six major military airframe production lines in the 1960s. He finds that within a year of completing a government contract each production line is awarded a new one, usually for a weapon which is similar while superior to the one which the production line has just stopped producing. For example, between 1966 and 1986 Lockheed-Georgia stopped building the C-141A and was awarded the contract to build the C-5A. Kurth argues that follow-on imperatives can be witnessed in seven of the ten production contracts awarded from 1960 to 1970.[2] Kaldor argues that this follow-on imperative has led to a peculiarly conservative form of technological innovation in weapons acquisition, which she calls baroque technical change, whereby new weapons are characterised by highly cost-ineffective, incremental improvements which are needed to keep the industry going and not for their added military capability (1981; 1986). She points to the Trident submarine as an example of baroque technical change. This submarine is larger and faster that its predecessors, the Polaris/Poseidon submarines. However, this size and speed are not in the Trident submarine's advantage: its increased size makes it easier to detect, especially when it travels at its top speed of 25 knots, which is, in any case, still 5 knots slower than that of attack submarines (Kaldor, 1981, pp. 7–12).

The size of the military industries may be seen to provide political, as well as economic, incentives for politicians to fund weapons acquisition. Ever mindful of elections, members of Congress seek to secure defence contracts for their districts and thus jobs for their constituents

(Smith, 1988). This is known as 'pork-barrel' in the United States. Recent studies have offered sophisticated critiques of this explanation. James Lindsay argues that, with regard to the oversight of nuclear weapon programmes, legislators are not just focused on pork-barrel but may also seek to promote worthy policy (1991). Kenneth Mayer argues that pork-barrelling is based on the myth that legislators are able to influence the awarding of defence contracts. Mayer also maintains that legislators promote this myth for their own electoral purposes (1991). These arguments will be dealt with later in this chapter.

Perhaps the most well known variant of the domestic process model is the 'military-industrial complex' (MIC) which Eisenhower warned of in his farewell address (cited in Buzan, 1987, p. 101). This explanation combines the bureaucratic determinism, economic interests and national politics explanations. In the US context, Gordan Adams has referred to an 'Iron Triangle', defined by Hedrick Smith as a 'symbiotic partnership between the military services, defence contractors and members of Congress', as the driving force behind weapons acquisition.[3] In a another version of the Iron Triangle, Judith Reppy argues that 'it is useful to think of the MIC as a set of interlocking networks organized around specific weapon development projects and bound together in dependent relationships' (1992, p. 61). Nick Kotz adopted a similar approach in his study on the B-1 bomber programme. He argues that the success of the programme was due to the high degree of co-operation between the Air Force, the prime contractor (Rockwell), and certain members of Congress (1988).

Approaches which focus on the internal determinants of state armament have difficulty explaining the dynamic character of this process. This is because these approaches all suggest that the weapons acquisition process is driven by invested interests, be they bureaucratic, political or industrial. While such approaches provide good accounts of continuity in policy, they are unable to explain policy change, such as radical innovations in weapons acquisition. Approaches which do attempt to explain innovation in weapons acquisition in terms of internal determinants focus on the role of technology and scientists in the process.

Technological Imperative Model

The belief that weapons technology has a momentum of its own is a common one.[4] According to a UN *Comprehensive Study of Nuclear Weapons*:

> It is widely believed . . . that new weapons systems emerge not because of any military or security considerations but because technology by its own impetus often takes the lead over policy, creating weapons for which needs have to be invented and deployment theories have to be readjusted (Spinardi, 1988, p. 129). .

Even where the pace of technology does not by itself drive weapons acquisition, the promise of technology is given voice by the scientists who become entrepreneurs and push their technologies upon an eager military establishment. Thus, according to Solly Zuckerman, former chief science advisor to the British Ministry of Defence, 'Ideas for a new weapon system derive in the first place, not from the military, but from different groups of scientists and technologists' (1982, p. 103)

The 'technology out of control' approach has been undermined by two comprehensive studies on the sociology of specific weapons technologies. Graham Spinardi and Donald MacKenzie argue that technological development cannot be explained in terms of natural trajectories. Social forces, in particular the flow of resources, shape technological development. The notion of 'technologists out of control' has also been questioned. According to MacKenzie:

> [technologists may] seek to shape, as well as to anticipate, and to meet, the criteria of those in power. They may even seek to alter power and who holds it . . . [but they] are not always the all-powerful manipulators that authors such as Lord Zuckerman sometimes seem to suggest (1990, p. 390).

Spinardi is even more circumspect with regard to the influence of technologists. Spinardi notes that there were instances when technologists sought to promote a technology, but he goes on to argue that: 'these are generally cases where the technologists convinced "the people in charge" that their existing [weapon programme] goals could be better fulfilled by a new device, *not* where they changed these goals to further a preferred technology' (1988, p. 202).

Thicket of Theories[5]

Approaches which concentrate on the external factors which determine weapons acquisition tend to end up examining why states arm, whereas those concentrating on internal determinants look at how states arm. Both questions need to be answered in order to understand why certain weapons are developed and acquired, and others not. Some studies have attempted to combine these two approaches.

In his comparative study of weapons innovation in the United States and the Soviet Union, Matthew Evangelista concludes that in neither state could the process be explained by one set of determinants alone. At different stages in the innovation processes one or the other was dominant but the overall processes themselves were determined by factors which were *both* internal and external to the state. Evangelista maintains that the process of innovation in each state can be divided into five stages stretching from technological breakthrough, through development, to production. He argues that, in the United States, the impetus for weapons innovation comes from technological and military interest groups. Threat assessments and strategic rationales only become important when these weapons are being pushed by the military sponsors from development into production (Evangelista, 1988, pp. 52–68).

Evangelista only concerns himself with innovative weapons programmes, that is, ones 'which entailed major restructuring of military organizations, significant changes strategy, or both' (1988, p. 11). Yet he recognises that mainstream programmes (that is, ones entailing only incremental changes in organisational structure and/or strategy) 'constitute the main activity of military research and development' (Evangelista, 1988, p. 51). Michael Brown sets out to address this limitation by examining the origins and outcomes of 15 post-war US strategic bomber programmes which by their very nature are mainstream programmes. Brown tests existing theories on weapons acquisition which he groups into four types: strategic, bureaucratic, economic and technological. He concludes that there is a lot of evidence to support strategic explanations and some support for bureaucratic accounts: military services were usually sensitive to any foreign military or domestic political developments and especially if these developments threatened their core missions. He finds little, if any, support for economic or technological arguments: defence contractors usually were not very active in the early development stages of mainstream programmes, and the performance requirements set by the services usually far outstripped technological developments (Brown, 1992, pp. 307–16).

In explaining where weapons come from, Brown's study is clearly impressive; but it is less so in explaining where they end up. Brown argues that the success of each programme, measured in terms of the gap between the actual cost, schedule and performance of each programme and their original targets, 'is a function of the interaction between its development objectives and the procurement strategy on which it is based' (1992, pp. 19, 23). The issue which Brown is addressing here is an interesting one and his analysis is mostly convincing. However, a more basic issue is that of the role strategic, bureaucratic, economic and technological pressures played *throughout* the life-span of these programmes and not simply in their genesis. Brown suggests what impact they had: he argues that strategic and bureaucratic pressures led the Air Force to pursue ambitious programme objectives and accelerated procurement strategies (1992, pp. 323–5; 334–7). But a more explicit framework which incorporates these explanations needs to be constructed. Furthermore, Brown's study only examines the acquisition of one type of weapon, namely strategic bombers. The insights his study reveals may or may not be applicable to weapons acquisition in the other military services, or even other Air Force programmes. This book will address this limitation by examining the origins and outcomes of four different types of weapons, with one from each service.

WHAT DRIVES WEAPONS ACQUISITION?

This book argues that three sets of issues drive weapons acquisition in the United States: strategic, institutional and budgetary. Strategic issues refer to the strategic rationale(s) for a weapon. Institutional issues are the organisational and presidential politics surrounding weapons acquisition. Budgetary issues have to do with the cost of weapons programmes. Any or all of these sets of issues may account for the origin, development and outcome of a weapon programme. It follows that strategic, institutional and budgetary issues must all be examined when explaining weapons acquisition in the United States.

Strategic Issues

The DoD claims that weapons are acquired to meet strategic needs. This claim will be tested in Chapter 2 by examining the strategic rationales for four weapons: namely, the A-12 stealth naval attack plane, the Divisional Air Defence System (DIVAD), the MX intercontinental ballistic missile (ICBM), and the B-2 stealth bomber. A strategic rationale is the declared military requirement and/or international political purpose of a weapon.

In each of the four cases, three questions will be addressed to establish whether or not the military requirement for that weapon is genuine. First, was the weapon intended to carry out a necessary military mission? A military mission is the specific wartime task assigned to particular military units. Obviously, if this task was unnecessary, then the military requirement for the weapon is questionable. Second, is the weapon capable of carrying out its military mission? Conceivably a weapon may be developed to fulfil a mission requirement which is beyond its capabilities. Third, were there other, more cost-effective alternatives for meeting this mission requirement? Even if the military mission proves to be necessary, and the weapon is able to carry it out, there may be other cheaper, yet equally effective, ways of meeting this mission requirement.

Weapons also serve international political purposes. This book will only look at the international political purposes of nuclear weapons and not those of conventional weapons. The primary purpose of nuclear weapons is to deter nuclear war. In spite of secret plans and public policies which are designed to demonstrate the utility of nuclear weapons, the fact remains that they have not been used in war since 1945. There is a tradition of non-use surrounding nuclear weapons (Schelling, 1980, pp. 260–1; Bundy, 1988, pp. 586–8) and there may even be a 'taboo' surrounding their use (Herring, 1992). As Eric Herring rightly argues, the bottom line is that, 'nuclear weapons are too dangerous to be useable. This is the reality, even though decision-makers who realize this feel they cannot admit it outright' (1991, p. 107). Hence military rationales are still given for the acquisition of nuclear weapons, and these shall be examined for the MX and B-2. However, the fact that nuclear weapons are intended to maintain deterrence, and consequently not to be used militarily, lends greater significance to their international political purposes. Conventional weapons, on the other hand, are used in war and this fact has a direct impact on their political purpose. Conventional weapons are judged by their performance in battle. If they do not work, or are redundant on the battlefield, then this would also undermine their international political purpose. The military requirement for the Patriots was less pressing than their political purpose; their ability (or inability) to knock down Iraqi Scuds was less important than their ability to keep Israel out of the Gulf War. However, if the Patriots had proven unable to shoot down any Iraqi Scuds then they would have done little to reassure the Israelis.[6]

The most significant international political purpose of nuclear weapons is to serve as symbols of state intent. Robert Jervis argues that symbols have always been central to international politics, but they had gained added importance in the nuclear era for two reasons.

First, nuclear weapons can only be used in an indirect manner to coerce a nuclear opponent. Unlike brute force, this process relies upon both sides engaging in mutual posturing and making subjective assessments about each other. In this case, strength is a function of perceived intentions as well as perceived capabilities. Second, since the world has never experienced a nuclear war, everything we believe about such an event must be highly speculative (Jervis, 1989). Nuclear weapons can also be used to try and gain leverage in negotiations with adversaries. On several occasions, US Presidents have justified the acquisition of a particular nuclear system on the grounds that it could be used as a bargaining chip with the Soviet Union. The problem with this second political role is that it is not always clear if the President is seeking bargaining leverage over the Soviets or Congress. A President may in effect be trying to cut a deal with Congress to conclude an arms agreement Congress wants in exchange for funding for a new nuclear system. Alternatively, a President may be offering to acquire a new nuclear weapon if the Senate will ratify an arms control treaty the President wants. In either case, the weapon is needed for a domestic political purpose, not a strategic one. So with the MX and B-2, two addition questions will be asked in each case in order to ascertain if the weapon was acquired to meet a genuine strategic rationale. First, was it needed as a symbol of state intent? Second, was it a genuine bargaining chip in the superpower arms negotiations?

Making judgements about whether or not a weapon is really needed is, of course, a subjective business: one person may see a genuine strategic rationale where another perceives a self-serving rationalisation. The purpose of the three questions on the military requirement for each weapon, and two questions on the international political purpose of each nuclear weapon, is to provide a number of tests for measuring the strategic rationale in each case. The extent to which a weapon passes each test will provide greater or lesser certainty in judging whether or not strategic issues can explain the origins, development and outcome of a weapon programme. For example, if it is determined that a nuclear weapon, such as the B-2, does not serve a necessary military mission, which it is incapable of carrying out, for which there are more cost-effective alternatives anyway, and it is not a symbol of state intent nor a bargaining chip in arms talks, then we can be pretty sure that strategic considerations had no impact on this programme. Chapter 2 shows that this is, in fact, the case with the B-2. Had the B-2 passed any of these tests then the picture would be more ambiguous;

had it passed a few of them then it would have to be concluded that the programme was affected by strategic considerations.

Institutional Issues

Institutional issues are about the self-interests of military organisations and the political hierarchy and how these interests affect weapons acquisition. Like most policy areas, weapons acquisition is a political process in that it is about determining the appropriate allocation of limited resources. Chapter 3 will consider who stands to benefit from this process and how such self-interest affects behaviour in the weapon acquisition process.

The bureaucratic politics model proposed by Graham Allison, and developed by Allison and Morton Halperin, provides the most useful framework for this examination. This model sees policymaking as a highly political exercise, in which policy comes from the pulling, hauling and bargaining between policy actors, and not from a rational process whereby the optimum policy is carefully selected from an exhaustive range of options. The bureaucratic politics model also suggests that policy actors can be motivated by narrow self-interest to pursue certain policies, or that parochial perceptions can lead them to hold a unique perspective on the national interest which may be completely at odds with competing notions of the national interest held by other policy actors (Allison, 1971; Allison and Halperin, 1989 [1972]; Halperin, 1974). In short, the bureaucratic politics model demands that attention be focused on the policy process, and on the interests and influence of actors within this process, in order to explain why and how particular policies are pursued. Chapter 3 will adopt this approach to explaining weapons acquisition.

While Allison's seminal book *Essence of Decision* received widespread praise for its breath and originality, it also attracted criticism from several quarters. Critics have attacked the loose manner in which Allison formulated his three models – the rational actor, organisational process and bureaucratic politics models – and the quality of the evidence which Allison produced to support his case. Two important criticisms stand out with regard to the bureaucratic politics model. First, Allison has been taken to task for the quality of his propositions: one pair of critics concluded that 'some of the propositions seem to be only ad hoc generalizations lacking clear derivation from the underlying model' (Bendor and Hammond, 1992, p. 317). Indeed Allison does as much to undermine as to prove the central proposition of the model that the policy choices of actors are based on their institutional position (Art, 1989 [1973], p. 443). Moreover, David Welch argues that the evidence that actors' preferences and/or perceptions 'correlate highly' with their institutional position is sporadic and inconclusive (Welch, 1992, pp. 128–31). Second, Allison is criticised for saying 'surprizingly little about the fact that executive branch policymaking takes place in a hierarchy' (Bendor and Hammond, 1992, p. 314). In particular, the assertion that the President must, and does, routinely bargain with subordinates has been questioned (Art 1989 [1973], pp. 441–7; Krasner, 1989 [1978], pp. 425–6). Welch maintains that it is the 'hierarchical distribution of authority' which determines the degree to which institutional position and bargaining matters to policymaking (1992, pp. 132–3).

This chapter will show that, when it comes to the role of the military services in weapons acquisition, policy preferences and perceptions not only correlate with, but are determined by institutional position. Furthermore, their influence over this process may be based on institutional position regardless of the policymaking hierarchy. However, it should be noted that there appears to be general agreement between the proponents and some critics of the bureaucratic politics model that the model is particularly well suited to explaining institutionally grounded policy issues involving budget allocations and procurement (Allison and Morris, 1976; Art, 1989 [1073], pp. 447–53; Welch, 1992, pp. 131, 135; Spinardi, 1988, p. 222).

This chapter will focus on the military services because they clearly have self-interest at stake in weapons acquisition. It will be shown that the services stand to benefit most from the process: weapons give them military capabilities which serve their service doctrines which, in turn, fulfil organisational needs. Service interests are defined, therefore, in terms of major military missions, such as defending Western Europe for the Army. Chapter 3 will begin by examining the self-interests of the services and identifying the core interests which the services will seek to advance by securing resources. This will provide the first question to be addressed in each of the four weapons examined in this book: did the weapon serve a core interest of a military service? If a weapon did serve a core interest of a military service then that organisation would have far stronger incentives to ensure that the weapon was acquired than if it merely served a peripheral interest. Establishing the presence of organisational self-interest is not enough, however. It is also necessary to show that the military services are able to advance the weapon programmes they favour even when such weapons lack strategic rationales. Through an analysis of the weapons acquisition process, Chapter 3 will show that services routinely engage in acquisition practices which are intended to ensure that weapons are acquired regardless of the strategic need for them or their cost-effectiveness. This provides the second question that will be addressed in each of the four cases: were any of these inefficient acquisition practices evident in the weapon programme?

The criticism that the bureaucratic politics approach 'obscures the power of the President' will be also be addressed in this book (Krasner, 1989 [1971], p. 420). It will be argued that the President may also be driven by self-interest to pursue certain policies regardless of national interest. In constrast, the bureaucratic politics model suggests that presidential control is a restraint on rampant bureaucratic politics and, as such, it ensures that sometimes policy does serve national interests; thus it depicts self-interested actors attempting to escape or circumvent presidential control so that they can serve their own narrow ends. This book argues that the President may also seek to look after his or her own interests. It will also be shown that while there are limits to presidential involvement in specific weapon programmes (given constraints on time and information), Presidents can overcome substantial opposition from subordinates in making policy decisions that have a dramatic impact on specific programmes.

It will be argued that Presidents only get involved in later stages of nuclear weapon programmes; they have neither the time nor ability to regulate the early stages of nuclear weapon programmes and they have no interest in overseeing the acquisition of individual conventional weapon programmes. Presidents may have self-interests at stake (no less than six distinct presidential self-interests are identified in Chapter 3) as nuclear weapon programmes enter their final stages, where they become more expensive and politically visible. This then provides the third and fourth questions to be addressed in the cases of the MX and B-2: did the programme attract presidential involvement and did the President have self-interested reasons for advancing or cutting the programme?

Budgetary Issues

Concerns about cost must be taken into account when trying to explain weapons acquisition. Weapon programmes are usually, by any measure, very costly. Chapter 4 will examine how much of an issue this is and how it affects weapons acquisition. Three questions may be asked with regard to the cost of a weapon programme. How much does it cost? Is it cost-effective? Will its costs spiral out of control? Each of these questions will be applied in turn to the four case studies. Particular attention will be paid to the perceptions of administration and DoD officials and members of Congress.

The conditions under which cost considerations are more likely to have an impact on weapon acquisition will also be discussed in Chapter 4. These conditions, which are collectively referred to as the budget climate, are the size of the defence budget and defence expenditure, and the degree of centralisation in the DoD acquisition and resource allocation policy structures. Each of these conditions indicate the level of concern about cost considerations and the likelihood that this concern will affect weapon programmes. Take the case of a budget climate which is generally unfavourable for weapons acquisition. Decreasing defence budgets indicate a reluctance in Congress and/or the administration to spend money on weapons acquisition. Increasing centralisation of DoD policy structures indicates a shift in influence over weapons acquisition away from the services which are unconcerned about cost towards civilian DoD officials who are more likely to be looking for good deals. The state of DoD policy structures also reveals much about the attitude of the Secretary of Defence and of Congress towards the role of the services; centralising policy structures indicates a declining trust in the services.

Budgetary Issues Do Not Include Broader Economic Interests

This book will not consider the impact of broader economic considerations, such as MICs, on weapons acquisition. Such military-industrial interests may explain the militarisation of US foreign policy just as economic imperialism may account for the globalism in US foreign policy. But explanations based on broader economic considerations are not useful when it comes to explaining the origins and outcomes of specific weapon programmes; military-economic interests should seek to promote all weapon programmes not specific ones. The concept of military-industrial networks, commonly referred to as 'iron triangles', combines the electoral worries of politicians with military-industrial concerns and thereby may explain why certain weapons are bought: some weapons are bought because they have influential political patrons whereas other weapons are not because they do not have such patrons. However, this approach is also flawed as it is based on the myth that politicians are driven solely by electoral concerns in policymaking and that they are able to use their position to promote weapon programmes.

Members of Congress are often portrayed as being obsessed with re-election. Ironically, incumbency is so high in Congress, that they have very good prospects for staying in office. Nevertheless, legislators, especially Representatives, still seek to maximise their re-election prospects by constantly campaigning. Hence, the conventional wisdom is that when it comes to defence policy legislators are more concerned with promoting parochial (that is, constituency) than national interests, that is, pork-barrelling. In most other areas of public policy this is to be expected; after all, legislators are supposed to be representing their constituents. However, when it comes to defence policy, national interest ought to take precedence over parochial because this is in the interest of their constituents as well as the rest of the country. The pork-barrelling perspective holds that, when it comes to weapons acquisition, legislators are more interested in whether or not a weapon will be built in their constituency rather than if it is needed or cost-effective (Smith, 1988, pp. 205–7; Gansler, 1989, pp. 118–19). James Lindsay argues that the opposite is in fact the case. He outlines four reasons why legislators may concentrate on policy rather than 'pork'. Firstly, they may want to 'advance their conceptions of good public policy'; the idea being that people have more than self-gain at heart when they enter politics. Secondly, legislators may be advancing their own electoral interests by responding to the concerns of constituents; although Massachusetts has sizeable defence industries, it is also strongly Democratic. Hence legislators representing this state would conceivably have good reason to oppose a weapon programme even if it was being partially built in Massachusetts. Thirdly, they may want to advance their reputation as a player in Congress, and in doing so increase their influence within Congress; there are numerous examples of Senators and Representatives (the respective former Chairmen of the House and Senate Armed Service Committees, Les Aspin and Sam Nunn, to name a couple) who have gained influence by virtue of their expertise in defence. Lastly, they may see such work as a way of gaining higher office; for example, Aspin went from the House to become (briefly) the Secretary of Defence and Senator Al Gore became Vice President under the Clinton administration (Lindsay, 1991, pp. 16–18).

Where's the Pork?

However, there is an even more devastating critique of pork-barrel politics, that is, that legislators merely pretend to be able to influence new weapons programmes when in fact they are unable to do so. In his impressive study on *The Political Economy of Defence Contracting*, Kenneth Mayer shows that 'nearly all of the political activity surrounding major defence contracts is largely for show and has little substantive impact on the process' (1991, p. 7). Mayer argues that when it comes to weapons programmes, members of Congress want to *appear* to be motivated by parochial (or 'pork-barrel') interests in order to show their constituents that they are attempting to secure jobs for their district. Lindsay also argues that legislators claim credit where it is not due and that such behaviour perpetuates the myth of pork-barrel politics: 'Observers typically notice credit claiming behaviour and jump to the erroneous conclusion that congressional parochialism shapes defence spending' (1991, p. 132). According to Mayer, legislators realise that, in reality, they have no hope of gaining support within Congress for one weapon programme if they do not have a convincing argument for doing so besides simply that of securing jobs; there must also be a genuine military, political or technical argument favouring the programme in order to attract congressional support. Legislators must nevertheless appear to be doing something. So they take credit when their district gains a contract, and when it loses one, they blame it on 'pork-barrel' politics (Mayer, 1991, pp. 143, 211–33).

Legislators do have some chance of keeping old weapon programmes going. Mayer distinguishes 'award advocacy' from 'funding advocacy', where the former refers to attempts by legislators to secure contract awards and the latter refers to legislating more funds for a programme. He argues that with funding advocacy legislators have some chance of influencing programmes in being by preventing the administration from scaling them back or cancelling them (Mayer, 1991, pp. 133–5, 144). But even here, the perception of legislators wasting money on obsolete weapons for simply electoral purposes is far greater than the reality. If things were otherwise, why is it, as Mayer notes, that 'the two most powerful congressional players in defence policy [in the 1980s], Sam Nunn Aspin and Les Aspin, represent areas with small stakes in defence contracting'? Significantly, these men do not appear to have sought to use their positions to secure additional defence contracts for their constituencies. In 1986 Nunn's state, Georgia, ranked 12th in the value of its defence contracts relative to the other 50 states, by 1988 it had dropped to 19th place. In 1986 Aspin's district, Wisconsin, ranked 280th relative to the other 435 districts; by 1987 it had dropped to 398th place (Mayer, 1991, pp. 215–16). However, Mayer does show that administrations and the DoD have manipulated the timing of defence contracting in order to support 'allies' in Congress in the run up to elections; in these instances, far more defence contracts than usual are awarded before elections (1991, pp. 203–7). But again, it is not clear how this affects the acquisition of specific weapons.

In short, this book will concentrate on narrow calculations about costs since these appear to be most relevant to the fates of individual weapon programmes. Furthermore, the chapter on institutional issues will not examine whether or not members of Congress are driven by self-interest to support or oppose a weapon. It has been argued that legislators have as much reason to seek to promote good public policy as constituency interests. Indeed, it is often in their self-interest to promote good public policy. More importantly, individual legislators are unable to mobilise support or opposition to a weapon in Congress unless they can present a good strategic or budgetary reason for doing so.

METHODOLOGY AND CASE SELECTION

In their 1976 survey of the literature on the arms dynamic in the United States, Allison and Morris concluded that there was 'an overwhelming need for many more careful, detailed case histories aimed at developing preliminary causal maps of the weapons development process'; this need still exists 20 years on. While recognising the difficulty of such as exercise, they nevertheless made three recommendations. First, they suggested that such studies should clearly define what aspect of the force structure they are examining, that is, what exactly is the dependent variable. In this case it is the outcome of individual weapon programmes. Second, they argued that the impact of single or clusters of factors on weapons acquisition needed to be determined. Finally, they recommended that chronology be used as 'an organizing device' in packaging hypotheses about weapons acquisition. This means that the decisionmaking process in weapons acquisition is best revealed through stories about weapon programmes (Allison and Morris, 1976, pp. 121–2). This book addresses need referred to by Allison and Morris and also adopts their recommendations.

Structured, Focused Comparison

Four case studies of weapon acquisitions will be analysed within a structured, focused comparison approach to establish the variables which determine the outcomes of the case studies and induce causal patterns which determine different outcomes (George, 1979, pp. 43–68).

This approach is comparative in that a number of case studies are analysed. It is focused in that it is only concerned with particular aspects of these case studies, that is, explaining the origins, development and outcomes of the weapon programmes. It is structured in that clearly defined terms and a standard set of questions are used in analysing all the case studies. The outcomes that we are concerned with are whether a programme succeeds, partially succeeds, or fails to produce a weapon which is acquired by the US military. The variables which determine these outcomes are the strategic, institutional and budgetary issues in weapons acquisition. The impact of these variables on the case study outcomes will be traced by applying three sets of questions (as outlined in the previous section) to each case study. The causal patterns which determine different programme outcomes will be discerned by examining how the three independent variables relate to each other.

This approach implicitly accepts the argument that history has much to offer in helping us to understand international politics (Gaddis, 1987; Trachtenberg, 1991, pp. 261–86). Positivist methodologies may provide better platforms for theory generation and evaluation but they ignore the benefits that holism has to offer. For holists, in order to understand behaviour, it must be seen in the context of the actor's own subjective understanding, and against a detailed cultural, social and historical background. Positivists in their search for objective causes ignore the subjective context of actions by individuals and institutions. As Jack Snyder puts it: 'Positivists trace patterns across many cases, setting context aside by holding it constant; holists trace patterns within cases, exploring connections between context and action'.[7] This book seeks to do both. It shall, therefore, build upon the strengths of historical analysis and social scientific methods by using a structured, focused comparison of a variety of historical case studies so that a system can be understood. Having a variety of case studies, that is, 'cases belonging to the same class that differ from each other', is essential in order to provide adequate possibilities for falsifying hypotheses (George, 1979, p. 60).

What is Being Explained?

This book seeks to explain three types of outcomes in weapon programmes: these are the successful, partially successful and failed acquisition of a weapon. A weapon may be said to have been successfully acquired if it is bought in numbers. The number of models (or units) acquired is important. If considerably fewer units are acquired than the service originally expected to get then the weapon may only be said to have been a partial success. As far as this book is concerned, for a programme to be a complete success at least 25 per cent of the original planned number of units have to be acquired. This figure is taken to represent the minimum number of units that a service would hope to get from a weapon programme. There are two grounds for expecting a service to ask for the greatest number of units from a weapon programme, both based on the assumption that militaries tend to plan for the worse. First, the service will expect there to be a greater rather than lesser demand for the weapon in war. The service can prepare for the worst eventuality by having the greatest number of weapons possible. Second, the service can also expect there to be likely political and budgetary pressures to reduce the unit requirement for a weapon programme. Thus by asking for the most units possible the service can expect to get at least the minimum amount of units that it believes it needs. While the actual minimum amount will vary from programme to programme, and from one service opinion to the next, a quarter for the original unit requirement will be taken as a reasonable expectation of success.

This book is not particularly interested in the performance of weapons after they have been acquired. This is because it is the process whereby the United States acquires weapons, and not the weapons themselves, which is under examination. Therefore, weapon performance will only be discussed in so far as it may reveal something about the strategic rationale for, or cost-effectiveness of, the weapon programme.[8]

Case Selection

Four case studies of weapon programmes will be examined in the book. This number is small enough to enable a historical examination of each weapon programme in sufficient detail while also providing enough variety to allow for rigorous comparative analysis. The weapons examined are from roughly the same period, that is, from the Carter to Bush administrations; all the case studies span at least two presidencies (either Carter–Reagan or Reagan–Bush) and one, the B-2, spans all three. The variety in the weapons examined is evident by glancing at Table 1.1. Two of the case studies are of nuclear weapons while two are of conventional ones. There is at least one weapon from each of the three military services. Most importantly, examples of successful,

partially successful and failed weapons will be examined so that a rigorous analysis may be made of the impact of strategic, institutional
and budgetary issues on weapons acquisition.

Table 1.1. Case Selection

Weapon	Programme outcome	Weapon type	Service sponsor
A-12 (1984–90)	Failure	Conventional	Navy
DIVAD (1977–85)	Partial success	Conventional	Army
MX (1976–88)	Success	Nuclear	Air Force
B-2 (1977–92)	Partial success	Primarily nuclear	Air Force

Research and Development (R&D) on the MX (for Missile Experi-
mental) programme began in 1976. The Air Force intended to buy 200
MXs but in 1985 Congress mandated that the Air Force could only acquire 50. One year later the first 10 MXs were deployed and by 1988
the Air Force declared that the programme had reached full operational capability (FOC) after it had received all 50 MXs.[9] Hence, the
MX was successfully acquired. On the other hand, the A-12 failed to
be acquired. The A-12 was a naval stealth bomber started in 1984 and
cancelled by Defence Secretary Dick Cheney in 1990 before the plane
had even entered production.[10] There are also two case studies of partially successful weapons acquisitions. The Air Force started R&D on
the B-2 stealth bomber in 1977, in 1983 the Reagan administration declared its intention to acquire 132 B-2s, but in 1992, under intense pressure from Congress, President Bush announced that the programme
would be terminated after the first 20 bombers had been acquired.[11]
The DIVAD programme also began in 1977. In 1981 the Army planned
to acquire 614 DIVADs and it awarded a contract to Ford Aerospace
to develop and build the first 280 or so units. However, in 1985 Defence
Secretary Casper Weinberger cancelled the programme before it enter
full-scale production leaving the Army with only 64 DIVADs.[12]

Sensitivity Analysis and Programme Outcomes

How sensitive would the analysis be to variations in the criteria for the
categories of success, partial success and failure? A successful weapon
programme was defined as one in which 25 per cent or more of the original units are acquired. This figure was chosen as representing what a service would reasonably expect to get from a weapon programme. But
what if the figure ought to be 33 per cent or even 26 per cent? Under

such circumstances, the one weapon portrayed in this book as a success would have to be considered merely a partial success: 50 MXs were acquired when the Air Force had planned for 200. However, there is no reason for raising the ceiling: even if the ceiling were raised above 25 per cent, while the MX would no longer classify as a successful programme, it would still be by far the most successful programme in the context of this book. The MX was clearly more successful at being acquired in relative numbers than the DIVAD and B-2: only about 10 per cent and 15 per cent respectively of the original DIVAD and B-2 unit requirements were acquired. Thus the ceiling for success could be lowered by a considerable amount, though again there is no reason to do so, and still the MX would have been the only entirely successful programme.

What this Book Does Not Reveal

The book might as well be subtitled 'the Politics of Weapons Cancellation in the United States' as only one weapon was successfully acquired: two others were only partial acquisitions and one failed altogether. This is unproblematic: this book is as much about how weapons flunk as how they pass. More importantly, this book makes no pretensions to be a scientific study nor does it claim to produce any statistical findings. The four case studies are only supposed to be representative of US weapons acquisition in so far as there is at least one weapon from each service and examples of both conventional and nuclear weapons are included. They are not intended to reveal anything about the amount or type of weapons that are acquired and that are rejected in the United States. The fact that the MX succeeded where the A- 12 failed says nothing about the relative likelihood of nuclear versus conventional weapons being acquired.

There is a problem, nevertheless, with regard to the population of cases in this book. A trade-off has to be made in any study of this kind between the number of cases analysed and the depth of the case study analysis. This book focuses on four case studies so that each case can be analysed in sufficient historical detail: this is integral to the structured, focused comparison methodology. In addition, by applying a number of set questions to each case study (and thereby increasing the number of observations) when testing for the impact of each independent variable, this book gets a lot of mileage out of its four case studies (King *et al.*, 1994, pp. 217–30). On the downside, however, the full variety of possible weapon programmes will not been covered. In particular, this book will not examine any cases of weapons which never made it to full-scale development. This is significant, but only up to a point. It could be argued that the military services do not support every weapon which takes their fancy but rather they cull strategically or technologically weak weapons and keep the best. However, there is evidence to suggest that this is unlikely to be true. The findings in this book reveal that three of the weapons examined had no strategic purpose and/or did not work, yet in each case the services tried everything to get them acquired. Why, then, should they act differently with any other programmes? Joint service weapons have also not been examined. It would be interesting to study how institutional issues operate in this context. More case studies would not only have allowed a greater variety of weapons to be examined but also provided greater opportunity to test arguments and check casual patterns. This book argues that regardless of strategic and budgetary considerations, a weapon programme will not get started without the support of a military service. Perhaps there is a weapon which was started without any service support; and perhaps it is a joint service programme, that is, joint service because no individual service was willing to develop it. On the whole, however, the four weapons examined in this book contain enough variety to enable rigorous testing of the central argument of this book, namely, that all three sets of issues – strategic, institutional and budgetary – must be analysed when explaining why certain weapon programmes succeed and others fail.

2 Strategic Issues

To what extent do strategic issues explain weapons acquisition? In addressing this issue, three questions will be applied to each of the four case studies. First, was the weapon intended to carry out a necessary military mission? The strategies underlying the military missions for each weapon will be briefly examined when answering this question: if the strategy is suspect, then so must be the military mission. Second, was the weapon capable of carrying out its military mission? Given that it takes several years to develop a weapon, its military mission may well change. The weapon ought to be able to adapt accordingly. Third, were there other, more cost-effective alternatives for meeting this mission requirement? Since nuclear weapons also serve international political purposes independent of their military missions, two additional questions will be addressed when examining the strategic rationales for the MX and B-2. First, was it meant to serve as a symbol of national resolve, to ward off enemies and reassure allies? Second, was it needed as a bargaining chip to wring concessions out of the Soviets in arms negotiations?

A-12 AVENGER

On the surface, the rationale for the development of the A-12 can easily be justified on strategic grounds. Originally designed in the late 1950s, the Navy's standard medium attack aircraft, the A-6 is arguably becoming obsolete.[1] Many A-6Es, the latest version of the A-6 which were first introduced in 1972, were by the 1980s restricted to non-demanding flight manoeuvres as a result of wing cracks. Such aircraft remained incapable of combat operations until they were re-winged (or retired).[2]

The A-12 was therefore needed to meet an established mission requirement, that is a medium attack aircraft for the Carrier Air Wings (CAWs). Nevertheless, the exact requirements the A-12 was designed to fulfil may, upon closer examination, be found to be questionable. Significantly, was there a genuine need for an aircraft that incorporated such advanced stealth technologies?

The Over-Demanding Maritime Strategy

Navy Strategy demanded very capable aircraft. In the late 1970s a self-styled 'renaissance' occured in the Navy as the service began to think and talk about strategy. This resulted, in the early 1980s, in the development of the Maritime Strategy and its promulgation throughout the service under the guiding hand of the Chief of Naval Operations (CNO) Admiral John Watkins and with the strong backing of the Navy Secretary, John Lehman (1988, pp. 129–30). The Martime Strategy was designed to give the Navy a more offensive wartime posture; it was essentially a package of three offensive missions – power projection, horizontal escalation and counterforce coercion. Power projection involved seeking out and destroying enemy forces, particularly the Soviet Navy and its land-based facilities. Horizontal escalation referred to attacking Soviet vital interests outside Europe. Counterforce coercion referred to threatening the Soviet ballistic missile submarine (SSBN) fleet. The main burden for carrying out these missions was to fall on the Navy's aircraft carrier battle groups (CVBGs), each one consisting of a large decked carrier and a number of escort ships.[3]

All three offensive missions were criticised for either being too risky, largely irrelevant, and/or a waste of naval and national resources. It was argued that using naval forces to attack land forces and bases on Soviet territory would not have had any real impact on the outcome of a ground war in central Europe. The same was also said of attacking Soviet vital interests outside Europe: what was the point in capturing Cuba or Vietnam if West Germany fell to Warsaw Pact forces? Since it was the battle for Central Europe which mattered, it was argued that defence dollars would be much better spent on tactical air and ground forces dedicated to the defence of North Atlantic Treaty Organisation (NATO) territory. Power projection was seen as contributing to NATO's defence by neutralising the Soviet naval threat. However, critics argued that this could be achieved in a much more cost-effective manner through defensive operations using mines, frigates and attack submarines rather than offensive operations using CVBGs.[4] The main criticism of counterforce coercion was that it could inadvertently trigger a nuclear war. The US Navy's intention was to be able to tilt the balance of nuclear forces in favour of the United States by destroying part of the Soviet SSBN fleet. It was argued that the Soviets could simply react by using nuclear weapons against vulnerable CVBGs. This was a reasonable fear: after all, NATO threatened to use nuclear weapons against Soviet forces should the alliance start losing a European war.[5]

Critics were concerned with more than simply wasted funds, they also argued that moving CVBGs near Soviet territory, as envisaged under the Maritime Strategy, would unnecessarily put US naval forces in jeopardy by playing to Soviet strengths. The point was, according to

Lehman, for the Navy to 'sail in harm's way', to 'go into the highest threat areas to defeat the Soviet [naval] threat'.[6] The 'harm's way' strategy (or 'forward strategy') would have created severe problems for CVBGs, to say the least. This point is amply demonstrated by one much discussed and criticised wartime operation, namely an offensive against the Soviet Northern Fleet which was based on the Kola Peninsula and in the surrounding Barents Sea. This fleet was seen as presenting the greatest threat to NATO's sea lanes of communication. Furthermore, over half the Soviet SSBN force was based off the peninsula.[7] Under the 'harm's way' strategy, CVBGs escorted by attack submarines were supposed to enter the confines of the Barents Sea and attack the Soviet Northern Fleet.

It was doubtful that CVBGs could even have survived in the Barents Sea, let alone have defeated the Soviet Navy. The Soviets would easily have detected any approaching CVBGs and have been able to mobilise defensive forces. At 1,600 miles the CVBGs would have been within range of 90 per cent of the Soviet Union's land-based bombers, whereas the carrier bombers only have a range of about 500 miles. This would have given the Soviets up to two days to launched repeated air and sea attacks against the carriers while the CVBGs tried to close the distance. The carriers would also have been sitting ducks while their aircraft bombed Soviet bases and airfields (Turner and Thibault, 1982, pp. 126–7). Not only would carriers have been very vulnerable, but the local balance of forces would have favoured the Soviets. The Soviets could have reassigned units from other areas to reinforce the aircraft in the Kola Peninsula, whereas the CVBGs would have had a finite number of planes. The Navy bombers would also have had to contend with the considerable Soviet air defences around the Kola Peninsula (Mearsheimer, 1986, pp. 36–9; Lind, 1988, p. 58). In a statement to a subcommittee of the House Armed Services Committee in 1985, retired Rear Admiral Eugene Carroll concluded: 'The Soviet Navy is strongest in the very seas through which Secretary Lehman argues that a US naval offensive should be prosecuted. It is in fact hard to see how such an offensive could succeed.'[8]

While most serving admirals endorsed the 'forward strategy' in public, the views they expressed in private appear to have been far less supportive. As one senior congressional staffer (specialised in national security affairs) reportedly put it, 'they may not say it publicly, but many aircraft carrier skippers pale at the thought of taking their giant ships into the waters of the Barrents'.[9] Indeed, former Admiral Stansfield Turner claimed some years before that he had 'yet to find one

Admiral who believes that the US Navy would even attempt it' (1982/83, pp. 456–7).

The Maritime Strategy demanded high performance from all carrier-borne aircraft. Furthermore, unlike the Navy fighters, the new bombers would have to face Soviet ground-based as well as airborne defences. In 1984 when the A-12 was first proposed, the Navy was placing particular stress on power projection as the primary mission of the Maritime Strategy. While this was replaced by coercive counterforce in 1986, power projection continued to be recognised as a core mission. In 1988, when the first development contract for the A-12 was awarded, the DoD reaffirmed that: 'The US Fleet is built around the aircraft carrier and operates primarily in [CVBGs, which are] the US Navy's principal conventional deterrent, presence, and power projection instrument.'[10] Since the Maritime Strategy, a strategy which made no military sense, established the requirement for a very 'stealthy' aircraft to replace the A-6, then it must be concluded that the mission requirement for the A-12 is not convincing.[11]

Just as the development of the A-12 cannot be explained in terms of strategic issues, neither can its cancellation. The mission requirement for the A-12 did not change between 1984 and late 1990. Lehman's resignation in February of 1987, and the replacement of Admiral Watkins by Admiral Carlisle Trost (not Lehman's choice) the same year, raised speculation that the Maritime Strategy might not last long.[12] By 1987 the Navy appears to have reacted to criticisms that its forward strategy was too risky. Instead of sending CVBGs into the Barrents Sea, the Navy began talking of controlling the Norwegian Sea, and while attacks against the Kola Peninsula were still envisaged, the carriers were to be kept out of, and not placed in, 'harm's way'.[13] Both Admiral Trost and Lehman's successor, Navy Secretary James Webb, were broadly supportive of the Maritime Strategy, although both indicated that it would have to become more flexible, so that regional and fleet commanders could interpret it more loosely.[14] In sum, by 1990 war with the Soviet Union seemed even more remote, yet if it had come the CVBGs were still expected to conduct operations against targets close to Soviet territory. As one study noted in late 1991, such operations would still have been extremely risky (Daniel, 1993, p. 40).

Questioning the Need and the Technology

One test of whether the A-12 was cancelled because there was no military requirement for it is the mission requirement of its successor, the

A-X. By 1990, the most likely threat was no longer considered to come from the Soviet Union but from Third World adversaries.[15] Indeed, six CVBGs were engaged in combat operations against Iraq when Cheney killed the A-12 programme. If future military threats to US interests will come from an as yet unknown Third World enemy, then the flexibility offered by carriers is desirable. This is especially so considering the financial and political investment required to base forces overseas. This view was shared by Cheney who strongly believed that despite budget cuts, the United States would 'want to continue to be the pre-eminent naval power in the world' in order to deal with Third World threats. Furthermore, both chairmen of the congressional armed services committees, Nunn and Aspin, indicated in 1990 that they favoured retaining funding for the Navy's power projection capability.[16] This still leaves the question, does the US Navy need stealth aircraft to bomb Third World states? Cheney stated in 1991 that 'we will still need to develop a next-generation strike airplane for our carrier force to replace the aging A-6'. He added that 'stealth technology will be required'.[17] But how 'stealthy' does the A-X have to be? Navy officials were reportedly divided on whether the level of stealth should be 'very low observable' (as in the case of the A-12) or simply 'low observable'.[18]

Around this time some critics in Congress began to question both the effectiveness of, and requirement for, stealth aircraft. They advocated a greater reliance on tried and tested radar-jamming, as opposed to radar-evading, technologies.[19] The call for a return to relying on defensive avionics was strengthened by persistent press reports in 1990–1 that the Air Force's B-2 stealth bomber could not escape radar detection as easily, or as effectively, as had previously been promised.[20] Furthermore, it was reported in 1992 that the Air Force's F-117A stealth fighter had not performed as well as had initially been believed either. According to a Republican member of the HASC, Andy Ireland, the Air Force had admitted that the F-117A had to be escorted by radar-jamming (or electronic counter measures) aircraft because the stealth fighters were being tracked by Iraqi air defence radars. As Representative Ireland noted, this defeated the whole purpose of having the stealth planes:

> Having Stealth airplanes escorted by planes with electronic jamming equipment is the antithesis of Stealth. Electronic jammers are like a bell on a cat's collar. They announce the creature's presence to every target in the area.[21]

Moreover, inside sources told Representative Ireland that Navy E-2C aircraft were able to track the F-117A from more than 100 miles away.[22]

The F-117A's tarnished war record could well have reinforced the case in the Navy for the A-X to be very stealthy. However, given the equally disappointing performance of the B-2, which was supposed to be more stealthy than the F-117A, the F-117A inability to evade radar was probably symptomatic of the limitations of stealth technologies. Moreover, as details regarding the shape and composition of stealth aircraft become more available to radar engineers, they are more likely to be able to develop a radar that can acquire these elusive aircraft.[23]

The mission requirement for a very stealthy naval bomber to replace the A-6 was not convincing. The flawed Maritime Strategy did indeed require enormously capable aircraft, but this was to carry out operations that were so hazardous as to be almost suicidal to both the aircraft and their carriers. By 1990, when the A-12 was cancelled, the Navy was far less concerned with conducting operations against the Soviet Navy than against possible Third World opponents. This latter type of operation was a less demanding one for naval bombers. This new set of circumstances may account for the uncertainty within the Navy over how stealthy the A-X needed to be. Uncertainty was also generated, however, by new evidence suggesting that the F-117A and B-2 were not as effective as originally thought. This may have led some Navy officials to conclude that they needed an A-X which was more stealthy than the Air Force's stealth planes, but critics in Congress began reaching another (more persuasive) conclusion: stealth technologies would never be as good as originally promised. Alternatives were not readily available, the Navy needed a new bomber, but an alternative plane could have been developed which incorporated tried and tested radar-jamming technology.

SGT YORK DIVAD

As with the A-12, the development of DIVAD also, on the surface, appears to have been driven by strategic issues. According to the US Army, DIVAD was desperately needed to upgrade the service's ageing short-range air defence (SHORAD) systems. SHORAD systems are designed to protect command posts, and battlefield support and field units (such as armoured and mechanised units) deployed in the forward half of the division area (about 10 kilometres from the frontline) from aerial attack. The Army had three front-line SHORAD systems in the late 1970s, with a fourth added in 1981. The M-167 Vulcan and M-48

Chaparral were both procured in 1966. The Vulcan was armed with a six-barrel 20 mm Gatling Gun with a range of 1,200 metres. The Chaparral carried four heat-seeking missiles with a range of about 5 kilometres. A manportable shoulder-fired version of a Chaparral missile was introduced in 1979, designated the Redeye. This was slowly replaced from 1981 by the Stinger, an upgraded version of the Redeye. All these systems had shortfalls which DIVAD was supposed to address. The Chaparral, Redeye and Stinger systems were all vulnerable to enemy attack. The former vehicle was not armoured and the latter two systems could not be fired from within an armoured vehicle. Furthermore, both the Chaparral and Redeye missiles lacked the speed to hit very fast Soviet fixed-wing aircraft and both lacked the infra-red sensitivity to effectively target approaching aircraft.[24] The Vulcan lacked sufficient range to be really useful in an battlefield air defence role.[25] So the new DIVAD was needed to augment the Army's deficient SHORAD capability.

The Soviet Threat Shifts from Planes to Helicopters

How serious was the threat from Soviet aerial attack on US ground forces? Analysis by the Army's Training and Doctrine Command (TRADOC) in 1985 predicted that up to one quarter of all US Army losses in a short, intense battle could come from Soviet aerial attack.[26] The Soviet aerial threat came in two forms: low flying fighter bombers[27] and hovering helicopter gunships. The primary air threat that DIVAD was originally designed to meet in 1977 was from fighter bombers. By 1980 this priority had switched to helicopter gunships.[28] The Warsaw Treaty Organisation (WTO) had greater numbers of fighter bombers than NATO, but NATO warplanes were qualitatively better than those of the Warsaw Pact.[29] As one independent analyst argued:

> NATO . . . fighter-bomber aircraft would likely have done more damage against Pact ground forces than vice versa . . . With the exception of the small number of 'Frogfoot' [the Soviet version of the USAF's A-10] aircraft deployed in the 1980s, Pact tactical fighter bombers were not well suited to [the close air support][30] mission. Moreover, the Pact seemed more concerned with attacking NATO's tactical nuclear assets and airbases than using TACAIR to affect the ground battle (Posen, 1991, p. 103).

This view fits with the conclusion reached by Western military analysts in the early 1980s that Soviet military doctrine was orientated towards achieving strategic objectives, in particular the neutralising of NATO's tactical nuclear capability, rather than operational objectives as is the case with US Army doctrine (Donnelly, 1983, pp. 121, 124, 130).

The growing concern with Soviet helicopters was heightened by the Soviet Army's deployment in Afghanistan in 1980 of its most up-to-date helicopter gunship, the Mi-24 Hind-D.[31] By 1985 the DoD was clearly worried by the increasing quantity and quality of Soviet helicopter gunships.[32] Very little was known in the early 1980s about the effectiveness of helicopter gunships against armoured vehicles. Only one such engagement occurred during this period, when Israel invaded the Lebanon in 1982. This experience suggested that the US Army had good reason to be concerned, as Israel gunships proved very effective at knocking out Syrian tanks.[33]

This distinction between fighter bombers and helicopter gunships is very significant. Each was designed to attack US ground forces in different ways and so each required a different response from air defence units. Soviet fighter bombers could have attacked in two ways. They may have approached the target at a low altitude, then climbed steeply to a high vantage point (600 to 2,300 metres), from which to locate the target and release their weapons in a dive. In this 'pop-up' profile, Soviet fighter bombers would have been vulnerable to air defence AD fire. Thus, they were more likely to have approached their targets in 'laydown' profile which would have minimised their exposure to air defences, that is, flying as fast as possible (between 350 to 500 knots) towards the target at a constantly low altitude of about 150 metres. Helicopter gunships would have used a very different attack technique. Unlike fighter bombers which have to approach their targets within 1,500 metres, helicopters can stand off and fire their missiles up to several kilometers away. Soviet gunships were also expected to hide behind terrain obstacles only popping up briefly to locate and fire upon their targets. These very different attack patterns required different capabilities from US SHORAD units. Longer range is more important against helicopters than fighter bombers; infra-red heat-seeking missiles are less effective against helicopters since they emit far less heat than fixed-wing aircraft; and hovering or slow moving helicopters are much more difficult to acquire either visually or by radar. Radar returns from helicopters are obscured by terrain features (this is called 'ground clutter'). Terrain features, especially hills, would also have constrained the air defenders' low altitude field of vision.[34] In short, helicopters are far more difficult to locate and destroy than planes.

This view was not shared by all. According to one account, this anti-helicopter mission did not provide a convincing rationale for DIVAD because 'experience [in Vietnam] has shown that even a $600 rifle can do the job', and because Afghan rebels had proved able to shoot down Soviet Hinds using Redeyes and machine-guns (Easterbrook, 1982, pp. 107–8). This argument is crude and inaccurate. There is a big difference between counter-insurgency and counter-armour missions for helicopter gunships. In the case of the former mission, the helicopter must fly low and close to enemy positions in order to acquire and hit targets, whereas in the case of the latter mission the helicopter may hide behind cover kilometers away, only exposing itself briefly to fire at its targets. Certainly a helicopter has no armour, so its survivability depends upon not being targeted, which is difficult in counter-insurgency but easy in counter-armour missions.

DIVAD Can't See Nor Shoot Helicopters

So although DIVAD was originally developed to combat fighter bombers, this threat was overtaken in 1980 by that of helicopter gunships. Did DIVAD develop to meet this new threat? Apparently not. According to Weinberger, ultimately it was DIVAD's inability to meet this new mission priority which led to its cancellation in 1985.[35] This would seem to suggest that DIVAD had been developed for strategic reasons, and cancelled when the military requirement changed beyond the capabilities of the weapon. Yet this new mission requirement emerged in 1980 when DIVAD was still being developed. So why did the DIVAD programme not evolve to meet this new threat? The answer is simple: the weapon's very design prevented it from doing so. The Army required that DIVAD incorporate AD guns and an AD radar as well as being mounted on an armoured chassis. It was also decided that, where possible, existing mature components would be incorporated into the design. This was seen as necessary for a highly concurrent programme, that is, one which would allow the DIVAD to proceed straight from the prototype stage to production without prior rigorous testing. The Army argued that concurrency was considered highly desirable as DIVAD was urgently needed. Pro-defence members of Congress naturally accepted this argument. Indeed, it would seem that the Army's decision to use mature components in the DIVAD came from a suggestion made by a staff member of the SASC in early 1977.[36]

The Ford prototype which was eventually chosen in 1981 met these basic programme requirements: twin 40 mm Bofors L-70 guns, a

Westinghouse AN/APG-66 (also known as the doppler) search and track radar, all mounted on an M-48 tank chassis.[37] And therein lay the problem. As has already been noted, radar has difficulty locating hovering helicopters due to their small signature and ground clutter. The doppler radar had been taken from the F-16 fighter bomber and adapted to a ground environment.[38] Obviously fighter radars are able to acquire other fast-moving fixed-wing aircraft but it was widely recognised that such radars had severe problems locating hovering helicopters.[39] It should have come as no great surprise then that the attempt to adapt the doppler radar to this new mission requirement failed.[40] Furthermore, in the early 1980s US intelligence estimated that the new anti-tank guided missile (ATGM) which was carried on Soviet helicopter gunships, the AT-6 Spiral, had a range of 5–6 kilometres. The Boffors L-70 guns only had a range of about 4 kilometres.[41] So even if DIVAD could acquire enemy helicopters, they could hit it but it could not hit them.

This is not to argue that there was no mission for a new SHORAD system. As with the Navy and its Maritime Strategy, the Army had also developed a new doctrine in the late 1970s and early 1980s. The previous doctrine which had been adopted in 1976, called Active Defence, was heavily criticised (both from outside and within the service) for giving the Army a far too static and defensive posture in Western Europe. In response to these criticisms, and a new appreciation of the strenghts and weaknesses of Soviet Army formations, a new doctrine was developed by TRADOC called AirLand Battle (Romjue, 1984, pp. 5–15). Unlike Active Defence, AirLand Battle called for a fluid deployment at the foward edge of the battlefield area (FEBA). In particular, the new doctrine called for deep attacks to be conducted against reserve enemy forces in the Soviet rear in order to prevent them from reaching the main battlefield area, at least until the initial wave have been neutralised. Deep attacks, which were to be conducted by US aircraft, artillery and electronic warfare systems, were to be used to create opportunities for manoeuvre operations by US Army units to exploit weaknesses in Soviet formations.[42] Hence, AirLand Battle doctrine established the need for an armoured mobile air-defence system which could travel with these manoeuvre forces and provide air-protection for them in the FEBA. As has been noted, existing SHORAD systems lacked this capability. This mission requirement was explicitly recognised by the DIVAD programme manager in 1980 when Army doctrine was shifting from Active Defence to AirLand Battle.[43]

The Army Fancied a High Tech Gun

It would seem then that there was a mission requirement for a new armoured mobile SHORAD system and that DIVAD was the wrong weapon for the job. Why was it chosen then? The Army had two other alternatives to DIVAD: a low technology AD gun-based system, or a new AD missile on an armoured chassis. There were two military reasons why the Army Air Defence Center favoured a gun over a missile system. First, AD missiles had problems acquiring helicopters. Second, the new Soviet AD gun, the ZSU-23-4, appeared to have performed extremely well in the 1973 Arab–Israeli War. As it happens, when the Army Air Defence Center tested a captured Egyptian ZSU-23-4 they discovered that it was not very accurate and was unable to shoot down manoeuvring drones (Easterbrook, 1982, pp. 102–3). It was nevertheless very effective at forcing pilots to abort their missions. It did this not by destroying aircraft but by discouraging and damaging them. As one senior staff member of the SASC commented, 'our pilots are terrified of ZSU-23s . . . primarily because of the volume of lead they can put up, it's not because of the accuracy of the system'.[44] Unfortunately drones could not be scared off. As will be argued in the next chapter, institutional considerations led the Army to require that a sophisticated AD gun system be developed, one which could shoot down instead of simply scare off enemy planes, and so one quite unlike the ZSU-23-4.

There was no real military requirement for a sophisticated, high-technological gun system. More to the point, had the Army chosen to develop a low-technology system then it would have got a much more cost-effective weapon. The most complex subsystem in the DIVAD, and so most difficult to develop, was the radar. It was also the most costly. The doppler radar and associated processing equipment amounted to an astonishing 55 per cent of the DIVAD's unit cost. This high unit cost had military implications. According to Congressional Budget Office (CBO) estimates the Army needed to procure 70–80 new SHORADs per division in order to ensure two engagements per helicopter standing off up to 6 kilometres away. This was because terrain obstacles in the European theatre obscured the line-of-sight/fire of SHORAD units, so limiting the total area each unit could cover. Yet the DIVAD programme was only intended to provide 36 units per division. The CBO argued that the expense of each DIVAD would have prohibited the procurement of the weapon in greater numbers.[45]

Instead of radar the new SHORAD system could have used a passive detection system such as a forward looking infra-red system (FLIRS).

The are several advantages with radar: it can observe approaching targets from 360°; it can detect targets at greater ranges than passive systems; and it works better in bad weather. The ability to spot targets coming from any direction would be useful for manoeuvre units engaging in operations close to or behind the enemy's frontline. Yet, while radars do not require line-of-sight to acquire aircraft, AD guns require a line-on-fire in order to be able to hit approaching aircraft. Hence, the fact that radar can detect obscured enemy aircraft is largely irrelevant for a gun-based SHORAD system. The all-weather capability of radars is equally questionable. Aircraft, as well as AD systems, have problems operating in bad weather. Thus, as the CBO noted, 'aircraft are not likely to fly in the type of weather that would prevent a FLIR from working'.[46] Indeed, there were certain disadvantages with radar. AD radars can alert enemy aircraft to their presence by emitting radiation. This may not have presented a direct threat to DIVAD itself as according to Army instructors the system was able to 'cover itself up', thereby eliminating any radar signal, and to target the incoming ATGM.[47] Nevertheless, the enemy aircraft would still have been given the opportunity to avoid the DIVAD. The Army could have had a far cheaper alternative which, as a result, could have been bought in far greater numbers had it chosen a FLIR instead of a radar for DIVAD. Indeed, General Dynamics were developing a SHORAD system in 1982 that incorporated twin 35 mm guns on an armoured chasis with a laser range-finder and a FLIR instead of radar (Easterbrook, 1982, pp. 118–19).

In conclusion, it would seem that there was a military requirement for a new SHORAD weapon, and this was reinforced by the shift to a new Army doctrine in the early 1980s. However, this military requirement changed between the late 1970s and early 1980s and DIVAD was unable to adapt to meet it. Therefore, while strategic considerations can account for the origins of DIVAD, they cannot explain why the weapon was developed in the manner in which it was.

The weapon was eventually terminated for strategic reasons; it did not work as advertised and so was deemed to be unable to meet the specified military requirement. Army and DoD officials claimed that the DIVAD was performing well in initial operational tests.[48] However, these operational tests were added to the programme under the Weinberger's orders, as some earlier tests had not been carried out, and there were allegations that the Army had rigged the tests anyway and that it had fed misleading information to the DoD.[49] Perhaps not surprisingly, Weinberger ended up believing the assessment of analysts from the Office of the Secretary of Defence (OSD) over that of the Army, which concluded that the DIVAD offered only marginal improvement on the Vulcan and that it was unable to meet the threat from helicopters.[50] Strategic issues do not entirely explain the programme outcome, however. The Soviet air threat switched from fighter bombers to helicopter gunships in 1980 yet DIVAD was not terminated until 1985. It is reasonable to expect that it would take some time for the Army to test DIVAD against this new threat and come to realise that it was unable to meet it; however, five years is a bit much. It was during these extra five years that the Army acquired 64 DIVADs. Thus, in the context of this study, this period of grace meant the difference between total failure and partial success for DIVAD. The next chapter will explain why DIVAD was developed in the way it was and how it managed to survive until 1985.

US NUCLEAR STRATEGY

Some discussion of US nuclear strategy is required in order to properly assess the strategic rationales for the MX and B-2. It is not entirely clear what US nuclear strategy is and who makes it. Analysts have focused mostly on the distinction between declaratory policy and employment policy, and the role played by Presidents and their closest advisors in both. Declaratory policy consists of public statements about how the United States would use its nuclear forces, while employment policy refers to secret directives on actual nuclear weapons usage in war issued by the President down the change of command to military planners. Particular attention has been paid to the gap that has existed between these two policy areas in the past. Nuclear employment policy appears to have evolved over the last few decades with increasing demands for ever greater discrimination in targeting options. In contrast the development of declaratory policy appears to be characterised by shifts back and forth between Mutually Assured Destruction (MAD) and nuclear warfighting.[51] In the past three decades this gap between declaratory and employment policies has closed, however. While there was considerable disparity between the declared and intended use of nuclear weapons in the early 1960s, gradually this disparity faded so that by the early 1980s declaratory policy genuinely reflected employment policy (Sloss and Millot, 1984).

Some other analysts have pointed to what they believe to be a far more significant gap between employment policy on the one hand,

and nuclear target lists and operational planning on the other. Since 1960 nuclear target lists and operational plans have been contained in a nuclear war plan, called the Single Integrated Operational Plan (SIOP). Officially, the President and Secretary of Defence may play a large part in shaping the SIOP in that the war plan is supposed to be based on employment policy.[52] In reality it would seem that, for the most part, the civilian authorities had only marginal influence over target lists and operational plans. In his seminal history of US nuclear strategy, David Alan Rosenberg found 'serious discrepancies between strategy and operational planning' in the 1950s (1981/82, p. 17). More recently Janne Nolan (1989) and Bruce Blair (1993) have highlighted the lack of effective civilian control over the drawing up of nuclear targeting lists and operational plans. According to these accounts, military planners in Strategic Air Command (SAC) and the Joint Chiefs of Staff (JCS) basically ran the show and, consequently, presidential directives on employment policy did not affect the broad thrust of the SIOP.

This section will start by analysing developments in declaratory policy and employment policy under Nixon, Carter and Reagan; from this, the mission requirements for the MX and B-2 that were debated among policymakers can be distilled and listed. Given that there is no fine distinction between the two types of policy, one will not be drawn. Indeed, as has been noted already, the gap between declaratory and employment policy had closed by the 1980s. This section will then go on to discuss the likely gap between employment policy and the actual SIOP during this period and whether or not this could be expected to produce different, actual mission requirements for the MX and B-2.

Nuclear Strategy from Nixon to Reagan

Upon entering office, Nixon, Carter and Reagan each ordered a review of nuclear strategy which eventually led to them issuing a directive on nuclear employment policy. In Nixon's case the review was initiated by Defence Secretary Melvin Laird. This led to Nixon issuing National Security Decision Memorandum (NSDM) 242 in January 1974 which eventually resulted in the approval of SIOP-5 by the President in December 1975. Under NSDM-242, the SIOP was supposed to be revised in two significant ways. First, military planners were supposed to build in Limited Nuclear Options (LNO) for nuclear weapons employment. This effort started in 1969 when Henry Kissinger, then Nixon's National Security Adviser (NSA), persuaded the President that effort had to be put into providing more employment options for the National

Command Authorities (NCA) than were contained in the original SIOP. Second, increased emphasis was to be placed in the SIOP on targeting Soviet nuclear and general purpose forces and command facilities, and a new emphasis was to be placed on targeting Soviet industry. Specifically, US nuclear forces were required to able to destroy 70 per cent of the industry that would be needed by the USSR to enable it to recover after a nuclear war (Ball, 1986b, p. 71–4). Nixon's second Defence Secretary, James Schlesinger, declared in 1974 that the United States could destroy more than 30 per cent of the Soviet population and 75 per cent of Soviet industry in retaliation for a general nuclear attack.[53]

An 18-month Nuclear Targeting Policy Review (NTPR) was started by the DoD under the incoming Carter administration in summer 1977.[54] The NTPR made two main recommendations. First, in addition to even greater emphasis on the 'effective' targeting of Soviet nuclear and general purpose forces, it called for a shift in the targeting priorities, with the counter-recovery mission being downplayed and concentrating specifically on war-supporting industry, and a new emphasis on directly targeting the Soviet leadership. Second, it advised that since the Soviet nuclear doctrine contemplated the possibility of fighting a prolonged nuclear war, the United States should develop the capability to fight one.[55] These recommendations were gathered together in the countervailing strategy by Carter's Defence Secretary, Harold Brown.[56] The countervailing strategy was codified by Carter when he issued Presidential Directive (PD) 59 in July 1980 and, by the following year, this was supposed to have led to the nuclear war plan being revised accordingly in SIOP-5F (Ball and Toth, 1990, pp. 67–8). According to Walter Slocombe, Brown's Deputy Under Secretary of Defence for Policy Planning, the countervailing strategy specifically called for the United States to 'improve its ability to conduct a sustained [nuclear] exchange' (1981, p. 23).

A review of targeting policy was started by the incoming Reagan administration in the spring of 1981. By October, Reagan had issued National Security Decision Document (NSDD) 13. The main goal established by NSDD-13 for the SIOP was for the United States to be able to *prevail* in a protracted nuclear war with the Soviet Union; under PD-59, it only had to be able to *fight* such a war.[57] NSDD-13 led to the development of SIOP-6 in October 1982. In a change from previous practice, Weinberger then issued new guidance to the JCS almost every year leading to SIOP-6 being updated several times. Under Weinberger, the SIOP was supposed to stress counterforce and counterleadership targeting. Soviet war-supporting industry was still to be targeted, but counter-recovery targeting was to be dropped altogether. The most radical subsequent changes in employment policy were introduced in October 1987. The resulting SIOP-6F, which was approved by Bush in 1989, gave even greater emphasis to targeting priorities expressed in SIOP-6 and required the United States to be able to threaten deeply buried and mobile Soviet leadership and nuclear forces with prompt attack (Ball and Toth, 1990, pp. 68–71).

Table 2.1. Targeting Priorities in US Nuclear Employment Policy

Target Type	Nixon: SIOP-5	Carter: SIOP-5F	Reagan: SIOP-6	Bush: SIOP-6F
Leadership	Targeted	Top priority	Priority target	Top priority
Nuclear forces	Top priority	Top priority	Top priority	Top priority
Other military	Targeted	Targeted	Targeted	Targeted
Recovery	Top priority	Targeted	Not targeted	Not targeted
War industry	Not specified	Targeted	Targeted	Targeted

Table 2.1 provides a guide to the targeting priorities that successive administrations tried to integrate into the SIOP. From this, we can discern the kind of mission requirements that policymakers expected the MX and B-2 to be able to fulfil. US nuclear forces were required to provide improved hard target capability, promptness, and survivability. Survivability was needed if the United States hoped to be able to fight a protracted nuclear war. Promptness (i.e. the ability to rapidly deliver nuclear warheads on designated targets) was considered necessary for counterforce and counterleadership targeting, especially against mobile targets. Better hard target capability was also sought in order to more effectively threaten deeply buried Soviet nuclear forces and leadership bunkers.

Actual Mission Requirements

The Cold War SIOP was drawn up by military planners in the Joint Strategic Target Planning Staff (JSTPS) based in Strategic Air Command (SAC) Headquarters at Offutt Air Force Base in Omaha, Nebraska (Ball and Toth, p. 65, fn.1) How much heed did they pay to guidance from the Defence Secretary and directives from the President? Not much it seems. Blair argues that the SIOP was 'virtually etched in stone' and that the 'political authorities' were 'bound by the contours of the war plan rather than the other way around' (1993, pp. 42–3). Military planners had considerable discretion in interpreting guidance from the civilian masters: 'The war planners of JSTPS and JCS basically determined whether the SIOP provided for enough damage to the Soviet target base to satisfy national guidance' (1993, p. 44). Since the primary goal of the SIOP was to achieve a high level of damage expectancy against the Soviet Union in a nuclear war, that is, to destroy the full range of targets in the war plan, US nuclear forces were prepared to carry out massive strikes against the Soviet Union under the SIOP. In addition, military planners believed that nuclear retaliation was not practical as the US nuclear force structure would in be no shape to execute the SIOP after it had absorbed a Soviet first strike. Thus, in the early 1970s, the SIOP adopted a Launch On Warning (LOW) posture for US nuclear forces which subsequently became known as the 'midnight express' within SAC (Blair, 1993, pp. 168–70, 173, 185).

These priorities in the SIOP clashed with some of those contained in the successive employment policies of the Nixon, Carter and Reagan administrations. Most significantly, all three administrations were concerned with building in options for launching more discriminating nuclear attacks. Civilian policymakers wanted LNOs to give them more options in a crisis. However, the JSTPS were loath to 'waste' weapons on limited strike options that, at best, served no apparent military purpose and, at worse, could interfere with the execution of massive preemptive strikes (Nolan, 1989, p. 258). Hence, they were very slow to include LNOs in the SIOP; at first they offered to execute the SIOP in stages thereby creating LNOs of sorts, later they included so-called 'LNOs' which were actually large-scale attacks using up to 100 weapons (Blair, pp. 42–3, 294). In particular, Nolan shows that civilian policymakers in the Nixon and Carter administrations failed in their attempts to get military planners to insert genuine LNOs in the SIOP (1989, pp. 112–39).

In addition to a clash of priorities, a gap grew between employment policies and the actual SIOP because some aspects of these employment policies made little operational sense. According to Nolan, this problem stems, in part, from policymakers ignorance of the technicalities of nuclear targeting and operational planning. Consequently, Nuclear Weapons Employment Plans (NUWEPs) were often so vague that the JSTPS had no choice but to interpret them as their saw fit (Nolan, 1989, pp. 251, 255). Take counterleadership targeting. Based on the assumption that there is nothing that people value as much as their own skins, the Soviet political leadership (which according to DoD estimates in 1980 numbered about 110,000 people[58]) was a priority target set under the countervailing strategy. The intention was also to be able to threaten to remove the political leadership's control over their own country.[59] First of all, it was by no means clear that US intelligence could even find them, or determine which elements of the leadership were in which bunkers. Brown himself admitted in his Fiscal Year 1981 Posture Statement that the DoD had managed to identify 'relatively few leadership shelters' (Ball, 1986a, p. 22). In addition, given the likely Soviet response, Blair notes that a counterleadership strike would have had to be accompanied by a full counterforce strike (1993, p. 43).

There was also an obvious tension between the protracted war-fighting capability established under PD-59 and the LOW posture adopted in the SIOP. A protracted nuclear war would have had to be limited at first in order to last any length of time, and so one would not have expected the United States to launch a massive nuclear strike in the opening shots of the war. A LOW posture was adopted in the SIOP precisely so as to enable the United States to fire off a massive counter-attack while Soviet nuclear weapons were in flight and before they hit the US nuclear force structure. In all likelihood, the tension between these two mission requirements was never resolved.

There is some evidence to suggest that the requirement for a protracted war-fighting capability was adopted as a political measure, to bolster the US deterrent, rather than as a military measure designed to improve the United States' chances in a war. Right from the beginning there was not even agreement in the Carter administration as to what was meant by a protracted nuclear war. The General Accounting Office (GAO) reported in 1981 that there was 'no consensus [within the DoD] on how long a protracted period might be'.[60] In addition, there was considerable dispute within the Carter administration over the desirability of establishing this mission requirement. Carter's first Secretary of State, Cyrus Vance, declared at the time that the claim to be able to fight a prolonged nuclear war was 'fallacious and totally unrealistic' (Scheer, 1982, pp. 11, 135). Vance's viewpoint was shared by the Chairman of the JCS (CJCS), General David Jones, who, on his retirement in 1982, criticised the effort to acquire a protracted war capability as a waste of money: for General Jones there was not 'much chance of nuclear war being limited or protracted' (Arkin and Pringle, 1983, p. 176). Most importantly, according to Raymond Garthoff, Harold Brown saw the countervailing strategy as primarily designed to enhance deterrence rather than prepare the United States for war (1985, pp. 789–90) This view is supported by public statements by Brown in which he accepted that it was doubtful that a nuclear war would remain limited or last very long but maintained that US preparations to fight a protracted nuclear war would nevertheless enhance deterrence.[61]

Rosenberg's outstanding history of early nuclear operational planning in the United States supports Blair's account of events. Throughout the 1950s, while the JCS had some say over the targets and objectives of the nuclear war plan, ultimately it was SAC which dominated the drawing up of target lists and operational plans (Rosenberg, 1981/82, pp. 8–10; Rosenberg, 1983, pp. 18–19, 37; see also Kaplan, 1983, pp. 40–2, 104; Pringle and Arkin, 1983, pp. 24, 30). This situation was institutionalised in 1960 when Eisenhower gave SAC command of the JSTPS which had been newly created to draw up the first SIOP (Rosenberg, 1983, pp. 4–5). The first SIOP institutionalised SAC's operational plans, which had existed for a decade, for US nuclear forces to destroy the entire Soviet target base in a single massive pre-emptive strike (Rosenberg, 1981/82, p. 11; Rosenberg, 1983, pp. 36, 64–9).

However, it would appear that civilian policymakers became far more active in overseeing the development of the SIOP from the late 1980s onwards. Nolan argues that with the support of Defence Secretary Weinberger, OSD officials were able to force the JSTPS to co-operate in the drafting of NUWEP 97 which gave detailed guidance on targeting and operational planning to the JSTPS. Nolan maintains that this effort also resulted in the creation of new procedures for civilian oversight of the SIOP and, finally, in the inclusion of genuine LNOs in the war plan (1989, pp. 251–5, 261). Nolans account is confirmed by a 1991 GAO report which noted that OSD officials closely co-ordinated with the JSTPS and JCS in drafting the NUWEP, so as to avoid the JSTPS misinterpreting the Defence Secretary's guidance, and that the JSTPS briefed OSD officials on the target list in the SIOP before submitting the war plan for approval.[62] All this, in turn, suggests that the gap between employment policy and target lists and operational plans may have narrowed somewhat.

The conclusions of this section are fairly obvious: employment policy did not determine the SIOP during the Cold War. That is not to say, however, that all aspects of employment policy were ignored by the JSTPS. SAC did occasionally try to placate civilian policymakers by making some concessions but these did not result in changes to the broad thrust of the SIOP; thus, the 'LNOs' that were integrated in the SIOP before 1987 were not limited at all. More significantly, the JSTPS would have had few problems accommodating in the SIOP some of the targeting priorities that were identified in employment policy. The counter-recovery and counterleadership missions emphasised in

NSDM-242 and PD-59 respectively, merely involved adding more targets to the SIOP or prioritising existing targets. Adding more targets simply gave SAC added reasons to request more capabilities (Nolan, 1989, p. 117). Placing emphasis on particular categories of targets was pretty meaningless in operational terms anyway as the SIOP covered the entire target base. Moreover, it was impossible in practice to select certain types of targets for attacks without hitting others: for example, as has already been mentioned, a massive counterforce strike would have to accompany any counterleadership attack. The employment policies of the Nixon, Carter and first Reagan administrations probably led to an expansion of the Soviet target base. Given this likelihood, and the fact that SAC intended launching a massive LOW strike against the full range of targets in the SIOP in the opening shots of a nuclear war, weapons which promised improved hard target capabilities and promptness would have been welcomed by SAC planners. On the other hand, the LOW posture meant that nuclear weapons were not required to be survivable. Greater survivability in the US nuclear force structure was central to the development of a protracted warfighting capability. Yet it would seem that this mission requirement, while important to policymakers, was ignored by operational planners.

MX PEACEKEEPER

SAC was originally interested in developing MX for its superior hard target capabilities. About the same time, in 1967, the Institute for Defence Analyses released its *Strat-X Report*, which assumed that the Soviets could develop a first strike capability against the US ICBM force and, from this basis, it examined various survivable basing modes for ballistic missiles.[63] This concern for the survivability of the ICBM force was adopted by SAC and, in 1972, it announced that the two basic programme requirements for the MX were increased hard target capabilities and missile survivability.[64]

What Window of Vulnerability?

Not surprisingly, the MX programme got caught up in the wider debate on ICBM vulnerability. In the mid to late 1970s analysts, such as Paul Nitze, and a prominent hawkish pressure group on national security, called the Committee on the Present Danger, argued that, by the end of the decade, the Soviets would gain a decisive counterforce capability and therefore advantage if the United States did not respond appropriately. The Committee had been set up in 1976 to highlight what its members perceived to be the threat of Soviet strategic superiority. It preached that a 'window of vulnerability' was opening up which would enable the Soviets to make international military and political gains (Scheer, 1982; Lebow, 1984; Bundy, 1988, pp. 556–9). About the same time Nitze argued that if the Soviets were able to destroy the entire US ICBM force with just a fraction of their own ICBM force then this would give them a favourable post-exchange force ratio which would then be used to intimidate the United States into not retaliating. He argued that the threat of this scenario would enable Soviets to coerce the United States in crises (1976; 1976–7). The 'Nitze Scenario', as it became known, was deeply flawed in one sense: it was far more believable that the United states would retaliate after a Soviet first strike regardless of the force ratio. However, as Richard Betts argues, if the United States hoped to threaten or use a nuclear first strike, say, to defend Western Europe – something which the Nitze Scenario did not deal with – then projected post-exchange ratios become more significant (1987, p. 193). As it happens, in terms of the quantity and quality of their nuclear weapons the Soviets were indeed catching up with the United States but they were hardly on the verge of 'nuclear superiority' (whatever that meant). So why the hawkish hysteria?

The answer lies in the politics and confusion which enveloped the meaning of nuclear parity and superiority. Richard Betts argues that by the early 1970s US policymakers realised that they would be unable to maintain their position of nuclear superiority over the Soviet Union. The Nixon administration therefore declared in 1970 that the two superpowers had reached a stage of parity: this was known as the Doctrine of Sufficiency. However, the administration never made clear what was meant by sufficiency (or parity). Nixon gave it contradictory meanings by implying that it referred to the United States having sufficient forces to deter a Soviet attack on the US continent and, at the same time, having sufficient forces to intimidate the Soviets in future superpower crises. Betts identifies two meanings: parity in terms of the ability to inflict population damage and parity in terms of nuclear weapons. By the early 1970s the superpowers had reached parity in terms of the first definition but the United States was still superior in terms of the second one. Confusion was allowed to continue over the meaning of sufficiency because it suited the Nixon administration: it enabled them to negotiate the Strategic Arms Limitation Talks (SALT) I Treaty with the Soviets on the basis of parity while, at the same time, telling critics in Congress that the treaty did not threaten US superiority (which was essentially true). Notwithstanding these assurances to Congress, it was implied that parity referred to equal ability to inflict population damage. The relative superiority of the US nuclear arsenal was generally downplayed so that Nixon could declare that parity had arrived (Betts, 1987, pp. 182–188). Betts argues that:

> [This] oversight subsequently enabled hawkish critics to cite Soviet gains in the balance of forces during the late 1970s, which were to a large extent catching up in net technical indexes, as movement beyond the parity existing at the beginning of the decade (1987, p. 188).

Therefore, even though the Soviets were just reaching parity, hawks in Congress (such as Senator Henry Jackson and his aide, Richard Perle) took this as evidence of the Soviets reaching superiority.

The Carter administration tried to set the record straight by pointing out that Soviet nuclear forces were inferior to US ones for most of the 1970s and that the Soviets had, in fact, just caught up with the United States by the end of the decade. However, the administration did see trouble over the horizon: it was implied that the Soviets could continue on to achieve nuclear superiority. Defence Under Secretary William Perry reported to Congress that the Soviets '[h]ad in the last five years gone from a position of marked inferiority to one of essential equivalence, and they show no signs of stopping'.[65] Much of the focus of concern for defence officials were the Soviet ICBMs which were far larger than US ICBMs and therefore could carry heavier payloads. This was nothing new: the Soviets had always built larger ICBMs as they were less accurate than the US ones and so they had to drop larger warheads on their targets. What worried US analysts were intelligence reports in late 1977 which identified significant advances in Soviet missile accuracy, along with the fact that by this time the Soviets were also placing Multiple Independently Targeted Re-entry Vehicles (MIRVs) on their ICBMs (Hampson, 1989, pp. 122–3; Holland and Hoover, 1985, p. 142). Indeed Perry's testimony before the SASC in 1979 suggests that, while the DoD was not surprised by the rate of growth of Soviet MIRVs, they had been taken off guard by the speed with which the Soviets had made advances in ICBM accuracy.[66] The Soviet Union was, therefore, able to place many smaller, more accurate warheads on the same large missiles. Under such circumstances Soviet advantages in throw-weight[67] would enable them to destroy all US ICBMs using only a small fraction of their own ICBM force.[68] Initially in 1978 the DoD declared that the USSR could develop this capability by the early to mid-1980s.

However, by the following year, new assessments on Soviet ICBM accuracy led the DoD to suggest that this threat would emerge sooner than later.[69]

Table 2.2. *Composition of US and Soviet Nuclear Forces in 1980*

| | Delivery vehicles | | Total warheads | | Throw weight | |
	US (%)	USSR (%)	US (%)	USSR (%)	US (%)	USSR (%)
ICBMs	51	56	24	75	33	70
SLBMs	32	36	50	20	25	15
Bombers	17	6	26	5	42	15

Source: Brown, *Annual Report, FY81*, p. 89.

But what did this mean for the US nuclear force structure *as a whole*. Table 2.2 shows the composition of both US and Soviet nuclear arsenals in 1980. The US would have lost just over half of their delivery vehicles had the Soviets destroyed the US ICBM leg but this represented only one-quarter of all the warheads and one-third of the total throw weight of the US nuclear triad. That still left a lot of nuclear megatonnage to throw back at the Soviets in retaliation. Therefore, '[f]or the window of vulnerability argument to work, its proponents must simply ignore America's submarines and bombers' (Scheer, 1982, p. 71). Indeed Defence Secretary Brown concluded in his 1980 report to Congress that:

> the hypothetical ability of the Soviets to destroy over 90 percent of our ICBM force cannot be equated with any of the following: a disarming first strike, a Soviet advantage that could be meaningful in an all-out nuclear exchange; a significant contribution to a damage-limiting objective; or an increased probability of a Soviet surprise attack.[70]

In short, Brown had little difficulty dismissing the Nitze Scenario.

Why Worry about ICBM Vulnerability?

So what was all the fuss about? Brown gave two reasons for why the United States should nevertheless be worried about the vulnerability of its ICBMs which again had to do with the perception and the reality of US military capabilities. The first reason was that the US could not afford to let the Soviets 'have a monopoly of any major military capability' if it wanted to maintain the perception of a balance of power

between the superpowers. Maintaining 'essential equivalence' was identified by Brown as the next most important role for the US nuclear
triad after deterrence. Brown argued that 'We need forces of such a
size and character that every nation perceives that the United States
cannot be coerced or intimidated by Soviet forces.'[71] This was already
a commonly held belief; indeed, it was the United States and not the
Soviet Union which had in the past manipulated the threat of nuclear
usage for the purpose of intimidation.[72] What Brown may have meant
was that the United States needed to be able to continue trying to
coerce the Soviet Union in a crisis. This was less likely to be the case if
the projected post-exchange ratio favoured the Soviet Union and, as
such, it may have caused problems for US extended deterrence. Brown
did not discuss this, however.[73]

The second concern had to do with the maintenance of deterrence.
Brown argued that the US could 'live temporarily with the vulnerability
of one TRIAD leg, so long as the other two were in working order'. He
maintained, however, that the US would be 'ill-advised to accept that
vulnerability as a permanent condition', as the other two legs of the
triad could themselves become vulnerable in the future.[74] Therefore, as
Defence Secretary Brown declared before a Senate hearing in 1980,
'[w]e are going ahead with the development and deployment of the
MX system, so as to make the land-based component of the triad survivable'.[75] However, in a speech to the Naval War College in August
of the same year, Brown admitted that the only Soviet threat to the
US strategic nuclear submarine (SSBN) force was a 'hypothetical' one
(Scoville, 1981, p. 74). Indeed, as one comprehensive study argued two
years later, it was extremely unlikely that the Soviets could even have
hoped to develop the capability to threaten the US SSBN force (Garwin, 1983). Furthermore, as will be discussed in later in this chapter, the
United States was also engaged in a strategic bomber modernisation
programme that was designed to ensure the post-launch survivability[76]
of the air-based leg of the triad. In his Annual Report for Fiscal Year
1982, Brown expressed particular confidence in advances in air-
launched cruise missile (ALCM) and stealth technology which promised to enhance the potential of the bomber leg.[77]

Bigger Is Not Always Better

Greater importance was placed on MX survivability as a result of PD-
59 and NSDD-13. Not only was this programme requirement perceived
to be needed to meet an established policy objective, namely maintain-

ing an effective triad of nuclear forces, it was also perceived to be needed to meet the new objective of being able to fight a protracted nuclear war. There were four options for making the MX more survivable than its predecessors: concealment, mobility, hardening, and defence (Toomay, 1987, p. 196). Submarine-launched ballistic missiles (SLBMs) are secured from attacks by concealment below the oceans. Strategic bombers rely on mobility to get into the skies before they are attacked. Minuteman silos were hardened to decrease (although not by much) their vulnerability, and for a while part of the ICBM force was protected by the Safeguard anti-ballistic missile (ABM) system. At the same time the Carter and Reagan nuclear employment policies demanded improved capabilities from the MX. It had to be more accurate and carry more warheads than its predecessor in order to provide a greater hard target capability.

The MX was also designed to meet a third programme characteristic: it had to be big. Specifically, the MX had to be the largest ICBM allowable under the SALT II Treaty.[78] The new Soviet missiles, the SS-18 and SS-19, were expected to be even bigger than the old ICBMs they were replacing. It was estimated that the SS-18 would be able to carry 8 to 10 'high-yield' (i.e. large) MIRVs and the SS-19 up to 6. According to Congressional Budget Office (CBO) calculations in 1978, '[u]nder the likely SALT II ceilings, the Soviet Union could deploy 308 SS-18 missiles [which amounted to 3,080 warheads]; only 250 would be required to target two warheads on each of the 1,000 Minuteman silos'.[79] In addition, under the SALT II Treaty, the Soviets were allowed 512 SS-19s and SS-17s which could deliver 3,072 warheads, and 380 single-warhead ICBMs (Scoville, 1981, p. 98). The SALT II Treaty limited each side to 820 MIRVed ICBMs (the United States had 550 MIRVed ICBMs at the time), and placed a upper limit on the size of ICBMs. The Treaty also limited each side to 2,400 delivery systems (includes ICBMs, SLBMs, bombers and cruise missiles) in total (George, 1990, p. 90). Under these circumstances, it was argued that the US should build the largest MIRVed ICBM allowable, as this would maximise the amount of warheads in the US inventory (Chayes, 1987, p. 156).

This third characteristic is also related to the previous one in that, as has been suggested, the potential yield and number of MIRVed warheads may be related to the size of the ICBM. Larger ICBMs can have greater hard target capabilities than smaller ones with the same accuracy. A large new ICBM would also neutralise the Soviets' theoretical advantage in exchange ratios. These three characteristics can be inconsistent with each other. The larger the missile, the more difficult it is to hide and/or move. In this sense, the programme characteristics that are designed to take account of arms control constraints, and to support the new hard target counterforce mission requirement, could impede the development of those that were desirable for the established requirement of survivability.

Saturating the Target Base

The Air Force and the DoD also originally wanted a new MIRVed ICBM in order to be able to cover more Soviet targets, and in particular, hard targets. Each of the guidances signed by Schlesinger in 1974, Brown in 1980, and Weinberger in 1982, led to more targets being added to the National Strategic Target Data Base (NSTDB). Under Schlesinger, SIOP-5 was given greater target flexibility and concentrated on retarding the Soviet Union's ability to recover from a nuclear war. Browns guidance led to SIOP-5F de-emphasising counter-recovery targeting, although this target set was still retained, to the war plan covering more Soviet leadership and military targets. Counter-recovery targeting was dropped altogether from SIOP-6 under Weinberger, although the NSTDB was still expanded to cover a greater range of military, political and economic targets. As a result of these developments the number of targets in the NSTDB increased from 4,100 in 1960, to 25,000 in 1974, to 40,000 in 1980, and finally to 50,000 in 1982 (Ball and Toth, 1990, pp. 67–71; Ball, 1986b, pp. 80–1; Ball, 1982–3, p. 36; Richelson, 1986, p. 129).

Schlesinger was particularly keen on acquiring new weapons, especially the MX, which he believed were needed to implement the new demanding nuclear employment policy (Holland and Hoover, 1985, p. 132). DoD studies conducted in the mid-1970s on counter- recovery targeting revealed a major shortfall in the capabilities of US nuclear forces (Sagan, 1989, p. 46). This gap between the number of targets in the SIOP, and the ability of SAC to cover them, grew throughout the 1970s and into the 1980s. According to Scott Sagan, this situation encouraged both the Carter and Reagan administrations to accelerate the MX and Trident D-5 programmes (1989, p. 52). Indeed, the Commander-in-Chief of SAC (CINCSAC), General Richard Ellis, informed Brown that SAC would be unable to implement PD-59 until 1986, by which time 'sufficient numbers of ALCM, Trident and MX missiles' would have been acquired (Richelson, 1986, p. 132). The Reagan administration's commitment to closing this gap was indicated by the adoption of a Nuclear Weapons Employment and Acquisition Master Plan in 1982 (Ball, 1982–3, p. 59; Sloss and Millot, 1984, p. 26; Ball and Toth, 1990, pp. 86–7). Whether this plan was primarily designed to rationalise nuclear force planning or to provide convenient rationales for individual weapon programmes is not clear, but what is clear is the Reagan administration's failure to acquire enough deliverable warheads to cover the full target base (Arkin *et al.*, 1984).

Given the amount of overkill built into the SIOP, this gap was arguably unimportant. Viewed retrospectively, in light of the two major culls of the NSTDB conducted by the JSTPS in the 1980s, it was clearly unimportant. According to the Air Force Chief of Staff, General Larry Welch, 'literally thousands of targets [had] been dropped from the SIOP' when the counter-recovery mission was abandoned in 1982 (Sagan, 1989, p. 53). Desmond Ball and Robert Toth cite defence officials as saying that this mission had badly distorted the SIOP: nuclear weapons were wasted on targeting marginal industrial facilities, some major facilities had three nuclear weapons targeted on them when two would have done, and it proved impossible to calculate if this mission could have been successfully carried out (1990, pp. 70–1). Thousands of minor military targets were also dumped after Weinberger issued a new guidance in 1987, reducing the NSTDB from 50,000 to 14,000 targets (Ball and Toth, 1990, p. 72). So while some defence officials and Air Force officers, especially in the JSTPS, may have wanted a new MIRVed ICBM to cover the expansive target base, this requirement was driven by their bias towards overkill in the SIOP.

Increased Capability Before Survivability

As far as SAC and Schlesinger were concerned, the MX was required for its hard target capability. This clearly appears to have also been the case under the Ford administration when the programme requirements were established. Writing in 1987, ten years after he retired as CINC-SAC, General Russell Dougherty made the following observation:

> In the mid-1970s when the need for [the MX] was first established . . . the requirement was driven by strategic needs, modified by fiscal and development realities . . . Mobility and survivability were not then considered as driving needs, and the initial designs had the new, large MX going into fixed silos at Grand Forks (p. 156).

According to the former Under Secretary of the Air Force under the Carter administration, Antonia Chayes, the Ford administration made a 'hasty choice for capability over survivability'. She argues that 'the lack of a solution to a survivable basing mode led to a recommendation for silo basing in order to get the new missile into full-scale engineering development' (1987, p. 155). It would seem, therefore, that right from the early programme stages the MX missile design and basing mode were treated almost as two separate problems. The Air Force wanted a new highly accurate high yield MIRVed ICBM to be developed and deployed as soon as possible. The basing mode problem was not allowed to hold up the missile development programme.

Chayes claims that it was not until the late 1970s that 'the search for a survivable basing mode began in earnest'.[80] Certainly by this stage it was generally recognised that, as the GAO put it to Congress in 1981, '[t]he driving need for the MX is increased survivability'.[81] The MX development programme was delayed for two years under Carter while the new administration tried to come to grips with the basing problem, but there were also arms control and budget considerations which encouraged Carter to hold up the MX programme. Eventually Carter did authorise the Air Force to proceed with full-scale engineering development of the MX in June 1979, but *three months* before he announced a mobile basing mode.[82]

Why did the President finally change his mind? By 1978 pressure was building from his advisors to develop the MX for strategic reasons. As has been noted, the DoD became alarmed with the growth rate of Soviet MIRVs and improvements in missile accuracy. The National Security Council (NSC) staff which, in 1977, was against MX on the grounds that it would hinder arms control, was by 1978 in favour of developing the missile in case the United States failed to negotiate MIRV limits with the Soviets in the SALT II talks. However, there were also presidential political reasons for Carter's about-turn on this issue, namely, he was also under domestic political pressure to build MX. He was due to sign SALT II with the Soviet Union in Vienna in July 1979, and was very keen to placate conservative critics in the Senate and the military who had indicated that they would not support the Treaty unless the MX was acquired (Hampson, 1989, pp. 122, 124, 127). These presidential political considerations will be discussed in more detail in Chapter 3.

The mobile basing plan which Carter had endorsed for MX, called Multiple Point System (MPS) was rejected by the incoming Reagan administration on technical and political grounds. As will be discussed in the next chapter, it was hugely complex, expensive and unpopular in the states in which it was to be based. However, Reagan's Strategic Modernisation Programme appeared to ignore the vulnerability problem by recommending that the MX be placed in existing silos. The MX missile programme was only delayed because Congress refused to fund it until a survivable basing mode had been found. Reagan's solution in 1983 was to adopt the recommendations of the Scrowcroft Commission report which argued that the vulnerability of ICBMs was not so significant after all, as the Soviets still had to contend against the other two more survivable legs of the US nuclear triad.[83] The same point was repeated in 1985 by the CJCS, General John Vessey, in a statement to the Senate Defence Appropriations Subcommittee (SDAS).[84] Congress did eventually agree to fund MX in 1983 but only after Reagan had promised to implement two of the Commission's recommendations, namely, to negotiate an arms reduction treaty with the Soviets and to acquire a small mobile ICBM.[85] Finding a survivable basing mode for the MX became even more important for Congress in mid-1985 as legislators were concerned that the administration was already reneging on its promise to implement the Scowcroft Commission recommendations.[86] After what appears to have been much reluctant effort, the DoD finally did come up with the Rail Garrison concept in late 1986 which Congress accepted.[87]

As with Ford and Carter, the Reagan administration appears to have treated the MX missile programme separately from the basing programme. But for Congress, the administration would have been content to acquire 200 MXs and place them in existing silos while it figured out how to make them more survivable.

Providing Redundant Capabilities

This apparent disregard for the survivability requirement does not by itself indicate that these three administrations and the Air Force were not motivated by strategic issues to support the MX. There were also the other new requirements for prompt and hard target counterforce capabilities which the MX was supposed to meet.[88] It is worth asking though, did the Air Force need a new ICBM to meet these mission requirements? Table 2.3 outlines the US ICBM force structure which existed in 1980. Two changes occurred in the 1980s; namely, all the Titans were decommissioned in a five-year retirement programme from late 1982 to early 1988 and 50 MXs were deployed between 1986 and 1988. Since all existing ICBMs could already retaliate promptly, the Air Force did not need a new ICBM for this capability. But most of the existing ICBMs lacked the necessary combination of accuracy and high warhead yield to destroy hard and very hard targets, such as Soviet

ICBMs and leadership bunkers. The Titans were too inaccurate, and the warheads carried on the Minutemen were too small.

Table 2.3. ICBM Force Structure (1980s)

Missile	Number	Deployed	Warheads
Titan	54	1963	Single
Minuteman II	450	1965	Single
Minuteman III	550	1970	Three (MIRV)
MX	50	1988	Ten (MIRV)

* All Titans were decommissioned between 1982 and 1988

Source: GAO Report, *Countervailing Strategy Demands Revision of Strategic Force Acquisition Plans*, p. 28; GAO Report, *ICBM Modernization; Availability Problems*, p. 2; Arkin *et al*, 1984, p. 7.

However, in 1979 the Air Force began deploying a new re-entry vehicle (MK12A) with a larger warhead (W78) on 300 of the Minutemen III. The W62 warhead carried by the other 250 Minutemen III had a yield of 170 kilotons compared with 335 kilotons for the W78 (Arkin *et al.*, 1984, p. 6). Furthermore, some improvements were made to the guidance software of Minutemen III.[89] The MX promised to be even more accurate. It could also, in theory, carry the same 1.2 megaton W56 warhead as the Minuteman II, thus giving it an overall greater hard target capability than even the improved Minuteman III (Brown, 1990, p. 134). However, the MX was expected to carry the same warheads, or ones of a similar yield, as that carried by the Minuteman III. The MX was configured to carry the W78. The new warhead (W87) that was being designed especially for the MX was only expected to have a baseline yield of 300 kilotons, which could be upgraded to 475 kilotons (Arkin *et al.*, 1984, p. 7). It would appear, therefore, that in the early 1980s there was not the requirement to be able to deliver a very large warhead very accurately on target. So it is arguable that the improved Minutemen III could meet *both* new mission requirements. Indeed, this is precisely what Brown argued in 1980 when he stated in his report to Congress that 'because of accuracy and yield improvements, the Minuteman III will by the mid-1980s give us a considerable counter-silo potential, even without MX [and that] the unique feature of MX is that it provides this capability in a survivable basing mode'.[90] It is true that Minuteman III could not have made up for the shortfall in SAC's ability to cover the target base but, as has been argued, this did not provide a sufficient rationale for the acquisition of a new large ICBM.

MX Was Booked on the 'Midnight Express'

Congress's obsession with MX survivability, and the Air Force's nonchalance about it, is easily explained. Legislators didn't know that SAC had adopted a LOW posture, its 'midnight express'. As noted previously, planners in SAC thought that the idea of retaliation after absorbing a Soviet nuclear strike was wholly unrealistic as it would leave the US nuclear force structure in no shape to execute the SIOP; hence the 'midnight express'. For SAC, MX survivability would have been ensured by simply launching the missiles before they were hit by a Soviet first strike. While Air Force and administration officials admitted that the capability existed to carry out such an option, they denied that LOW had been adopted as the basic US nuclear force posture; they lent the impression instead that the intention was to ride out a Soviet attack and then retaliate.[91] Understandably, since Congress did not know about the 'midnight express', legislators could not see the point of deploying a large MIRVed ICBM that would be vulnerable to a Soviet first strike (Blair, 1993, p. 177). For some military planners, MX vulnerability was even desirable in that it reinforced the logic of LOW; the President would be faced with no choice but to launch the MXs before they were hit, and this would be evident to the Soviets (Nolan, 1989, p. 276).

The existence of the midnight express, while horrifying in terms of its implications for accidental nuclear war, still provides no clues as to the military requirement for the MX. If the MX was going to be launched on warning of a Soviet attack then there was no need for it to be survivable. If it was not, but rather held in reserve to fight a protracted war and maybe for counterleadership targets, then it did have to be survivable. The genuine need for survivability is questionable in that, as has been argued, PD-59 was designed to enhance deterrence rather than change the SIOP. At the same time, however, survivability was the only genuine military requirement for the MX; Defence Secretary Brown admitted as much. Existing weapons in the US nuclear force structure could already cover the full range of targets in the SIOP. SAC did not have enough weapons to cover the full number of targets, but the target base was unnecessarily massive anyway. A LOW posture would not have necessarily added to or reduced the target base nor would it have increased the number of hard targets: since the 'midnight express' was to be a counterstrike in response to a Soviet attack, and not a US first strike, it would have been aimed at the same target base as would have been the case under a retaliatory strike.

Demonstrating Resolve and Encouraging Arms Control

It can be argued that despite the fact that a largely redundant set of military requirements drove the MX programme, strategic considerations still explain why the MX was acquired. As has been discussed, the strategic ends the new ICBM was meant to serve were not simply military ones, they were also international political ones. On different occasions the MX was seen as an important symbol of national resolve and as a bargaining chip in strategic arms talks with the Soviets.

As was argued earlier, the MX was sought to help redress a growing perception of a nuclear power imbalance between the Soviets and the United States. It was felt that Soviet advances in warhead numbers and missile accuracy would translate into a common international perception of US strategic inferiority, leading to Soviet over-confidence and aggression, and making US allies restless and nervous. Brown did not fear that the Soviets would actually gain any real military advantage. Brown's two immediate predecessors, Donald Rumsfield and Schlesinger, both also expressed greater concern with maintaining Soviet and allied perceptions of a superpower balance of power than with a real advantage the Soviets may gain by modernising their ICBMs. According to Steven Kull, it was Schlesinger who 'enshrined' this overriding concern with the perception of essential equivalence 'as official US policy' in his FY 1975 and FY 1976 reports to Congress (1989, pp. 121-3).

Weinberger was also, to a lesser extent, concerned with maintaining the perception of a balance of power in the eyes of the allies as well as Soviets.[92] He even declared that, 'in some sense, the political advantages of being seen as the superior strategic power are more real and more usable than the military advantages of in fact being superior in one measure or another' (Jervis, 1989, p. 197). Indeed, demonstrating national resolve was one of the main reasons given in the Scrowcroft Commission Report, which was adopted by the Reagan administration, to justify deployment of the MX.[93] This was also the Air Force's position in 1983.[94] In March 1985 the President and his officials again drew the attention of members of Congress to the symbolic importance of MX.[95]

MX was also, on occasion, touted as a possible bargaining chip. Indeed, in testimony before the Senate Foreign Relations Committee (SFRC) on behalf of the Scowcroft Commission, Schlesinger claimed that this was the MX's original purpose.[96] This may have been the OSD's position, but it is doubtful that the Air Force were solely, mainly, or at all interested in acquiring a new ICBM for this reason. It most certainly was not the case under subsequent administrations, when the bargaining chip rationale was used by opponents and proponents of the MX to justify their own agenda, an agenda that was more concerned about the outcome of the MX programme than advancing arms control.

The Carter administration came into office hoping to kill the MX programme, but it still wanted to get something in return. Hence Carter sent Vance off to Moscow in March 1977 with a bold offer to trade the MX for deep cuts in Soviet heavy ICBMs (Holland and Hoover, 1985, p. 88). A month later Carter made some noises about accelerating the MX programme following the Soviet rejection, but he then turned down a subsequent request by the DoD to move the missile into full-scale development (Hampson, 1989, pp. 121–2).

The Reagan administration originally declared its intention to reverse the position of strategic 'inferiority' by engaging in a major strategic modernisation programme and not through arms talks with the Soviets (which it considered to be pointless). So MX was not to be negotiated away. However, in an about-turn in 1983 the administration presented the missile as a crucial bargaining chip in the Strategic Arms Reduction Talks (START) in order to prevent Congress from killing the programme. In a SFRC hearing into his Commission, General Brent Scrowcroft argued that the 'MX was essential in order to induce the Soviets towards negotiations which would permit us and encourage them to move in the direction of stability'.[97] So the MX was being presented as something which would eventually encourage stability in the strategic force postures of the two superpowers. Two years later when the MX was once again in trouble on Capitol Hill, the Reagan administration urged Congress not to 'undercut' the US bargaining position at the START talks (which were due to resume a week later) by cancelling MX.[98]

The bargaining chip rationale for the MX is not convincing. Carter tried to use the MX as a bargaining chip because he wanted to get rid of it in the first place. Reagan used the bargaining chip idea just to win over Congress which was sceptical about the military utility of the weapon. It is very doubtful that Reagan, or his advisors, actually believed that the MX should be negotiated away.[99] Certainly this was how the Soviets saw it at the time.[100] Indeed, on 26 February 1985, just one week before Reagan's appeal for congressional support for the

MX, Shultz clearly told the SASC that MX was not a 'bargaining chip'.[101] So the bargaining chip argument was used as an excuse by both the Carter and Reagan administrations: neither saw it as a genuine strategic rationale.

An Important Symbol

The MX was supposed to meet two basic programme requirements: to enhance the survivability of the ICBM force and to provide increased hard target capabilities. These two requirements should have been treated as integral, but they were not. Successive administrations treated the missile and basing mode as two separate programmes, and did not allow problems with the latter programme to hold up the former. As a result, the MX programme was in fact driven by the increased capabilities requirement. Hard target capabilities were needed for the counterforce and counterleadership missions, prioritised under the Carter and Reagan nuclear employment policies, but a *new* ICBM was not required to fulfil these mission requirements. SAC wanted the MX for its warheads, in order to be able to cover more targets in the SIOP: indeed General Vessey reportedly exclaimed, 'We need those warheads on the MX so bad, I'd put them in the Pentagon parking lot' (Nolan, 1989, p. 275). But, as subsequent culls to the target base showed, there was far too much overkill in the war plan: SAC could have done with far fewer targets and warheads.

The requirement of survivability is equally questionable. What was the point of spending billions of dollars on placing the MX in a survivable basing mode if SAC intended on launching the MX on warning of a Soviet attack? In any case, the Air Force and successive administrations clearly did not treat survivability as a genuine mission requirement. It was not treated as such when the MX programme requirements were being established under Ford, nor when the programme proceeded into full-scale engineering development under Carter. Likewise, the Reagan administration proved in its numerous attempts to get Congress to fund production of the missile, that they were not too bothered how or where they based it. It was a perplexed Congress – perplexed because they did not know about the 'midnight express' – which forced the administration to find a survivable basing mode.

The bargaining chip rationale for the MX was not a strong one either, but the symbolic importance of MX is convincing. The Ford, Carter and Reagan administrations were all concerned with maintaining the perception of US power. The MX was genuinely considered by these administrations to be an important symbol of US resolve and military power. Hence, it would seem that strategic issues do go some way to explaining why the MX was acquired.

B-2 STEALTH BOMBER

The B-2 was designed to fulfil the Air Force's requirement for a strategic *penetrating* bomber for the next century. From the mid-1980s through to the 1990s this role has been carried out primarily by B-1Bs and some B-52Hs.[102] The Air Force planned to retain B-52Hs in the strategic force structure well past the 1990s, but as stand-off cruise missile carriers. The B-2 is intended to take over from the B-1B as the Air Force's primary penetrating bomber, allowing B-1Bs to be assigned less well defended targets.

Did SAC Need a New Bomber?

The then Secretary of the Air Force, Donald Rice, declared in 1990 that 'penetrating bombers are the most potent triad system because they provide the best combination of accuracy and weapon yield compared to any current and projected system' (p. 108). This assertion raised an obvious question: even if it is essential to have a penetrating bomber, is it necessary to build a new one for the 1990s? The Air Force testified before Congress in 1981 that the B-1B would be 'an effective strategic system for 25–40 years'. By 1986 (the same year the first B-1Bs became operational) the JCS were maintaining that the B-1B should have been able to penetrate Soviet air defences 'well into the 1990s'.[103] These statements do not necessarily conflict, as in 1981 the Air Force may have also been referring to the B-1B's role as a cruise-missile carrier.

Michael Brown argues that the 'best kept secret in the Air Force is that the B-1B has shaped up to be a very impressive strategic system' (1990, p. 131). This viewpoint was expressed in 1988 by Rice's predecessor, Edward Aldridge, Jr, who declared that 'one of the most popular myths [was] that the B-1 is a lemon'. Aldrigde went on to argue that the B-1B broke '13 records for speed, payload and distance in 1987'.[104]

However, there were confirmed reports of serious problems with the B-1B, which led the Air Force to withhold payments of $250–300 million to the manufacturers. The first squadron of B-1Bs had been declared operational on 1 October 1986, but as the Air Force freely admitted at the time, the B-1B bombers still suffered from persistent problems with fuel leaks, flight controls, defensive and offensive avionics, and from being overweight. These design flaws reduced the B-1B's range, cut its payload of cruise missiles, and forced it to fly at higher altitudes than it was supposed to, not to mention leaving it vulnerable to attack by Soviet fighters.[105] This led the HASC and SASC to hold hearings into the B-1B in early 1987, and this in turn led Congress to direct the Defence Secretary to submit a plan for testing the bomber's faulty defensive avionics (or electronic counter measures [ECM]) and to provide an independent assessment of the B-1B's ability to penetrate Soviet air defences. The Air Force identified over a dozen possible improvements to the B-1B, some of which had been carried out by 1988. If all these improvements are made to the B-1B, they will add up to 25 per cent of the original (baseline) cost of the plane, or $7.4 billion (Brown, 1989, p. 36). General John Chain, then CINCSAC, declared in 1987 that the fuel leaks and faulty flight controls had been fixed and were never serious problems anyway.[106] The GAO confirmed in 1989 that progress had been made in correcting some of the plane's deficiencies, but not its defensive avionics.[107] A GAO analyst testified before a House subcommittee hearing in March 1991 that these technical problems would cost $1 billion and take ten years to rectify.[108] Even then B-1B's deficient ECM system would be less effective that originally planned, but this was considered not so worrying after all as the Soviet air defences had not developed as well as expected either.[109]

However in mid-1991 Secretary Rice distributed a letter to Senators informing them that cracks had been found in the skeletons of several B-1Bs. The timing of this statement raises questions about its accuracy: it was released shortly before the Senate was due to vote on whether to authorise the purchase of four additional B-2 bombers.[110] Even if the B-1B problems were ironed out, and its life-span as a penetrating bomber was extended by equipping it with more effective defensive avionics, this would still have left SAC without a penetrating bomber beyond the early 2000s.

Not only was it necessary to assess the performance of the previous bomber in order to determine if there was a requirement for a new one, but it is also necessary to assess the other options which existed for threatening Soviet strategic assets. It could easily be argued that developments in other new weapon programmes undermined the supposed unique attributes of the B-2. If it is acquired, the next generation of cruise missile, the advanced cruise missile (ACM), will be stealthier than the B-2. The present generation of cruise missile has only 10 per cent the radar cross-section (RCS) (i.e. the amount of energy an air vehicle reflects back to the radar) of a B-1B, or twice that of a B-2. The cruise missile's terrain-hugging flight pattern makes it extremely difficult for air-defence radars to acquire it. The ACM will be even more difficult to detect. One estimate predicts that it will have half the RCS of a B-2 (Lepingwell, 1989, pp. 84–6). Although highly critical of the Air Force's acquisition strategy and cost estimates for the ACM programme, a recent GAO report nevertheless concluded that: 'Flight testing completed through May 1990 indicated that the ACM can meet most of its operational performance requirements, including range and accuracy.'[111] Furthermore, the Trident D-5 SLBM will be better able than the B-2 to survive a surprise nuclear attack and have the accuracy to disable hard targets (Wit, 1982, p. 168; Slocombe, 1985; Cote, 1991; Spinardi, 1994, p. 151).

Very Hard and Mobile Targets

The Air Force did not justify acquiring the B-2 simply on the grounds that it would increase SAC's chances of defeating Soviet air defences. The new penetrating bomber was to be assigned two types of targets that cruise missiles, ICBMs and SLBMs are ineffective against; namely 'very hard targets' (VHTs), and mobile or relocatable targets (RTs). VHTs and RTs had gained a far higher targeting priority as a result of reforms conducted to SIOP-6 between 1982 and 1987. The nuclear weapons employment guidance issued by Secretary Weinberger in 1987 led to two key developments: a 'prompt counter-C3' (typically VHTs and some mobile targets) capability being incorporated in the SIOP and a DoD-wide master plan designed to target Soviet mobile targets (Ball and Toth, 1990, pp. 69–78).

The number of Soviet mobile targets swelled in the late 1980s, in particular mobile ICBMs and C3 facilities. According to the DoD, the Soviet Union had deployed approximately 100 road-mobile single warhead SS-25s by 1987, and was beginning deployment of its new rail-mobile ten-warhead SS-24s the same year.[112] These two types of missiles were expected to form more than half the Soviet ICBM force by the mid-1990s.[113] Air Force estimates predicted that half of *all* Soviet strategic targets, and two-thirds of the Soviet ICBM force, would be mobile by the turn of the century (Ball and Toth, 1990, p. 77).

The Air Force maintained between 1986 and 1988 that the B-2 would be ideally suited to the task of locating and destroying mobile targets.

The B-1B had been considered for the job in 1985–6, but the Air Force determined that the B-2 would be far better able to locate Soviet RTs. Certainly, no other US strategic weapon was capable of doing this at the time (Ball and Toth, 1990, p. 80). However, as the Air Force was to admit in late 1988, neither was the B-2 (Brown, 1989, p. 14). It therefore downplayed this mission for the B-2 until mid-1989, when Air Force Chief of Staff, General Larry Welch, declared that the B-2 still offered the best chance of successfully targeting Soviet RTs (Ball and Toth, 1990, pp. 80–1). Furthermore, in March 1990 the CINCSAC, General John Chain, testified before the HASC that destroying mobile targets was a primary mission of the B-2 (Brown, 1990, p. 133). However, neither Welch nor Chain indicated any major technological breakthrough in the B-2's on-board sensors when they reasserted that the bomber would be used against mobile targets. In fact, the B-2 lacked the very FLIR and radar sensors which were needed for locating and identifying RTs (Ball and Toth, 1990, p. 89). Furthermore, there was considerable confusion over a programme which was supposed to put a new satellite in space to help the B-2 spot mobile targets.[114]

VHTs include deeply buried command and control centres and submarine facilities. General Welch declared in 1988 that the B-2's main mission would be to bomb very important VHTs (Brown, 1989, p. 14). According to Air Force officials, the ALCM-Bs, MXs and Trident D-5s lack the combination of warhead accuracy and yield necessary to ensure destruction of these targets. Warhead yield refers to the explosive power of the nuclear warhead. The Air Force estimates that B-2s are about twice as effective at knocking out VHTs as the other systems above (Rice, 1990, p. 106). Critics have attacked this assertion on three accounts. Firstly, the Air Force calculations do not distinguish between short range attack missiles (SRAMs) and gravity bombs, even though the B-2 is designed to carry both. SRAMs are designed to be launched at a target from a safe distance, but they only have a warhead yield of 170 kilotons (less powerful than that of a cruise missile), compared to 1–2 megatons for the standard B83 gravity bombs. Since VHTs are bound to be heavily defended, an attacking B-2 may have chosen to use SRAMs even though B83 bombs would have a greater chance of destroying the target. Secondly, some MX and D-5 missiles can be equipped to deliver large warheads with a yield comparable to B83 gravity bombs carried by the B-2. The MX and D-5 can be equipped with four and three 1.1 megaton W56 warheads respectively, instead of ten and eight 300–475 kiloton W87 warheads respectively. Finally, there were in fact only a small number of Soviet VHTs which would have required such high-yield weapons to be targeted against them (Arkin *et al.*, 1984, pp. 6–7; Brown, 1990, p. 134).

Although some VHTs are being covered by MXs and D-5s, official dissatisfaction with the accuracy/yield combination of the warheads carried by these missiles led to Defence Secretary Frank Carlucci authorising a earth-penetrating warhead programme. A rigid penetrating warhead designed to be carried by the next generation of manoeuvrable re-entry vehicles (MARVs) was under development and was due to be deployed on MXs and D-5s by the mid-1990s (about the same time as the first ten B-2s were to have been delivered to the Air Force). Research was also being conducted into transforming the B83 bomb into a shallow penetrating warhead. A 'rigid' earth-penetrating warhead is a hardened device designed to burrow hundreds of feet into the ground using the force of its impact. A 'shallow' earth-penetrator only breaks the surface by a few feet before detonating. As an interim solution 20-year-old B53 bombs were also reactivated. These 9 megaton warheads would have been delivered by penetrating bombers (Ball and Toth, 1990, pp. 75–7).

It was considered technically possible then, by the late 1980s, to successfully destroy most VHTs by either using regular MX and D-5 warheads, or higher yield missile warheads and B83 gravity bombs. However, some VHTs were not believed to be held at risk by these weapons, and these targets were considered important enough to warrant an earth-penetrating warhead programme. In the short term, the role of penetrating bombers was seen as vital in that they were assigned to deliver those weapons (B83 and B53 gravity bombs) that most threatened important VHTs. In the longer term, it could have been argued, penetrating bombers would become far less important to the United States' ability to threaten Soviet VHTs as the next generation of MX and D-5 missiles would be equipped with earth-penetrating warheads.

Finding New States to Bomb

Clearly the B-2 was originally designed to be a strategic nuclear bomber. In particular, the Air Force argued that it was needed to maintain a crucial mission requirement, that is, to penetrate a modernising Soviet air defence system and bomb well-protected and elusive targets. The failed coup by hard-liners in the Soviet Union in August 1991, and the subsequent break-up of the Soviet Union, has undermined any rationale for a new strategic nuclear bomber. Russia does not represent a direct military threat to US security. Nor for that matter do any of the other three nuclear armed republics: Ukraine, Byelarus and Kazakhstan. The United States finally declared this to be case in mid-1992. The Secretary of Defence did argue in February 1992 in his Annual Report to Congress that these republics still possessed a 'robust strategic nuclear force' and could still 'revert to closed, authorized, and hostile regimes'.[115] This perspective was backed up by drafts of the DoD's Defence Planning Guidance leaked to the press in early 1992 which indicated that the Pentagon still considered some republics of the former Soviet Union to present a military threat to US security.[116] However, the White House and State Department immediately released statements admonishing the Pentagon's position · and rejecting these documents as not representative of administration policy.[117] A new document was quickly released by the DoD which stressed co-operation and not conflict with these new republics.[118]

The main security concern for the United States is to ensure that Russia maintains control over its shrinking stockpile of nuclear weapons and to encourage the de-nuclearisation of the other republics. It is difficult to see how military force could help the United States achieve these aims. It is through diplomacy, and maybe economic incentives, that the United States will have to concentrate its efforts (Miller, 1992). Even if the United States needed to bomb Russia, it is doubtful that it now needs a new bomber to penetrate what will for some time be a demoralised, disorganised and under-funded air defence force.

Even before the August coup the Air Force was beginning to change its tune on the B-2 and stressing its potential as a conventional bomber. Indeed, in one of his earliest references to the stealth bomber, Secretary Brown noted in his Annual Report for Fiscal Year 1982 that it 'must be considered not only in the role of strategic penetrator, but also in the broader context of world-wide force projection and cruise missile carrier missions'.[119] But the Air Force was not interested in either of these latter two roles for its new stealth bomber, hence its officials were originally quite happy to point out that the B-2 was not designed to be used as a conventional bomber or a cruise missile carrier. In 1990 General Chain, CINCSAC, testified before the HASC that 'because of the value of [the B-2] I can't see putting very many at risk in a conventional conflict' (Brown, 1990, p. 136). This point was also made (more crudely) by Jeffrey Record, a senior fellow at the conservative Institute for Foreign Policy Analysis, in 1986. Noting that the United States 'may have rather large nonnuclear bombing requirements in the future', Record argued that nevertheless 'you're not going to use a $500 million aircraft to bomb some wogs in Iran'.[120] Interestingly, Air Force Secretary Rice disagreed with this argument at the time. Rice argued that the United states had flown 'advanced technology SR-71 reconnaissance aircraft for several decades into "harm's way" '. However, Rice was unable to argue persuasively that the B-2 was needed as a conventional bomber: he maintained that it would enable US leaders to 'punish an enemy with the least risk to American lives' and that '[w]ithout the B-2, the United States would be forced to choose between maintaining the nuclear deterrent force of [the] small fleet of [B-1B] bombers or using some portion of them in a conventional role' (1990, pp. 110–11). The United States could have used the highly capable B-1B bombers, escorted by ECM aircraft, to minimise the risk to pilots on bombing missions. Moreover, the United States was unlikely to need all the B-1Bs to maintain the nuclear deterrent at the same time as wanting use some of them to bomb some developing state, and if it did need all the B-1Bs for the deterrent (if, say, the developing state it was about to bomb had been a Soviet client state) then SAC would probably have insisted that all the B-2s be kept as well to maintain the deterrent: in which case the conventional bombing mission could well have gone to carrier-based bombers.

By early 1991 the Air Force view had changed in line with Rice's, and the service began stressing the stealth bomber's conventional war-fighting role, declaring that this was as important as its nuclear capability. The effectiveness with which the bomber could have been used in the Gulf War was highlighted to Congress by the Air Force in order to support its case. At the same time SAC began to emphasise its conventional strategic bombing role, and the B-2's central importance to this set of mission requirements. Lt. General Charles Horner, Chief of Air Operations in the Gulf War, testified before the House Defence Appropriations Subcommittee (HDAS) (in April 1991) that the B-2 would have been invaluable during the Gulf War. He noted the obvious, that 'the B-2 combines the range and payload of the B-52 with the advantages of stealth F-117 that proved so valuable in *Desert Storm*'. General Lee Bulter, CINCSAC, told the House subcommittee that the B-2 was the cornerstone of the 'greatly expanded role I envision for SAC's conventional capabilities'.[121]

But does the Air Force need a new multibillion dollar conventional strategic bomber? The B-1B was not used in the Gulf. The rumour was that the Air Force was not confident that the B-1Bs were in full working order, and wanted to avoid the embarrassment of losing one in the conflict. The Air Force maintained that the B-52s were able to meet the mission requirement and could be spared from SAC's nuclear deterrent force, whereas B-1Bs could not. The B-52 bombers that were used most successfully in Desert Storm had been in service (thanks to extensive retrofitting) for 36 years.[122] It is interesting to note that in a 1987 RAND Corporation study commissioned by the Air Force which argued for the establishment of a US conventionally armed heavy bomber force, it was presumed that the B-52 would fulfil this role for at least another ten years (Hosmer and Kent, 1987, p. 34). The B-52s were able to operate with impunity in the Gulf with the assistance of allied air support. Indeed some evidence suggests that they were as likely to be shot down by their own air defence forces as by those of the Iraqis. A flight of B-52s was apparently mistaken for a Scud missile attack by US satellites, and allied fighters were only prevented from attacking their own returning bombers by the intervention of an Airborne Warning and Control (AWACS) aircraft (Rochlin and Demchak, 1991, p. 264). The Iraqi air defence forces were clearly outnumbered and outclassed by the allied air forces (Mason, 1991, pp. 212–13). Future US military operations against 'Third World' air defence forces may not enjoy the unique advantages they did in the Gulf. The fact remains, though, that present Air Force combat aircraft are already a generation ahead of anything possessed by any developing country. They therefore do not require numerical superiority or electronic counter-measure intelligence to overwhelm (let alone penetrate) the air defence forces of such countries.

No Strategic Purpose

Unlike the MX, it is not possible to argue that the B-2 was needed to demonstrate US resolve, and like the MX, it clearly was not bought so that it could be bargained away. It is perhaps for this reason that no mention is made of either of these two roles in any of the newspaper or academic articles on the B-2. The fact that no official alluded to these roles seems to indicate that the B-2 was never intended to play a symbolic or a bargaining chip function. This is hardly surprising considering that the stealth bomber was developed in strictest secrecy and its very existence was not acknowledged until 1980. Moreover, the United States had superiority in strategic bomber capabilities whereas many policymakers perceived an emerging US inferiority in ICBM capabilities. The B-2 was not needed, therefore, to plug the perception of a developing bomber gap. As the United States was not concerned about developments in the Soviet strategic bomber force structure, the B-2 was not needed to wrangle concessions from the Soviets in arms negotiations.

Given that it served no international political purpose, strategic issues cannot explain why the B-2 programme started and cannot explain why it was a partial success. The strategic justification for the B-2 has always been pretty thin. Established weapons could meet established mission requirements, and of the new military requirements, the B-2's ability to locate and destroy RTs was questionable[123] and most VHTs could be destroyed by other (cheaper) weapons in service or due to enter service. The collapse of the Soviet Union has made the complete lack of need for the B-2 blindingly obvious. The conventional bombing role is simply not convincing. In any case, spending tens of billions of dollars on 20 conventional bombers does not give you much 'bang for the buck'.

CONCLUSION

Strategic issues do not appear to explain much about the weapons examined in this chapter (see Table 2.4). The two stealth bombers come out in the worst light. Both were given unrealistically demanding mission requirements during the Cold War, a suicidal bombing mission for the A-12 and hunting down elusive targets for the B-2, which neither were capable of carrying out. These over-demanding missions have been replaced by an under-demanding one at the end of the Cold War, namely bombing Third World states, for which stealth bombers are not needed. There was no alternative for the A-12, as the existing naval bomber was obsolete, but some of the B-2's nuclear missions could have been carried out by other weapons in the US nuclear force structure; similarly, its conventional missions can be carried out by other bombers. The failure of the A-12 cannot be explained in terms of strategic issues as its successor is also to be a stealth bomber. Given that there was no good reason to buy it, strategic issues cannot explain the partial success of the B-2 either.

Strategic issues can explain the origins of the DIVAD programme. There was a genuine need for a new mobile armoured battlefield AD system, and this mission requirement was reinforced by the Army's new AirLand Battle doctrine. However, when the mission requirement changed in 1980 from combating fighter bombers to defending against helicopter gunships, DIVAD was unable to adapt accordingly. Strategic issues cannot account for the development of DIVAD because the

Army chose to develop a fancy AD system when a simpler, more functional system would have been more effective and adaptable; it so happens that General Dynamics were developing just such a system, thus there was an alternative to DIVAD. The programme outcome cannot be explained in terms of strategic issues either because it took five years for the weapon to be cancelled, far too long when it was clear that DIVAD was unable to meet the new threat, during which time the Army had already acquired 64 units.

Table 2.4. Strategic Issues in Weapons Acquisition

	A-12	DIVAD	MX	B-2
Mission requirement	None	Yes	None	None
Within capabilities	No	No	No	No
Alternatives available	No	Yes	Yes	Yes
Symbol of resolve	NA	NA	Yes	No
Bargaining chip	NA	NA	No	No
Strategic issues	Irrelevant	Origins only	Some relevance	Irrelevant

There was no military requirement for the MX. It was designed to give more warheads, greater hard target capabilities, and increased survivability to the ICBM force. However, it was not really needed for any of these reasons: SAC wanted more warheads simply to feed the massive overkill built into the SIOP, the improved Minuteman III had as much hard target capability as the MX, and survivable basing was operationally irrelevant as SAC intended on promptly launching the MXs on warning of the Soviet attack. The MX was frequently touted as a bargaining chip, particularly under by Reagan administration, but all the evidence suggests that nobody seriously thought that the MX ought to be acquired so that it could be traded away. However, it would seem that the MX was considered by successive administrations to be an important symbol of US resolve. It has to be said that this is not a very strong reason for spending billions on acquiring the MX, but it is nevertheless a genuine one.

The overall picture painted by this chapter is really quite shocking. Only the most sceptical observer would expect strategic issues to be so irrelevant to weapons acquisition. Yet a detailed analysis of the strategic rationales of each of the four case studies reveals that only the outcome of the MX programme can be explained in terms of strategic issues, and just about so at that.

3 Institutional Issues

The four military services – the Army, Air Force, Navy, and Marines Corps – and the President stand to gain and lose most, in terms of resources, from the weapons acquisition process. For the services, the resources are actual weapons. Obviously, without weapons, the services have no purpose; more weapons give the services more capabilities and increase their role in national security. For the President, the resource is his political reputation. Association with a successful programme adds to this reputation; similarly a President's reputation may decrease if he is associated with a troubled programme. For this reason, Presidents will only get involved with nuclear programmes, because that is expected of them, and they will try to tailor their involvement so as to avoid damaging their reputation. The services and the President also have the greatest ability to influence weapons acquisition without having genuine strategic reasons to justify their actions. The services gain tremendous influence by being permanent actors in this policy area, whereas political appointees come and go, and by controlling the detail of weapons development. Presidents are far less involved in weapon acquisition but they can still exercise a dramatic, if cruder, influence over individual nuclear weapon programmes.

This chapter will start off by examining service interests in, and influence over, weapons acquisition. Two questions will be developed from this discussion and applied to each of the case studies. First, did the weapon serve a core interest of a service? Second, did the service develop the weapon in a manner intended to maximise its chances of being acquired rather than to improve efficiency in weapon design and development? Two additional questions will be developed from an examination of presidential interests in, and influence over, nuclear weapons acquisition and applied to the MX and B-2 cases. First, did the weapon programme attract presidential involvement? Second, did the President have self-interested reasons for advancing or cutting the programme?

THE MILITARY SERVICES

The military services claim to strive to protect the nation but they also clearly strive to protect themselves. Most organisations seek survival, for its own sake, and in order to enable them to carry out tasks for the benefit of others.[1] Organisations will frequently seek survival through expansion. Greater resources enable the organisation to carry out more tasks, gain greater influence, and therefore become more indispensable. According to one student of US national security policy, this does not mean that organisations are 'mindlessly aggressive and imperialistic', but that they 'expand as necessary to monopolize capabilities and resources perceived as essential to fulfil organizational goals' (Clarke, 1984, p. 253).

It is important to point out that organisational survival may indeed benefit others and, more importantly, that organisations may seek to expand for this reason. Thus, a service may seek to maximise its share of the defence budget not simply because it wants to survive for its own sake, but also for the sake of the state. For instance, the Air Force may want a new bomber not simply to maintain its bomber fleet but also because it genuinely believes that this would serve national security. In the context of this book, it is unnecessary to distinguish whether service support for a weapon is based purely on self-interest or on perceptions of the national interest. Indeed, I argue that 'service interests' are very much defined by the interests of the dominant groups within the services *as well as* the beliefs held in those groups about what contribution the service ought to make to national security. What really matters is whether or not the services are driven by self-interests or self-images to acquire specific weapons even when there is no strategic requirement for these weapons. This means that the discussion in this chapter is very much related to the conclusion of the previous chapter; which was that in only two of the case studies were there genuine strategic reasons for starting the weapon programme, and in only one of these was there a genuine reason (albeit a weak one) for continuing to develop and acquire the weapon. In the absence of a strategic reason, the origins, development and outcomes of the other programmes still need to be explained.

Service Identity

How does an organisation define itself? Halperin develops the concept of 'organisational essence' to explain how organisations define their goals and, in turn, themselves. The essence of an organisation is 'the view held by the dominant group in the organization of what the missions and capabilities should be' (Halperin, 1974, p. 28). How is the dominant group's view disseminated within an organisation and how does it come to be accepted by that organisation? Stephen Peter Rosen comes up with convincing explanation. He portrays the military services as 'complex political communities in which the central concerns are those of any political community: who should rule, and how the "citizens" should live'. Rosen maintains that '[m]ilitary organizations have this political character to a greater degree than other institutional organizations because military organizations are divorced from the rest of society' (1991, p. 19). Rosen further argues that military innovation, that is, a service changing what it does and how it does it, 'requires an "ideological" struggle that redefines the values that legitimate the activities of the citizens' (1991, p. 20). It may be said, then, that the viewpoint of the dominant group within a military service is translated into the values that are encompassed in, and promoted by, a service 'ideology'; this way the values are disseminated within the service, and come to be generally accepted. In this sense, the 'ideology' becomes the fundamental expression of the service essence. A service strategy, to the extent that it is designed to promote the purpose of the service, may thus be seen as a service ideology. From this perspective the loyalty of individual members to their respective services is easy to comprehend. Community identity, shared values and ideology all serve to reinforce the natural tendency for individuals to adopt the perspective of the organisation for which they work.

Notwithstanding the strength of service identity, the services contain subunits, or branches, which also have their own identity. Indeed it is for this reason that Rosen describes the services as complex political communities. Each branch is defined by a particular military mission (or function), and by extension, 'its own culture and distinct way of thinking about the way war should be conducted' (Rosen, 1991, p. 19). Officers identify themselves in terms of these branches (Huntington, 1961, p. 407). Thus the Army contains armour, cavalry, infantry, artillery, aviation, airborne, air defence, logistics and special forces officers; the Marine Corps also contain armour, infantry, artillery officers and different types of aviators; the Navy has carrier pilots, submariners, and surface ship commanders; and the Air Force has pilots who fly strategic bombers, tactical bombers, fighter planes, ground attack planes, transport planes and officers who sit in missile silos. Service branches also tend to be based around specific types of weapon. So in the Army, armour and cavalry officers fight from main battle tanks (MBTs) and infantry fighting vehicles (IFVs), artillery officers fire self-propelled howitzers and rocket launchers, and aviators fly transport helicopters and helicopter gunships.[2] Hence separate branches may share the same military mission but still be distinguished by the military capabilities they embody. Indeed, their different capabilities may lead them to support different ways of achieving the same mission. Silo officers may argue that strategic bombers are redundant to counterforce targeting while bomber pilots may argue that they provide capabilities which are indispensable for such a mission.

Each branch has its own notion of not only its own role in war but also the wartime role of the other branches in its service (as well as the other services). Not surprisingly, this can lead to intraservice rivalry as the branches battle it out to promote their own perspective. In the late 1950s interservice warfare broke out in the Army between those branches that favoured focusing on the Army's traditional role, conventional warfare, and those branches which argued that the Army should create a role for itself in strategic deterrence (Halperin, 1974, p. 34). Naturally, in promoting their respective military missions, branches are also seeking to maximise their share of their service resources. Thus the intraservice Army dispute of the late 1950s was heightened by the fact that the development of long-range nuclear missiles was draining funds from equipping forces to fight a conventional war (Huntington, 1961, p. 406). However, because of the strength of service identity, officers are usually more loyal to their service than their branch. Comparing officers to citizens and services to nation states, Samuel Huntington argues that:

> Normally it is easier to change sectional or class affiliations within a nation state than it is to change citizenship from one state to another . . . [thus] intraservice controversy is mitigated by the relative ease of transfer among the various functional organizations within a service. The lines between the functional groupings within a service are never as clearcut as the lines between the services (1961, p. 407).

For military officers, service identity matters above all else.

Core Functions

The services seek to protect their 'organization essence' by exercising their autonomy, and by maintaining and enlarging their functions and the resources necessary to carry out these functions. Autonomy is sacred for the services. This is their right to determine how they should prepare for, and fight in, war, as expressed in their service strategies. This, in turn, entitles the services to determine their functions and required capabilities. Each service has one or more core functions, and a number of peripheral functions. The core functions of the Air Force are air defence, aerial bombardment and nuclear deterrence. Nuclear deterrence has, since the late 1950s, also been a core function of the Navy, along with power projection and control of the seas. Unlike these two services, the Army and Marines only have one core function each, which is conventional land warfare and power projection respectively (Clark, 1984, p. 256; see also Halperin, 1974, pp. 28–35; Builder, 1989). Core functions are valued above peripheral ones and are protected at all costs. This is understandable as a service largely defines itself by its core functions. As far as the Air Force is concerned, its overriding purpose has always been strategic aerial bombardment, and since the early 1950s, nuclear deterrence (Brown, 1993, pp. 29–67; Builder, 1989, pp. 67–73; Kaplan, 1983). In contrast, peripheral functions are largely unimportant to a service and tend to be neglected. Peripheral functions may even be sacrificed in order to maintain sufficient resources for core functions (Clark, 1984, p. 253).

It should be noted that the services will rarely, in fact, encroach upon each other's core functions. Indeed, according to Smith, the military services operate as a 'military turf cartel' in that they have formed 'a pact not to intrude upon each other's turf or challenge each other's missions' (1988, p. 265). This tacit agreement to bound their competition is reinforced by the more formal 1948 Key West agreements which gave sole responsibility for certain functions to specific services (Hendrickson, 1988, pp. 108–9). The main purpose of this 'cartel' is to ensure that interservice strife does not give politicians and civilian bureaucrats (especially those in the DoD) too much opportunity to interfere in the affairs of the services (Huntington, 1961, pp. 156–7).

On occasion an interservice dispute will nevertheless occur over a core function. In the 1980s the Navy threatened an Air Force core function by developing and acquiring the Trident D-5, a counterforce SLBM. Up to this point, the Navy's strategic deterrent was not capable of counterforce targeting, and so it did not threaten the Air Force monopoly on this mission. Trident D-5 changed all this by promising to be accurate and powerful enough to destroy hard targets and, by so doing, threatened to rob the troubled MX of its task. However, certain branches in the Navy were divided over the wisdom of a direct confrontation with the Air Force. Throughout the 1970s, the branch response for developing SLBMs, the Special Projects Office, were against such a bold move, fearing that it could threaten their programme, while the Trident Project Office and Navy strategic planners (some of whom were apparently 'tired of Air Force jibes about the

Navy's little firecrackers') wanted the greater missile capability. The Navy was also under tremendous pressure from McNamara and Schlesinger, and their respective OSD staffs, to develop and acquire a hard target capability for their SLBMs (Spinardi, 1988, pp. 166–74; 1990, pp. 159–72). Not only does this case show that one service may, on occasion, challenge another's core function, but it also suggests that the relationship between the services and OSD is quite dynamic and complex. It tends to be competitive. But the Secretary of Defence and his bureaus may find themselves in dispute not with a service, but with specific branches within the service. Furthermore, they may end up taking sides in an intraservice dispute. This case would suggest that, by so doing, the OSD may be able to decide the outcome of certain intraservice disputes.

Service Interests and Influence in Weapons Acquisition

A military service cares most about protecting its organisational essence, which means securing resources for its core functions. When it comes to weapons acquisition, a service will most vigorously promote those weapons which serve its core functions: hence, the Air Force is particularly keen on acquiring more bombers, the Army on more tanks and the Navy on more aircraft carriers.

The services are able to promote their institutional interests in weapons acquisition because they have more influence over the process than any other actors. Service influence over weapons acquisition comes from their ability to outlive administrations and from their ability to control the detail of weapons programmes. The services appear to enjoy considerable advantage by being more permanent features of the policy landscape than their political masters. Administrations come and go but governmental organisations remain. This is especially important in the case of weapons acquisition. The time it takes to acquire a new weapon is so lengthy that no one administration can oversee the process but a service can. Service campaigns on behalf of a weapon can therefore outlast administration directives to cancel it. The B-1 programme is a case in point. This bomber programme was started under Nixon, cancelled under Carter and acquired under Reagan. Although Carter tried to kill the B-1 programme outright, all he was able to do was to ensure that it was not acquired under his presidency. The Air Force was still able to fund development of the bomber under Carter and wait for a new President to come into office.[3] As will be discussed below, the services are able to control the detail of weapon programmes by determining programme requirements and through their management of acquisition programmes. This enables them to determine the cost and pace, and often thereby the outcome, of acquisition programmes. Service influence is also a function of service unity. A service will have more influence over a weapon programme when no branches in that service oppose the position adopted by the service hierarchy than when there are one or more dissenting branches. As was suggested above, outside actors may be able to exploit intraservice competition, in this case by supporting the dissenting branch against the hierarchy.

THE PRESIDENT

The President's interests are not synonymous with those of the United States. This point may be obvious, but it leads one to ask what are the President's interests and when do they, as opposed to national interests, drive presidential policy. This chapter is not only concerned with interest but also influence. While numerous studies on the presidency may disagree on the precise nature of presidential power they all agree on one point: the President is far from all-powerful. The size and complexity of executive government make presidential rule improbable. The division of authority within the executive, and between the branches of government, make presidential rule impossible. Instead, Richard Rose argues that 'the President is not so much laying down the law as he is selectively seeking to make policies where and when he can' (1991, p. 164; see also Hilsman, 1987, pp. 104–26; Ragsdale, 1993, pp. 4–9). For Rose, this encourages Presidents to preserve their power by only exercising it in a discriminate and cautious manner (1991; 1976, p. 167). Thus, the maintenance of power may be said to be the President's primary self-interest (Halperin, 1974, p. 63; Neustadt, 1980).

A Stranger in a Strange Land

It is precisely because the President is not all-powerful that Richard Neustadt argues in his famous study on *Presidential Power* that the President must persuade other actors in government to support his policies (1980). Thus Allison argued that the President must bargain with his own subordinates. The President does not have the power to simply command them to obey. But what of loyalty and duty? Do subordinates not feel obliged to faithfully serve their President? As one critic noted,

'There is a tendency in *Presidential Power* to picture the President as a lonely fighter against all others . . . Is it so inconceivable that some persons may genuinely want to help the President?' (Sperlich, 1975 [1969], p. 425).

Loyalty is based on relationships and duty is reinforced by them. Yet most subordinates have not even met their President let alone formed a relationship with him. Even those subordinates that do have regular meetings with the President may find it difficult to form a personal, or even working, relationship with him. Ford could not stand his Defence Secretary, James Schlesinger, and leaped at the opportunity to fire him in late 1975 (Isaacson, 1992, pp. 623, 669–71). Even those subordinates who might be expected to form close relationships with the President may be unsatisfied by the nature of the relationship. Some of Reagan's closest advisers were frustrated by the President's remoteness (Smith, 1988, p. 587; Cannon, 1991, pp. 172–6).

Indeed, Presidents, especially incoming ones, may be thought of as strangers in a strange land. Not only do they have no prior experience which can adequately prepare them for presidential office, but they must also contend with numerous government bureaucracies which each have multiple institutional and personal interests that may be at odds with those of the President.[4] The ignorance of new Presidents tends to be particularly pronounced in international affairs (Rockman, 1987, pp. 22–3; Williams, 1987, pp. 237–8). Based on his performance, after his first year in office, many presidential observers described Carter as amateurish (Davis, 1979, pp. 64–6). Reagan's complete lack of knowledge in general is legendary. According to Lou Cannon, Reagan's second NSA, William Clark, was simply astonished by how little the President knew about world affairs.[5] Indeed, Reagan's disregard for details was part of his electoral appeal just as Carter's lack of prior experience was his: Carter ran for office as an outsider untainted by the corruption surrounding the Nixon and Ford administrations; Reagan promised the broader vision which Carter, obsessed as he was with the detail of policy, was unable to provide (Davis, 1979, pp. 63, 66–7).

Incoming Presidents realise that on top of their inexperience, they must contend with competitive, or even hostile, government bureaucracies, and it is for this reason that each incoming presidential team supposedly appoints the President's 'own people' to the top 4,000 or so posts in the executive. For this reason also we talk of Presidents having 'administrations'. But with the exception of the Executive Office of the President, in reality Presidents do not really appoint 'their own people' to these posts. Cabinet secretaries are usually chosen for their political kudos or policy expertise and not because of some former relationship with the President (Rose, 1991, pp. 145–6; Ragsdale, 1993, p. 242). Kennedy preferred to appoint competent strangers than waste time trying to match friends and acquaintances with posts (Polsby, 1994, p. 4). He did not know McNamara or Dean Rusk before they were appointed as his Secretary of Defence and Secretary of State respectively (Rose, 1980, p. 146). Since he was an outsider, Carter was especially reliant on advice from strangers when it came to choosing strangers to fill government posts (Davis, 1979, p. 66). Lesser cabinet appointments may be based simply on the need to have a woman, black or Hispanic in the cabinet (Ragsdale, 1993, p. 242; Polsby, 1994, p. 4). These strangers which the President brings in to help run his administration are then faced with twin tasks, namely, to advise him and to represent their respective departments and agencies in government. These tasks may clash. More importantly, the President may feel that by advocating their agency position, a cabinet secretary is no longer loyal to the President's position. In any event, a President usually cannot trust his cabinet secretaries, deputy secretaries and under-secretaries to implement his agenda (Polsby, 1994; Cronin, 1975 [1970]).

The Great Persuader

The President's task, then, is to persuade others in government to cooperate. To do this the President relies on more than charm and logic, he also uses the status and authority of his office. In effect, through a process of bargaining with administration subordinates and legislators, the President seeks to persuade others that they should support his policies because their office or their interests require them to do so (Neustadt, 1980, pp. 27–9, 35). Presidents, and their advisers, spend much of their time building intra-executive alliances (Cronin, 1975 [1970], p. 365; Sarkesian, 1979, p. 25) or gaining the support of individual legislators for particular presidential policies (Sullivan, 1990). The White House may engage in log-rolling with other government actors in order to build support for specific presidential policies; the President's position on particular policy issues may be traded in the course of building intra-governmental support for favoured policies (Halperin, 1974, pp. 79–82).

Such acts of persuasion are time consuming. When the President must lean on someone, these acts also consume political capital. For this reason the President must carefully chose where, when and how to act (Rose, 1976, p. 151). By exercising their power in a selective, focused manner, Presidents are able to ensure that they have adequate information on which to base their decisions and are able to monitor the implementation of their decisions (Bendor and Hammond, 1992, p. 316; Krasner, 1989 [1972], p. 425; Art, 1989 [1973], p. 444). Presidents must also ensure that their policies are seen to succeed, or at least are not seen to fail. This is because the President's ability to persuade is based on his professional reputation and public prestige. If policies fail, then the President will be seen to be incompetent and his general popularity will suffer. Success, on the other hand, makes a President appear skilful and increases his popularity. Congress and subordinates are more likely to follow and less likely to confront a capable and popular President (Neustadt, 1980, pp. 64–79). Popular dissatisfaction with Carter's performance after his first year in office resulted in greater departmental and congressional assertiveness and severely weakened the President's ability to implement his agenda (Davis, 1979, pp. 73–6).

In short, Presidents seek to promote successful policies and avoid troublesome ones. Success is important not only for exercising selective power but also for staying in power. If they seek re-election, Presidents have even greater incentives to avoid costly policies. Indeed, it is likely that Presidents will grow more cautious as they approach their second presidential election campaign. By their third year in office, Presidents and their advisers are likely to assess whether new policy initiatives will help or hinder the President's re-election bid. By their fourth year, Presidents normally avoid difficult policies and stick with safe ones (Quandt, 1986, pp. 832–3). In the lead-up to their re-election, Presidents will seek, through mostly words but also deeds, to generate a popular image of themselves among the electorate, to deny major issues to rivals and to appeal to powerful interest groups (Halperin, 1974, p. 67).

Presidential Interests and Influence in Weapons Acquisition

Presidents can only deal with selected policy issues. Limited time and political capital prevent them from doing everything. More importantly (for them), they have strong self-interested reasons for being cautious and choosy when it comes to policymaking. Presidents who try to do too much risk getting less done and/or not getting re-elected. In the course of building support for favoured policies, Presidents and their advisers may give ground on other policy issues.

How does this relate to weapons acquisition? Whether or not a weapon programme attracts attention, including the President's, will be determined by the weapon's cost and its impact on national security.

Hence, Presidents are most unlikely to decide policy on specific conventional weapon programmes. Such programmes are rarely important enough to justify presidential involvement, and rarely do they capture much public attention. When conventional weapon programmes do become subjects of press and public debates, invariably because of cost, schedule or technical difficulties, the Secretary of Defence will usually handle any major decisions which need to be taken. The President can legitimately avoid handling a mess which he has little incentive to deal with anyway.

Nuclear weapons are another matter. The press and public are attentive to debates within the administration and Congress on such weapons. Most people realise the immense destruction these weapons can cause and that there is no defence against nuclear attack. This gives Presidents strong incentives to show interest in policy on nuclear weapons (Nolan, 1994, p. 35). If questions are raised in Congress, or the press, about problems with a nuclear weapons programme, the President will be expected to produce answers and, if necessary, solutions. Given these expectations, the President has little choice but to occasionally decide policy on specific nuclear weapons. However, unless the President has a strong personal interest in this subject or unless the weapon is central to a broader presidential policy, the White House will seek to keep his involvement as limited as possible; presidential interest will be determined by the level of public, press and congressional interest in specific nuclear weapons.

Nuclear weapons are not only important symbols of international politics but also national politics. Come election time, presidential candidates and Presidents may seek to promote two different images of themselves depending on circumstances. They may wish to portray themselves as warriors or as peacemakers (Halperin, 1987, pp. 67–8; Williams, 1987, pp. 221–8). Given press and public interest in nuclear weapons, portraying these images can easily be achieved by manipulating policy on such weapons. Promoting nuclear weapon programmes indicates a belief in military strength whereas promoting nuclear arms control and/or disarmament invokes the peacemaker image. The degree to which election and re-election concerns produces actual policy, as opposed to rhetoric, is questionable. Presidential election campaigns produce very few actual policies or even policy proposals. For instance, only 5 per cent of the proposals Kennedy put to Congress originated from his campaign pledges (Rose, 1991, p. 174). This is partly because candidates seek to ensure that nothing they say will offend potential voters or get them into trouble. Consequently, campaigns are largely about promoting image while neglecting issues, about concentrating on style at the expense of substance.[6] While policies rarely come from campaign statements, Presidents may still find themselves constrained by what they said while running for office.

When they do get involved in a weapons programme, what can Presidents do? While the services have massive influence over weapons acquisition by controlling the detail of the process, Presidents gain influence through their control over the broad allocation of defence resources. Congress may appropriate defence funds but it is the President who requests these moneys and, when he gets them, it is he who directs the military to spend them. As the case of the B-1 bomber programme demonstrates, while a President cannot always kill a programme outright, he can at least ensure that a weapon is not acquired under his tenure.

The President's ability to affect the detail of weapon programmes is limited. Halperin argues that the degree of presidential control over any policy issue is determined by the degree of presidential involvement, the complexity of the issue itself, and the range of potential policy implementators (1974, pp. 289–90). These conditions suggest that things do not look good for the President when it comes to the detail of weapons acquisition. Presidents usually have better things to do than follow the progress of individual weapon programmes, and even when they assess specific weapons, they are unlikely to be fully aware or informed of the possible programme options. Where possible, the services are likely to feed their civilian masters information which forwards their own position. Presidential awareness on this issue is hampered by the fact that weapon programmes are complex undertakings. In addition, the overall weapons acquisition process is itself immensely complicated. Finally, often the President cannot ask somebody else to acquire a weapon if he does not like the attitude of the relevant military service: he cannot ask the Army to acquire the nuclear submarine he wants if the Navy is being unhelpful.

OTHER POLICY ACTORS

The Secretary of Defence and the bureaus in the OSD do have considerable influence over weapons acquisition but their actions are unlikely to be motivated by self-interest. While they must not squander political capital carelessly in disputes with the services, they do not have to preserve their professional reputation or public popularity to the same degree as the President who faces a much broader range of competitors and issues. Furthermore, these actors do not have to campaign for re-election, as does the President.

It is possible that the Secretary of Defence may seek to promote the institutional interests of the DoD within US government. This is part of the job after all. Thus, in many ways, it was no great surprise that Weinberger, who had slashed state expenditure when he was California's budget director (under Governor Reagan), should become a forceful advocate of increasing the defence budget when he became Defence Secretary. However, pushing for larger defence expenditure in general is not the same as promoting funds for specific items. As Defence Secretaries have department-wide perspectives, there are no obvious institutional considerations which would lead them to support funding one weapon over another.

The same may be said of the OSD civilian bureaus, such as the Office of Programme Analysis and Evaluation (PA&E). It is possible that these civilian bureaus may seek to influence weapons acquisition in order to maximise their area of policy responsibility. But once again, this says little about why bureaus would seek to promote their own institutional interests by supporting specific weapons. The OSD bureaus may enhance their institutional standing by participating in the weapons acquisition process but, unlike the services, they do not benefit from the outcomes of these programmes. It may even be said that, since the task of most of these bureaus is to regulate and oversee policy and programmes in the DoD, they have a institutional interest in ensuring that these weapons meet genuine strategic requirements. In this sense, their professional reputation is on the line each time they support or oppose a weapon programme. So, while a bureau may be motivated by institutional interests to seek to influence a weapon programme, it is not clear how such self-interests would determine *what* outcome a bureau would seek to affect beyond ensuring that there is a good strategic rationale for the weapon.

Overall, the political appointees in the OSD are not so likely to adopt the institutional concerns of their bureaus and organisations since they are only in their posts for a few years. Career bureaucrats and military officers can be expected to spend almost all their working lives in their respective organisations. However, service secretaries, deputy secretaries and assistant secretaries are different. Anecdotal evidence suggests that they may seek to promote the institutional interests of their own services (Kotz, 1988, p. 184; Smith, 1988, pp. 256, 262–4).[7] This may be because they perceive it to be their job, if not in their career interest, to promote the institutional interests of their respective

services. Those service secretaries, deputy secretaries and assistant secretaries who have this attitude are likely to promote those weapons
favoured by their services.

MANIPULATING THE ACQUISITION PROCESS

The weapons acquisition cycle is supposed to begin with the identifica-
tion of a strategic requirement which existing weapons are unable to
meet. Options are then supposedly explored, among them new weapon
concepts, in order to fulfil this requirement. This may lead to the establishment of a weapon programme which, in turn, leads to the development, production and procurement of a new weapon. This acquisition
cycle formally occurs in four phases: concept formulation, validation
and demonstration, full-scale development, and production. Each
phase is separated by a decision point, called a 'Milestone', where the
programme is assessed and receives authorisation to proceed to the
next phase.[8]

The Milestone review structure was established by deputy Secretary
of Defence David Packard in May 1969. In the past, Milestone reviews
were conducted by a committee of high-level service and OSD representatives called the Defence Systems Acquisition Review Council
(DSARC). Every major defence acquisition programme[9] was reviewed
by the DSARC on three occasions (these are the 'Milestones'): before
it began development (Milestone I), before it went into full-scale development (Milestone II) and before it went into production (Milestone
III) (McNaugher, 1991, pp. 64–8; Mayer, 1991, pp. 58–9). On each of
these occasions, the services would present information on their programmes and, based on requirement, performance and cost considerations, the DSARC would recommend whether the programme ought
to proceed, or be delayed, or even (on occasion) be cancelled. This recommendation was then passed on to the Secretary of Defence who
would decide the programme's fate.

This Milestone review structure has remained largely intact up to today. In 1976 an additional DSARC review was instituted (Milestone 0)
in which authorisation had to be sought before a new programme
could even come into existence. Milestone 0 was dropped in 1981 by
Weinberger and subsequently reinstated after he left office. Two more
Milestones, IV and V, were added in 1987 and a new committee, the Defence Acquisition Board (DAB), with broader responsibilities and
membership was set up in place of the DSARC.[10]

According to DoD acquisition policy guidelines issued in 1991, the Milestone system is designed to ensure that five things occur in weapons acquisition: that all weapons are acquired to meet strategic requirements; that detailed performance requirements are not determined early in programmes; that cost-schedule-performance trade-offs are made in programmes; that weapons are adequately tested before entering production; and that fiscal constraints are constantly taken into account.[11] Furthermore, in their reports to Congress, Defence Secretaries Brown, Weinberger and Carlucci have all made assertions about their department's regulation of weapons acquisition which are consistent with those claims made in 1991 guidelines.[12] These claims have all been challenged by critiques of DoD regulation of the acquisition process (Dews and Rich, 1986; Gansler, 1989; McNaugher, 1989; Hampson, 1989; Mayer, 1991; Brown, 1992).

This book is fundamentally about the issue of whether or not weapons are truly acquired to meet strategic requirements: this question will not be addressed directly in this section but will be answered by the book as a whole. The issue of whether or not fiscal constraints are taken into account in weapons acquisition will be addressed in the next chapter. This section will focus on the three remaining assertions regarding detailed performance requirements, cost-schedule-performance trade-offs and adequate testing.

Detailed Performance Requirements Are Established Early On

Performance requirements state what the final product of a weapon programme must be able to do. In the case of the Air Force's nuclear-powered bomber and B-70 bomber programmes, which were started in the mid-1950s, the chosen plane was required to have a range of about 10,000 miles unrefuelled, or 13,000 miles refuelled, to be able to fly at between 60,000–75,000 feet, and to have 'the maximum speed possible' (Brown, 1992, pp. 200–1). Detailed performance requirements provide clear directions for service components and defence contractors to work with, but establishing them too early hinders discovery of the optimum way to meet a military requirement. The whole purpose of the early stages of a weapon programme is to explore what options may exist to meet the stated military requirement. These options narrow dramatically once detailed performance requirements are set (Rich and Dews, 1986, p. 32; McNaugher, 1989, p. 73). Thus, in the case of the nuclear powered and B-70 bombers, requirements were established before it was determined what was, and what was not, technologically possible. As it happens a plane could not be built in the end to meet the excessive range, speed and altitude requirements. It proved impossible to build a nuclear reactor small enough to fit into a bomber, let alone one that would not melt the plane and poison the crew with radiation. It was equally impossible to build a plane of the aerodynamic design and robust materials which an extremely high performance conventionally powered bomber demanded (Brown, 1992, pp. 193–229). This leads on to another good reason for avoiding setting the detailed performance requirements too early in an acquisition programme, which is that the programme outcome may be adversely affected. Had the Air Force waited until the feasibility of various technologies had been explored, then they would have had the opportunity to establish detailed performance requirements which were closer to science fact than science fiction.

If setting detailed performance requirements too early is not helpful, then why does it occur? The short answer is that the services, which control the timing and precision of performance requirements, favour it. The early determination and detail of performance requirements reinforce the impression that there is a legitimate and pressing military requirement for the new weapon (Brown, 1992, pp. 316–17). Furthermore, the consensus building which generates support for a weapon, both within the sponsor service and between the service and other governmental actors, also generates pressures for the early establishment of detailed performance requirements. As Thomas McNaugher notes, such pressures are based on institutional rather than strategic logic:

> Those who insist on detail in requirements . . . are not trying to make sense, at least at the level of the overall project. Rather, they are trying to protect the specific capabilities or technologies that matter to them. The more they can embed their own goals in detailed specifications, the surer they are that those goals cannot be traded away (1989, pp. 127–8).

So the more detailed the performance requirement, the harder it is to alter it (Dews and Rich, 1986, p. 33; Mayer, 1991, p. 47):

Even when they are altered, detailed performance requirements may be raised but are rarely, if ever, lowered. Again, this is for institutional reasons. For a start, as has been suggested, performance requirements frequently represent painstaking negotiations between the various governmental actors who have an interest in the weapon (McNaugher, 1989, p. 59). Lowering performance requirements would threaten capabilities in which various actors have interests whereas raising performance requirements only entails adding new capabilities. Not only could lowering requirements undermine the institutional alliance backing a weapon, but it would also lend the impression that the military requirement for the weapon was not so urgent after all. The services, therefore, will ensure that programme requirements are never lowered for the simple reason that to do so could be suicidal for a programme. The services may argue that, by regularly lowering performance requirements, the government would merely encourage defence contractors to take such requirements less seriously (Brown, 1992, p. 320). However, as the cases of the nuclear-powered and B-70 bombers demonstrate, there may be even stronger reasons for occasionally lowering performance requirements.

Not Making Cost-Performance-Schedule Trade-offs

It makes sense for trade-offs to be made between the cost of a weapon, its performance requirements and the programme schedule. It would be preferable for the US government if it could acquire the ideal weapon cheaply and quickly. However, it costs money and takes time to develop and build highly capable weapons; if greater performance requires innovating weapons technology, then programme cost and programme time will increase approximately in relation to the performance demanded.[13] Weapons take a long time to be developed and produced, but this process must still be kept as short as possible in order for the services to be equipped to meet military requirements as they arise and so that the services are not equipped with obsolete weapons.[14] Weapons are also generally very costly, but again their cost must be controlled as tightly as possible so that enough of them may be brought to adequately equip the services. Thus, it is often necessary, not to mention desirable, for cost-performance-schedule trade-offs to be made.

Contrary to policy, past experience suggests that such trade-offs are not made when they should be. Rather than making a trade-off between cost and performance, the services are likely to push for the greatest possible performance regardless of cost. Indeed, frequently performance requirements are set which only marginally improve the capability of the weapon while massively increasing its cost. This process of setting unnecessary and very costly performance requirements is referred to as 'gold-plating'. The Air Force's main fighter, the F-15, was gold-plated. By demanding that the plane have a top speed of Mach 2.5, when Mach 1.5 would have been sufficient, the service in-

creased the cost of each F-15 by $4.5 million and the overall pro-
gramme cost by $3.6 billion (all figures in FY 1987 dollars). If the lower
speed had been accepted then the service could have afforded to buy
950 instead of 800 F-15s (McNaugher, 1989, pp. 128–9).

Gold-plating may also come from the basic lure of high technology.
According to one recent study on arms production 'there is an empiri-
cally established general tendency among soldiers, bureaucrats and politicians in charge of procurement to favour the most sophisticated
technologies' (Brzoska & Lock, 1992, p. 6). Certainly this bias exists
among the military and defence policymakers in the United States.
This was one of the very tendencies with which the 'military reform
movement' took issue (Hendrickson, 1988; Fallows, 1981). Perhaps not
surprisingly, US defence policymakers (especially those in R&D policy) firmly believed that it was in advanced technology that the United
States enjoyed its greatest advantage over the Soviet Union.[15] It made
sense, therefore, for the United States to procure high technology weapons. This view was widely shared by more conservative defence analysts.[16] By the late 1970s and early 1980s there was even a sense of
urgency within the DoD about acquiring high technology weapons as
it was felt that the Soviets were catching up. The DoD Director of
R&D warned in 1976 that the Soviets could close this technological
gap by the 1980s, his successor stated in 1979 that the Soviets were closing the gap, and Weinberger declared in 1986 that the Soviets had
closed it.[17]

Two distinct sets of institutional pressures may also produced gold-
plating. The first set of such pressures has already been discussed,
namely, the consensus-building process which surrounds weapons programmes and which can encourage the raising of programme requirements as well as their early establishment. The Army's new IFV, the
M-2 Bradley is a good case in point. The Bradley was intended to replace the old M-113 armoured personnel carrier, and like the M-113 it
was originally required to be able to cross shallow rivers and to deliver
a nine-member infantry squad onto the battlefield. The infantry branch
raised the programme requirements of the Bradley in order to gain the
support of important actors with three distinct preferences: OSD analysts who were impressed with Soviet IFVs which were equipped with
both cannons and ATGMs; HASC members and Defence Secretary
Schlesinger who wanted to see the US Army packing more ATGMs;
and armour officers who called for a heavily armed and armoured
IFV capable of going into battle with their MBTs. By adding a cannon,
missiles and armour, the Army turned what was supposed to be a

cheap battletaxi into a mini-tank which was nine times more expensive than the M-113 it was meant to replace, yet was still too lightly armoured to take on enemy MBTs, too heavy to cross rivers (and to be easily transported in aircraft), and so cramped that it could only carry six soldiers (McNaugher, 1989, pp. 129–31; Stockman, 1986, pp. 296–302). Nevertheless, the infantry branch calculated that by adding extra arms and armour to the Bradley, it gave the weapon a far better chance of surviving on the institutional battlefield.

The second set of institutional pressures comes from the desire to promote programmes in their infancy so that they will survive to maturity. For the sponsors of weapons, it does not pay to be honest about the prospects for their programmes; programmes which promise to be costly and troublesome will get cut or killed. Instead a weapon sponsor tends, throughout the lifetime of their programme, to underestimate the final acquisition cost of their weapon and to overestimate the ultimate capability of their weapon. Thus additional capabilities are made to appear affordable (Gansler, 1989, pp. 145–6).

Inadequate Testing Before Production

Without testing and evaluation (T&E) the DoD would have no way of judging how a weapon programme was doing. T&E is central to how the DoD is supposed to regulate the acquisition cycle. The Milestone review structure is based on the idea that the acquisition cycle should be broken up into phases and that progress from one phase to the next should not be automatic but rather should be based on whether a programme has met the technical and performance specifications set for each phase. It is through T&E that the DoD is able to decide if these specifications have been met.

Weapons programmes are subjected to two types of T&E which serve very different purposes. Development testing and evaluation (DT&E) is designed to aid the engineering design and development of the weapon and to check that technical specifications have been met, whereas operational testing and evaluation (OT&E) is designed to 'determine the operational effectiveness and suitability of a system under realistic combat conditions'.[18] Basically, OT&E determines if a weapon can do the job it was intended to do, and if it can carry out this task without placing undue strain on battlefield support services.

These two types of T&E are not only different in purpose but also in how they are conducted. In OT&E the weapon is subjected to a field test; operational personnel test the weapon system in a realistic combat environment against a representative threat. In DT&E the personnel conducting these tests are usually technicians or civilian engineers, and the tests are carried out in laboratories or other such highly controlled environments.[19] This chapter is primarily interested in OT&E, since it is intended to help senior defence officials decide if certain weapons ought to be bought or not.

It is DoD policy that OT&E must precede weapons production.[20] This policy is reinforced by congressional legislation. In the 1984 Defence Authorisation Act, Congress established an independent office and Director of OT&E (DOT&E). The Act required that the DOT&E promulgate policy and procedures on OT&E, review and monitor all OT&E, and report to Congress on the adequacy of the testing and the test results.[21] In addition, the 1987 Defence Authorisation Act requires the DoD to develop competitive prototypes of weapons and subject them to OT&E before awarding a production contract.[22]

At the same time, however, DoD policy has also stressed another priority, that is, acquiring and fielding weapons as quickly as possible.[23] The main way of doing this is to allow a weapon programme to enter production before it completes full-scale development. This is known as concurrency. Concurrent programmes do indeed have advantages over sequential ones. As production is started before development has been completed, weapons may be acquired more rapidly than would otherwise be the case. This not only enables the services to meet emerging threats but also to take advantage of new technology before it becomes obsolete. As well as saving time, cost may also be reduced by consolidating or getting rid of duplicative tasks. Thus similar resources may be used in DT&E and OT&E which may be conducted side by side.

Against these advantages are considerable disadvantages to concurrency. In sequential programmes design flaws may be identified and rectified before the weapon enters production. In concurrent programmes such flaws may emerge in production models, which may then require extensive and expensive retrofitting, which may in turn lead to the production line being halted while production designs and techniques are altered.[24] As was noted in Chapter 2, the B-1B bomber emerged from a highly concurrent programme needing extensive retrofitting before it could come anywhere near meeting its original performance requirements.

That early OT&E is even more important for concurrent than sequential programmes should come as no great surprise. The point of early OT&E is to enable defence officials to make projections about a weapon's operational effectiveness and suitability *before* the weapon enters full-scale development and production start-up. This is important in all programmes because once a weapon reaches full-scale development it is usually acquired. This situation is suggested in a Navy instruction on acquisition which notes that Milestone II is the 'single most critical decision point, for it is here that the Navy makes a firm commitment to the programme; once started, it is difficult to turn back'.[25] Early OT&E is all the more important in concurrent programmes because full-scale development and production start-up overlap in such programmes, thus leaving no time between these two acquisition stages in which to complete OT&E, and making such programmes even more difficult to reverse once they reach this stage.

Both DoD policy and congressional legislation (1987 Defence Authorisation Act) allow programmes to enter production start-up before completing early OT&E. Indeed, of the four services, only the Navy has regulations requiring any OT&E at all before production start-up. Despite this, the GAO found that 'the Navy usually did not conduct OT&E' before full-scale development or production start-up.[26] Indeed, it would appear to be common DoD practice to allow programmes to start production without basing this decision on adequate OT&E data. A GAO report in 1985 was critical on this point: 'In all of the concurrently developed and produced weapon systems GAO reviewed, DoD did not obtain OT&E results critical to assessing mission performance before production start-up.'[27] In 1990, the GAO reported that things had not changed: DoD had 'made little progress in assuring that earlier OT&E is planned and conducted' and that 'the military services generally are not conducting or planning to conduct OT&E on weapon systems until after production start-up'.[28]

The services' casual approach to early OT&E may be explained by the real reasons for their attachment to concurrency. For if they were truly concerned with speeding up the acquisition process and reducing costs, then the services' would be far more rigorous about completing early OT&E, as this could save them time and money later. The services have strong institutional reasons for favouring concurrency in weapon programmes. By speeding up the acquisition cycle, concurrency enables programmes to rapidly enter full-scale development and production start-up. As was noted earlier, programmes which have reached this stage are rarely cancelled. It is at this stage that funds are sunk into a programme; full-scale development and production account for 26 per cent and 70 per cent respectively of the average costs of a weapon programme (Gansler, 1989, p. 157). By this stage most programmes will also have gathered a sizeable constituency of supporters. Hence, by the time a programme gets to full-scale development, many politicians and policymakers will already be looking to get returns on the money and political capital that has been sunk into that programme. Michael Brown argues that the services also find it easier to sell concurrent programmes to policymakers than sequential ones. Concurrency reinforces favourable assumptions in policymakers by implying that the military requirement for the weapon is urgent and that the weapon can be developed quickly and cheaply (1992, pp. 335–6). As the GAO puts it, for these reasons the services have 'a "build now and fix problems later" attitude': they 'want to move systems into production as quickly as possible in order to reduce the likelihood of them being cancelled'.[29]

Problems arise even when the services get around to conducting operational tests. Several GAO reports have noted 'serious inadequacies' in operational testing: 'Some tests were incomplete, and others were deferred or waived before key decision points. Also, tests were generally conducted in unrealistically favourable environments'.[30] On top of all this, the GAO also noted that, 'in some instances, timely test results were not provided to the decisionmakers'.[31] This behaviour confirms that the services are motivated by strong institutional interests to ignore, rather than uncover and resolve, problems in weapon programmes.

Conclusion: The Services Run the Show

DoD acquisition policy states that detailed performance requirements should not be set too early in a weapon programme yet in practice they are. It is also DoD policy that cost-performance-schedule trade-offs be made in weapon programmes but in reality performance is pushed at the expense of time and money. The adequate testing of weapons before they enter production is also stressed in DoD policy but again, in practice, production start-up frequently precedes OT&E. There are good reasons for these priorities in acquisition policy but the services have even better reasons for ignoring them.

The services share a primary objective which is to acquire the weapons they need to maintain their functions; the actual military usefulness of these weapons, the final cost of these weapons, and the amount of time it ultimately takes to make these weapons operable are of secondary importance. It is by steering their weapons through the acquisition cycle, and pursuing certain practices, that the services seek to ensure that their weapons are acquired. Hence, setting early detailed performance requirements, gold-plating, and concurrency without early OT&E are all examples of the services' ability to manipulate regulation of the weapon acquisition process to serve their own institutional interests.

A-12 AVENGER

The US Navy values large deck carriers above all its other assets and has done so for quite some time: carrier task forces have dominated US Navy strategy and force structures since the early 1940s (Lautenschlager, 1983, p. 32; Rosen, 1988, p. 158; Allard, 1990, p. 106). After World War Two, the Navy realised that carriers held the key not only to success in naval battles but in institutional battles as well. The principal post-war threat to the US Navy was not the Soviet Navy but the US Air Force (Builder, 1989, p. 77). It was obvious in 1945 that the US Navy was larger than all the other navies in the world put together: this led one Air Force general to declare that 'to maintain a five-ocean navy to fight a no-ocean opponent . . . is a foolish waste of time, men and resources' (quoted in Huntington, 1961, p. 377). However, carrier-based airpower offered the Navy new possibilities for power projection which then assumed a greater role in naval strategy than sea control. Airpower ended up saving the Navy instead of damning it: since the primary targets were to be on land and not at sea then the size of opponents' navies was largely irrelevant. Historically, the Navy has had two core functions, namely, sea control and power projection. While Navy strategy placed a different emphasis on these core functions during the Cold War, stressing power projection in the mid to late 1940s, and more recently combining the two functions in the Maritime Strategy, large deck carriers have been central to Navy strategy and force structures throughout this period. Naval proponents are quick to point out that large deck carriers are remarkably versatile and so able to disable any target whether it be located on land or at sea (Holloway, 1985; Jacobs, 1985; Friedman, 1987). Even when nuclear deterrence became the third core function of the Navy, it was the carriers which initially provided this capability from 1956 until the Polaris SSBNs took over this mission four years later (Lautenschlager, 1983, pp. 36–7).

The Navy Wants a Fancy New Bomber

The importance of the A-12 to the Navy is obvious in light of the fact that carriers are crucial for at least two of the Navy's three core functions. It is equally obvious that there is not much point to having carriers if you do not have bombers to launch from them. The naval medium attack aircraft is the service's main carrier-based bomber. However, as was shown in Chapter 2, the Navy urgently needed a replacement for its obsolete medium attack aircraft, the A-6E. It was also shown that carrier-based bombers played a central role in the Navy's Maritime Strategy and, in particular, in the 'forward strategy'. This made the need for a replacement for the A-6E all the more pressing.

By 1987, one year before a full-scale development contract was awarded for the A-12, the Navy abandoned the 'forward strategy', and by the end of the decade the Maritime Strategy was rapidly losing its relevance as the Cold War began to wind down. Despite this, the Navy still retained the requirement for CVBGs, this time to meet Third World contingencies, and so the requirement for a new naval medium attack aircraft stood. Indeed, shifts in the structure of Carrier Air Wings (CAWs) indicated that the importance of medium attack aircraft to carrier operations had, if anything, increased. In 1986 a CAW typically comprised nine squadrons totalling 86 aircraft, including two fighter squadrons of 24 F-14s, two light attack squadrons of 24 F/A-18s (or A-7s), and one medium squadron of 10 A-6s. By 1990 these ratios had evolved (with the addition of two extra planes), on the basis of a 1984 Navy CAW Composition Study, into three equal groups of 20 F-14/F-18/A-6s each. While this new mix was facilitated by the acquisition of the F/A-18, which is designated as a dual-purpose (that is, fighter and light attack) aircraft, this new composition still included *twice* as many A-6s as in the previous CAW.[32] Of course, the timing of the Navy's Composition Study may have had something to do with attempts to promote the A-12; the Study was conducted at the same time as the A-12 was being proposed as a replacement for the A-6E.

So the Navy needed a new plane to replace the A-6E, but why did it choose the A-12? It was argued in Chapter 2 that the Navy's awareness of the poor operational performance of the F-117A during the Gulf War may well have reinforced the service's inclination to develop a very stealthy aircraft. Notwithstanding this, the Navy already had strong institutional reasons for wanting to acquire a very stealthy bomber. The Air Force were developing at least two other stealth warplanes, the B-2 bomber and the advanced tactical fighter (ATF), both of which promised to be more stealthy than the F-117A.[33] The Navy could hardly aim to acquire a less stealthy aircraft than the Air Force. Moreover, within two years of the A-12 programme being started, the Navy may have come to believe that the A-12 would be the only stealth plane that they would be allowed to develop. In March 1986 the Navy Secretary agreed to look at the Air Force's ATF to see if it met his service's requirement for a naval advanced tactical fighter, and the Air Force Secretary likewise agreed to evaluate the Navy's A-12 to see if it fit his service's requirement for a stealth tactical bomber. Congress had insisted that the two services closely co-ordinate the development of their respective stealth planes in order to achieve 'commonalty and cross-service use' of these aircraft. The services must have realised that in all likelihood Congress would force them to acquire variants of each other's programmes. Since the Air Force ATF programme was developing apace, the Navy would have been very keen to see its own stealth aircraft programme develop. There is evidence to suggest that, consistent with the 'not-invented-here' syndrome, the Navy were not at all keen to buy planes that the Air Force had developed.[34] If the Navy was only really interested in acquiring weapons which originated from one of its own programmes, then the A-12 was its best hope of getting a very stealthy plane.

Navy Mismanagement

With regard to how the Navy managed the programme itself, there is no information available in the public domain detailing the early stages of the A-12 programme. The A-12 was initially classified as a 'special access programme' which meant that the DoD did not give release any information on the A-12 to the press nor to Congress at large; only selected members of the House and Senate Armed Services Committees and Defence Appropriations Subcommittees are given information on such programmes on a need- to-know-basis.[35] The DoD did not submit more widely available (but still classified and restricted) special access reports to Congress until 1988.[36] Navy spokespeople were unable to tell the press in 1989 what the A-12 even looked like.[37] Therefore, it is impossible to determine when detailed performance requirements were set. Nevertheless, the serious design problems suffered by the A-12 may have been due to detailed performance requirements being set too early.[38]

There is some evidence to suggest that performance was sought at the expense of cost and schedule. Certainly, the A-12 programme was gold-plated in its requirement for very costly excessive radar-evading capabilities when radar-jamming technology, or a less stealthy performance requirement, could have done the job. In addition, a report in the *Navy Times* in late 1990 revealed some of the other demanding A-12 performance requirements: the A-12 had to carry more ordnance and deliver it more accurately, as well as flying faster, farther, and longer without maintenance than the A-6E.[39] The fact that the programme experienced massive cost and schedule overruns would seem to suggest that the Navy paid more attention to weapon performance than to programme expense or timetable.[40] Indeed, according to the programme's prime contractors, one reason why they were unable to complete their full-scale development contract within cost and on time was quite simply the 'commercial impossibility of performance'.[41]

The A-12 was clearly a concurrent programme. The demonstration and validation phase of a programme, during which a weapon prototype is usually constructed, typically takes between two and seven years 'depending upon the complexity and the amount of technological advancement required' (Gansler, 1989, p. 156). The A-12, which was based on leading edge technology, flew through this phase in just four years with no prototype of the A-12 being built.[42] With no prototype on which to conduct tests, the decision to proceed with full-scale development was taken without the benefit of any OT&E.

Early OT&E did not precede production start-up either. Production start-up was included in the full-scale development contract awarded to General Dynamics and McDonald Douglas in 1988 but the first A-12 test flight was not scheduled before June 1990. By 1991 $100 million had been appropriated for production start-up even though the first test flight date had been pushed back to late 1992.[43]

Conclusion

The development of the A-12 can easily be explained in terms of institutional interests. Carriers were central to two of the Navy's three core functions as well as to Navy strategy. Hence, the Navy could be expected to support the A-12 programme under any circumstances; Navy support would be strong even in the absence of a real need for a new naval bomber. The requirement for the A-12 to be very stealthy can be seen in terms of interservice rivalry; the Navy wanted their stealth bombers to be as advanced as the new Air Force ones, especially if the A-12 was to be the only Navy-built stealth aircraft.

The A-12's acquisition strategy and programme structure reflected Navy interests. Detailed requirements may have been established early. High performance was almost certainly pursued without concern for cost and schedule. A highly concurrent acquisition strategy was chosen for the A-12 without provision for early OT&E. This enabled the Navy get $6.7 billion from Congress for the A-12, or about 10 per cent of the total programme cost, and spend just under half of it *without a single bomber being built*, let alone flown.[44] However, institutional considerations cannot account for the cancellation of the A-12. The Navy did not give up on the A-12 and, as the A-X programme showed, the DoD retained the requirement for a new Navy stealth bomber. Gold-plating the A-12 and rushing it into production did nothing to save it.

SGT YORK DIVAD

The origins of DIVAD cannot be readily explained in terms of institutional interests. The weapon did serve the Army's core function, conventional land warfare, and it was needed to implement Army doctrine, but it was not essential to either. The Army was engaged in an across-the-board modernisation of its force structure and so could be expected to pay more attention to those programmes which were vital to its core function and service strategy: such programmes included the M-1 Abrams MBT, the M-2/3 Bradley IFV, and AH-64 Apache helicopter gunship (Hendrickson, 1988, p. 80). It was these weapons, and not the DIVAD, for which the Army could be expected to fight tooth and nail. It was in response to widespread rumours that DIVAD 'rank[ed] low on the Army's priority list' that the Assistant Secretary of the Army responsible for acquisition, Jay Sculley, declared that the weapon 'has the total support and commitment of the US Army'.[45] However, Sculley was hardly going to say anything less than this, especially as he made this statement while addressing Ford Aerospace workers at the DIVAD's roll-out ceremony.

Furthermore, not everybody in the DoD was happy that DIVAD was a gun-based system. Missile advocates in the DoD reportedly leaped at every opportunity to undermine support for the weapon both within and outside the department.[46] This was confirmed by the Assistant Secretary of Defence for Development and Support, James Wade, who revealed in testimony before a congressional hearing into DIVAD that 'there was a fundamental flavour of some of the [OSD] staff . . . that a gun system per se was not the direction to go with'.[47] Given this, one would have expected the Army to have widened the consensus backing its new SHORAD system by designing one which incorporated both a gun and missiles.

Raising Expectations

Institutional considerations do account for DIVAD's development, however. It would seem that early detailed performance requirements were established in the DIVAD programme and it is clear that they were unnecessarily high. DIVAD was required to be able to detect, lock onto and fire at an enemy helicopter within eight seconds of the helicopter having popped up. In addition, DIVAD had to be able to do this while pointing 180° in the opposite direction to the helicopter. This detailed performance requirement was established in 1977 while the programme was still in concept formulation (phase 0).[48] According to one account, the need for an eight second reaction time was based on Army calculations that an enemy helicopter would be able to fire on friendly targets within 15 seconds and that it would take seven seconds for cannon fire to actually reach a helicopter hovering several kilometres away (Easterbrook, 1982, p. 108). This performance requirement was later challenged by the Army Deputy Chief of Staff for Research, Development and Acquisition, Lt. General Louis Wagner, in testimony before Congress: 'The Army didn't really have any enemy threat information to base [this requirement] on as far as I could tell when I went back and dug into how they came up with this specification in the first place.'[49] The General was also dismissive of another requirement which DIVAD was unable to meet, that is, the ability to engage enemy helicopters up to 4 kilometres away; he claimed that the DIVAD performance was 'satisfactory' at 'realistic ranges' of 2–3 kilometres.[50] General Wagner was not persuasive on this last point for, as was noted in Chapter 2, the ATGMs carried by Soviet helicopter gunships had a range of 5–6 kilometres.

The General's testimony revealed that setting early detailed performance requirements proved to be a mistake on the Army's part. So why did they do it? It would seem that the Army sought to promote the need for, and promise of, DIVAD by setting these detailed requirements early on. With so many, admittedly ageing, anti-aircraft systems already deployed, the Army had to show that DIVAD offered unique capabilities which were desperately needed. Thus, according to Lt. General Wagner, DIVAD promised to be able to do things which its predecessor could not: the DIVAD was to have all-weather capabilities and the ability to keep up with armoured units.[51] However, as has already been noted, Soviet aircraft had as much difficulty operating in bad weather as did US air defence systems. The need for mobility and armour may also be questioned. Not all armour and cavalry officers would like an air defence gun anywhere near them in battle; some fear that it would be more likely to attract instead of repel enemy aircraft.

When asked where he would deploy air defence units attached to his cavalry company, one commander told me that he would 'stick them on a hill' somewhere away from the rest of his company so as not to bring enemy aircraft bearing down upon his MBTs and IFVs.[52] Indeed, one critic contends that it is extremely difficult for helicopters to actually spot camouflaged ground targets from a few kilometres away, but that the Army had to exaggerate the threat helicopter gunships presented to ground units because it was seeking funds from Congress for the AH-64, its own helicopter gunship programme (Easterbrook, 1982, p. 108). Even if this were true, it is not at all difficult to spot a vehicle when it is shooting at you. In any case, OT&E revealed in 1984 that the DIVAD was unable 'to keep up with M60 tanks'.[53] This was particularly foreboding as DIVAD was designed to go into battle with M-1 MBTs which were able to travel far faster than M60s: 30 km per hour cross country as compared to 12 km per hour (Demchak, 1991, p. 60). Even if DIVAD was able to keep up with the M-1 it was likely to face the same problem as the Bradley, which was also supposed to go into battle with the M-1: that of not having enough armour protection to survive a direct hit from an enemy tank. Still, the Army felt that it had to promise all these things in order to get a new anti-aircraft gun.[54] As Wade told the Congress, because there was opposition to a gun-based system from within the OSD, DIVAD 'had to prove its worth'.[55]

The fact that unnecessary requirements were built into the DIVAD programme would seem to indicate that it was gold-plated. This was already suggested in Chapter 2 when it was pointed out that the Doppler radar, which in the end could not even distinguish helicopters from ground clutter, accounted for over half the cost of each DIVAD. It was also pointed out that radar guidance was not really needed and that the Army could have built a less sophisticated AD gun. Yet the service wanted the most complex gun, not only for its own sake, but also because it would be easier to sell to DoD officials and members of Congress. The US attachment to high technology means that, in order to succeed, weapons often have to be fancy as well as functional. As one senior staff member of the SASC argued:

We have a penchant in our country for knocking things out of the sky. So if it doesn't physically hit the target, we don't want it. The Soviets don't buy an air defence system for that. They buy it to prevent the pilot from carrying out his mission . . . by throwing a massive amount of lead in the air and hoping a pilot flies into it.[56]

So, even though the DIVAD was partly developed because the Soviets already had a similar system (the ZSU-23), this similarity was only skin deep.

Rigged Tests and Misleading Results

The Army chose a concurrent (in their terms, 'accelerated') acquisition strategy for the DIVAD ostensibly to save time and money. Risks commonly associated with other concurrent programmes were considered, in this case, to be minimal by the Army and OSD as the programme only used mature (that is, previously produced) components, or subsystems, and the contract awarded to Ford Aerospace was fixed-price, which meant that it was in the contractor's interest to remain within budget and on time.[57] On the whole, the programme costs remained stable but this had more to do with the fixed-price contract than the use of mature components. However, the programme did not proceed as quickly as originally planned: it was supposed to take six and a half years for DIVAD to be fielded, that is, reach initial operational capability (IOC), but by the time the programme was cancelled the Army was predicting that it would take ten years to acquire DIVAD. If this last estimate proved accurate, then DIVAD would have been acquired a few years quicker than at least seven other recent major weapons, but still, this performance was poor when compared with that of two other Army weapons developed under accelerated strategies, namely, the Multiple Launch Rocket System which took 6.2 years and Black Hawk helicopter which took 8.4 years to acquire.[58] The Army claims that using a concurrent acquisition strategy for DIVAD 'took about 5 years out of the normal development cycle [and] probably saved the taxpayers about $1 billion'.[59] These figures must be considered to be guesses at best. Even if they were accurate, in retrospect, they hardly represent savings considering how much time and money was wasted on developing a useless weapon.

As with all concurrent programmes, savings were to be made in the DIVAD programme by reducing testing and letting development and production overlap: operational and developmental tests were shortened and combined and the full-scale development contract awarded to Ford included production start-up. [60] As far as the Army were concerned 'further testing would cause a delay [which] could cost millions of dollars needlessly'.[61] The GAO argued that, far from being needless, further testing was essential and should have been carried out:

> As a result [of this acquisition strategy], critical information about the shortcomings in the *Sergeant York*'s ability to perform under realistic battlefield conditions was unavailable to decisionmakers until the system had entered its fourth year of production.[62]

The circumstances which led to this state of affairs are shrouded in controversy. Production start-up for the DIVAD was authorised at a DSARC meeting in May 1982. In what became known as the 'hotline allegation', it was claimed that the Army misrepresented developmental test data as if it was operational test data. It was further alleged that the effectiveness of DIVAD had been exaggerated, specifically that the weapon's lethality had been overstated by 300 per cent and that the speed with which it reacted to targets had been understated by 400 per cent. The Inspector General of the DoD, Joseph Sherick, looked into this allegation and concluded that while the information presented by the Army at the DSARC had been faulty, there was no evidence of deception. As it happens, the programme structure called for OT&E data to be presented at the DSARC meeting. Limited operational tests had been conducted in January 1982 but the evaluation of these tests was not completed until November despite instructions from the DSARC that they be done by March so as to have OT&E data available for the meeting two months later. When asked by Sherick about this, the Army gave no reason for this delay even though it was unusual, particularly in light of the DSARC instruction. This is all the more suspicious as evaluations of developmental tests which were conducted at the same time as the operational tests, and in which the DIVAD performed better, were completed in time for the DSARC. The Army claimed that detailed information, including raw OT&E data, was given in briefings before the DSARC meeting and that the charge of overestimating the DIVAD's effectiveness was based on an 'honest disagreement' between the Army and the PA&E analysts: the Army's interpretation of the tests show the DIVAD to have been more lethal and to have reacted more quickly than the PA&E's interpretation.[63] However, it should be noted that the Army Operational Test and Evaluation Agency had a history, stretching back to the early 1970s, of failing to provide realistic and timely test data and evaluations to DoD policymakers.[64]

There is evidence to suggest that the Army also rigged the first operational tests that it finally got around to conducting in July and August of 1984. No helicopter was made available to Army testers so they took a helicopter shell, put an engine in it, and mounted it so as to simulate a hovering helicopter. Army testers then claimed that it was necessary to hang reflectors on the helicopter because its small size and simulated motor gave it a far smaller radar signature than was expected from Soviet helicopters. Finally, after all this, DIVAD only locked onto the target on its third attempt.[65] Overall, the Army had no intention of conducting proper OT&E until *after* the full-scale production decision had been taken.[66] Thus, from the Army's perspective the July–August tests were only 'limited' operational tests.

Conclusion

The origins of DIVAD cannot be explained in terms of institutional issues. The Army had higher priorities than the DIVAD and there were policymakers in the DoD who disliked the very fact that it was a gun-based system. However, the programme structure and acquisition strategy, and so the development of DIVAD, were shaped by institutional concerns. The Army felt it had to promise to deliver a wonder gun.

Institutional considerations can also partly explain the outcome of the programme. By gold-plating the DIVAD, the Army forced it to live up to expectations it could not meet.[67] Instead of halting the programme when it ran into trouble, the Army insisted on proceeding into production albeit at a somewhat slower pace.[68] When the resources were not available to conduct proper operational tests, the tests were either delayed (by years) or effectively rigged. By these actions, the Army was able to acquire 64 DIVADs before it was finally cancelled.

MX PEACEKEEPER

The MX served a core function of the Air Force, and the core function of the most influential constituency in the service, SAC. Since its inception, SAC had proved willing and well able to defend its autonomy and core function. This was mostly due to the wartime abilities acquired by the Army Air Force and the capabilities entrusted to SAC in the postwar era.

SAC Power

At the onset of the Cold War, the newly formed Air Force was able to offer unique abilities deemed vital to US national security, namely, organisational experience of conducting wartime strategic bombardment and the capability to deliver nuclear bombs. The Air Force's SAC was given sole responsibility for these functions (Kaplan, 1983, pp. 40–2). The Air Force believed that nuclear weapons were central, not only to the survival of the United States, but also to their service. SAC rapidly gained confidence and competence (by their own measure) under its second CINC, General Curtis LeMay. Just as the Air Force gained ascendancy over the other services in the early Cold War period, so SAC ascended within the Air Force. Indeed, even though it was an Air Force administrative command as well as a specified command under the JCS, for much of the 1950s SAC acted independently of Air Force and JCS control (Kaplan, 1983, p. 104; Pringle and Arkin, 1983, pp. 24, 30). Ever since this time SAC has been well placed to define and defend its core function which was nuclear deterrence. As was noted in Chapter 2, the MX provided capabilities which SAC deemed crucial in order to cover the full target base in the SIOP.

The President's Problem

MX did not attract much attention from Presidents Nixon and Ford. The final decisions on the programme were taken by Defence Secretary Schlesinger, and his predecessor, Donald Rumsfield. Both men were strong advocates of the MX because they wanted SAC to acquire greater hard target hardware to implement the new nuclear employment policy NSDM–242. It was Rumsfield who pushed Ford into seeking congressional funding for full-scale development of the MX. Some legislators and congressional committees were concerned about the warfighting capabilities of the MX and about its survivability. However, these concerns were addressed to the Secretary of Defence not the President (Holland and Hoover, 1985, pp. 136–9). It was in Nixon's and Ford's self-interests not to get too involved in the MX programme. It was much better, from their perspective, to let the Defence Secretary handle the programme, especially if it was going to attract opposition from some quarters in Congress. Moreover, only Ford had any reason to get involved, and only in the last year of his presidency, when it was decided to move the MX programme into full-scale development. The importance of this stage in the life of any programme has already been noted, and so it would be reasonable to expect the President to ultimately decide whether a major nuclear weapon programme should proceed into this phase of the acquisition cycle.

MX was a problem for Carter. As far as the Air Force was concerned, the programme was only waiting on presidential authorisation before it entered full-scale production. However, Carter had expressed doubts about the MX during his election campaign and so, once in office, he could hardly be expected to simply reiterate the policy of the previous administration and support the Air Force's request. So Carter cancelled funds in Ford's last budget for MX full-scale development.[69] Carter was not only caught in a campaign bind; he was also personally concerned by the MX programme; he made no secret of his deep dislike for nuclear weapons (Carter, 1982, pp. 20, 66, 241).

Carter was initially more interested in making progress in arms control than in modernising the US nuclear arsenal. At the NSC meeting in June 1979 when it was decided to begin MX full-scale development, as at an earlier meeting in August 1978, Carter and senior administration officials concluded that MX would have to be acquired in order to win over the support of the JCS, the Air Force and conservatives in Congress for the SALT II Treaty (Holland and Hoover, 1985, pp. 143, 145, 147; Chayes, 1987, pp. 157–8). The support of the military is particularly important when seeking ratification of an arms control treaty. Since 1949, no arms control treaty has ever been ratified by the Senate without the support of the JCS (Miller, 1984, pp. 80–1; Stockton, 1991, p. 152). Needless to say, JCS opposition to such a treaty would surely kill it. In this case the CJCS, General David Jones, had made it clear that he would have had 'deep reservations' about supporting SALT II without the acquisition of MX (Hampson, 1989, p. 127; Stockton, 1991, p. 153). Carter let MX enter full–scale production for this reason. No decision was made on the basing mode at the June meeting because none was needed; since no basing mode had been found there was no basing development programme awaiting presidential approval. Indeed, on occasion Carter's concern for arms control clashed with the search for a survivable basing mode. An Air Force recommendation to the DSARC in December 1978 to proceed with developing a version of the Multiple Protection Shelter (MPS) system, called vertical-discrete MPS, was rejected by the President on the grounds that it depended completely on concealment for its survivability. Arms control required verification which meant revealing the location of US nuclear weapons once in a while. Carter finally announced in September 1979 that a different version of MPS which could be verified and moved rapidly to re-establish concealment, called horizontal-discrete MPS, had been chosen for the MX.[70]

The problem with any mobile basing system for the MX, aside from its sheer expense, was that it was going to take up huge tracts of land, use tremendous amounts of resources and affect communities which preferred to be left alone. Initial plans to deploy MX in a MPS system across Nebraska, Kansas and Colorado had to be abandoned in the face of fierce concerted public opposition. Despite a major Air Force public relations exercise, a subsequent plan to use the Great Basin region of Nevada and Utah ran into similar grief. Officials and public opinion in both states were originally supportive of the deployment. However, this all changed after the Air Force released its third Draft Environmental Impact Statement in 1980 which analysed the effect this deployment would have on the desert environment of both states: up to 40,000 square miles were going to be fenced off for the MPS system, 2.7 million tons of cement were going to be needed for the construction programme, and the MPS system was expected to use up 90 billion gallons of scarce water over a 20-year period. In addition, local American Indians were concerned about 313 sacred sites located within this area and the Mormon church, whose membership constituted 80 per cent of the population in both states, opposed the project because they feared that their communities would be wrecked by the 100,000 migrant workers that were expected to arrive with the construction project. When in 1980 Congress mandated the Air Force to explore the possibility of spreading the load of deploying the MX across four states, Nevada, Utah, Texas and New Mexico, this simply had the effect of spreading opposition to the programme to these other states. Needless to say, the DoD did not favour this. To top it all off, nobody much liked the idea that their state could one day be used to absorb a massive Soviet nuclear attack.[71] There were also substantial legal obstacles in the way of MPS deployment: the Air Force would have been required to abide by 38 different federal laws and numerous regulations, as well as numerous state and local laws and procedures. In addition, there would have been plenty of opportunities for private citizens and groups to bring lawsuits against the Air Force. One government study concluded that 'even without lawsuits . . . some Air Force officials fear that full compliance with the intricate network of legal requirements . . . could delay MX for years' (Holland and Hoover, 1985, p. 109).

Not surprisingly, when Reagan came to office he immediately dropped the MPS system. He had, in fact, been highly critical of it during his presidential election campaign and, in this case, implementing election rhetoric very much suited the President's self-interest (Wit, 1982). Reagan also had a personal interest in opposing MX MPS in that it was strongly opposed by Paul Laxalt, a Republican Senator from Nevada and the President's only close friend in Congress (Cannon, 1991, p. 165). The Reagan administration made sure not to repeat the mistake Carter had made; none of the basing options that they proposed exploring required much, if any, public land. Among the options considered by the Reagan administration were placing the MX on a plane, in a submarine, in existing silos, in super-hardened silos, deep underground, and lastly, bunching them closely together.[72] Even when it was decided (with congressional agreement) to temporarily put the MX in existing Minuteman silos in Wyoming and Nebraska, the Governors of these states asked Reagan to delay the deployment in order, among other things, to give more time to discuss the environmental consequences.[73] The mobile basing mode that was finally chosen, Rail Garrison, involved storing the missiles on rail cars on existing military property and only deploying them on the civilian rail network in times of emergency.[74]

While Reagan distanced himself from MX MPS he did not reject the MX missile itself: he embraced it. The MX was made the centrepiece of his administration's Strategic Modernisation Programme which was announced in October 1981. Reagan did not need MX to win over support for some arms agreement; quite the opposite, his administration declared its intention to improve the perception, if not reality, of US military strength before engaging in arms negotiations. For the Reagan administration the MX represented US military revival (Chayes, 1987, p. 160). As Chapter 2 concluded, the MX was important as a symbol of US determination and resolve. The importance of the MX to the presidency was indicated by the fact that its fate was decided by Weinberger and the President's Special Counsellor, Ed Meese, who did not consult the Air Force. According to one account, Weinberger and Meese based their decision on the MX solely on political considerations and, in particular, what they believed the President wanted (Cannon, 1991, pp. 165–71). When the military were told of the decision to temporarily deploy the MX in Minuteman silos, their opposition to it was ignored (Holland and Hoover, 1985, p. 218). Reagan fought tooth and nail to save MX whenever it ran into trouble in Congress and, in the mainstream quality press reports of such events, these executive–legislative disputes were presented as personal victories or defeats for the President.[75] Reagan had little choice: he had frequently stated quite clearly that MX was vital for national security.[76] Since Reagan's presidency was, in large part, based on reversing the supposed neglect of the defence establishment under Carter, he had to ensure that MX was acquired.

The Uncommon Missile

The sheer size of the MX made finding a mobile basing mode for it all the more difficult. Why did the Air Force not build a slightly smaller ICBM? There was considerable debate over the desired size of the MX under the Carter administration. SAC and the Air Force wanted the missile to be 92 inches in diameter, whereas Defence Under Secretary Perry, the State Department and the Arms Control and Disarmament Agency (ACDA) officials wanted the MX to be 83 inches in diameter (Holland and Hoover, 1985, p. 144). Perry favoured the smaller size requirement because it was small enough to fit into the Navy's new Trident SSBNs and so would have allowed both services to acquire a common missile.[77] SAC and the Air Force favoured the larger MX for the same reason: a 92-inch missile would not fit into the Trident launch tubes but could just about fit into the Minuteman silos.[78] SAC and the Air Force did not want to have to jointly develop a missile with the Navy or acquire a Navy built missile or, worst of all, see the vulnerability problem being solved by having their missiles based on submarines.

In the end the Carter administration authorised the full-scale development of the larger MX. Perry's deputy with responsibility for strategic programmes, Seymour Zeiberg, preferred the 92-inch missile. More importantly, so did Carter's NSA Zbigniew Brzezinski (Holland and Hoover, 1985, p. 144). He argued that the larger missile allowed the United States to take greatest advantage of the launcher and MIRVing limits being negotiated in the SALT II talks (Chayes, 1987, p. 156; Hampson, 1989, p. 124). Brzezinski also maintained that the size was very important in terms of the perception of US power; he firmly believed that the larger MX would have far greater symbolic impact since it would be equivalent in size to the SS-19 (Dunn, 1995). Thus, according to Chayes, 'Brzezinski made the size of the MX non-negotiable' (1987, p. 156). In all likelihood, Carter was indifferent to MX size. He had only agreed to let the programme proceed in order to secure the support of the military for the SALT II Treaty. So if the military wanted the larger missile then he would have been inclined to go along with this.

It Can Fly – But Does It Work?

The Air Force and DoD openly admitted that 'close to the maximum prudent degree of concurrency' was built into the MX programme.[79] Clearly, SAC wanted to acquire the new ICBM as quickly as possible. The original initial deployment date for the MX was 1982, that is, just ten years after the programme was started. In 1980 this date was pushed back to 1986.[80] The GAO reported a year later than this date for IOC was questionable as it allowed for very little slippage in a heavily overlapping programme schedule. As a result, roads and utilities for the MX bases were being designed before the location of these bases had been chosen, the programme called for roads and facilities to be constructed a year before the decision had been taken to produce and deploy the MX, and the programme only allowed for ten months to be spent obtaining land when this process normally took three years.[81]

The lack of early OT&E in the MX test plan was even more worrying. The DT&E plan included a flight test programme in which 20 missiles were to be test launched in four phases between 1983 and 1987. The OT&E plan called for 108 missiles to be test launched under operational conditions over a 15-year period. This OT&E programme was not due to start until December 1986, just after the IOC date, when ten MXs were due to be deployed at F.E. Warren Air Force Base in Wyoming.[82] Therefore the decision to produce and deploy the MX would have to be based on DT&E data. Phase III of the developmental flight test programme, when the 14th through to 16th missiles would be launched, was intended to test the MX performance and so may have provided some information relevant to the operational capability of the MX. Phase IV was specifically designed to provide an initial assessment of the operational performance of the missile; SAC crews were due to fire the final three missiles. However, phase IV was not due to start until 1987. While phase III was planned to begin in mid-1986 it was due to end at the same time as the first MX were being deployed.[83] Hence, the decision to produce and deploy the MX was based on *no* operational test data whatsoever.

How did concurrency affect the MX development? Early reports on the MX programme seemed to indicate that things were going well. A GAO report in 1985 noted that Air Force confidence was bolstered by the 'successful programme progress' and that 'To date, no major deviation to cost, schedule or performance milestones are evident.'[84] The first seven development test flights were widely seen as successful. They showed that MX accuracy had exceeded performance requirements. However, the failure of a missile component designed to add range to the MX (the stage III rocket motors extendible nozzle exit cone) in the third and seventh test flight caused half the missile's dummy warheads to miss their target areas.[85] The GAO noted at the time that if further test flights could not demonstrate that the problem with this component had been corrected, then it would have to be removed causing the MX to lose some range and thus target flexibility. The GAO warned that, overall, 'given the overlap between flight test activities and deployment activities, there could be little time for corrective action if unforeseen problems occur'.[86]

Problems did occur. The GAO reported in early 1989 that MX flight testing was two years behind schedule. At that time phase IV of the development flight testing still had to be conducted and operational test flights were not due to begin until the end of the year. The reason for the delay was simple: the Air Force was receiving fewer MXs than it had originally expected because of congressional reductions in the MX procurement budget, but the service was determined to stick to the revised IOC date of December 1986. As a result, missiles that were due to be used for test flights at Vandenberg Air Force Base were operationally deployed in Wyoming instead.[87] Ideally, since there was already so little early testing in the programme, priority should have been given to T&E over deployment. However, the services have institutional incentives to simply acquire new weapons first and worry about problems with them later, and the MX was no exception. The Air Force refused to delay the revised IOC because it was concerned that to back off from a long-established deployment date may give congressional opponents an excuse to cut acquisition funds for the MX.[88]

The lack of early OT&E produced two problems in the MX programme: SAC did not know how well the missile worked and the first 50 MXs which were deployed proved unreliable. The MX was incorporated into the SIOP based on data from the first seven developmental test flights; the critical performance characteristic was warhead accuracy. While this was consistent with JCS guidelines, the guidelines also state that 'developmental data may not be representative of the operational forces and should be replaced as soon as possible with operational flight test data'.[89] The delays in the flight test programme meant that this was not going to happen. Moreover, there were good reasons for SAC to be concerned about relying on data from the first seven test flights. The MX warheads proved to be *far less accurate* in the last nine developmental test flights (the ninth to seventeenth missiles). This was probably because the missiles were launched from a silo and used operational software during these later flights, whereas the missiles were fired from a launch pad and used developmental software in the first eight flights.[90] So the SIOP was assuming an unrealistically high level of accuracy in the 50 operational MXs.

SAC had declared full operational capability (FOC) once 50 MXs had been deployed in December 1988, but was unable to keep all the missiles on alert. This was partly due to a shortfall in the number of missile guidance and control sets (MGCSs) and inertial measurements units (IUMs). Both are required in order to operate an ICBM, yet because of reliability problems and repair times, the Air Force did not have enough of either to ensure that all 50 MXs remained on alert. Some missiles were also being kept off alert until a component failure in a 1988 test flight had been evaluated. As a result of these problems, each month roughly between 10 per cent and 30 per cent of deployed MXs were taken off alert during 1988.[91]

Just because the MX was perceived to be needed primarily for symbolic rather than operational reasons, it does not follow that the ambiguity about MX accuracy and unreliability of operational MXs were not so important after all. Acquiring a new ICBM which blatantly does not work only demonstrates incompetence and not resolve. Moreover, the Air Force's willingness to deploy the MX without knowing if it can hit its targets, or even fire for that matter, makes a nonsense of SAC's claim that it needed the new ICBM in order to be able to implement the SIOP.

Conclusion

The MX was clearly acquired for institutional as well as strategic reasons. The MX serves a core function of the Air Force, and the core function of SAC, the most powerful constituency in the Air Force. Detailed performance requirements were not established early on in the programme, but the Air Force did seek to protect its interests by developing an unnecessarily large missile (which would not fit into the Navy's submarines) and by using a concurrent acquisition strategy without providing for early OT&E.

Nixon and Ford had little to do with the MX. However, once the MX reach full-scale development, it attracted public and wider congressional interest and, therefore, presidential interest. Both Carter and Reagan had self-interested reasons to support the MX missile. Similarly, self-interest would have discouraged either from finding a satisfactory basing mode for the MX. Carter grudgingly supported it only in order to build support for his SALT II Treaty and so he was in no rush to resolve the basing issue. For this reason he also supported the development of a 92 inch missile for which it was going to be more difficult to find a survivable basing mode. Reagan gladly supported MX as a central element in his Strategic Modernisation Programme. However, his choice of basing modes appears to have been dictated by the desire to avoid domestic political and legal conflict rather than military advice. Moreover, once Reagan strongly identified himself with the MX he had a political interest in ensuring that the missile did not fail.

B-2 STEALTH BOMBER

The B-2 served two of the Air Force's three core functions: strategic aerial bombardment and nuclear deterrence. Given this fact, it is not surprising to find that institutional considerations do explain the origins and development of the B-2.

Service Support

As an institution SAC strongly identified with strategic penetration bombers. The creation of the strategic nuclear triad, with deployment of ICBMs and SLBMs in the 1960s, obviously weakened the case for continued bomber modernisation. Thus McNamara cancelled the B-70 bomber programme and ordered the acquisition of a small fleet of FB-111s (F-111s with enhanced range) to replace old strategic bombers which were being retired from service (Brown, 1992, p. 268). SAC saw things differently. Throughout all this, and despite being ultimately responsible for wartime operation of all the legs of the triad, SAC retained its attachment to strategic penetration bombers. Indeed Sagan argues that 'devotion to . . . the manned bomber led to a prolonged period of neglect for ICBM research and development' (1994, p. 89). This devotion was probably rooted in the experience of senior officers within SAC whose careers pre-dated the arrival of strategic ballistic missiles. These officers undoubtedly took their appreciation for strategic bombers with them into their parent service when they left SAC. As former SAC officers rose in Air Force ranks, they would probably have been inclined and able to promote SAC's interests. When General LeMay left SAC command in 1957 it was to become Vice-Chief of the Air Force, from where he was appointed Air Force Chief of Staff in 1961. It was from this position that he campaigned vigorously, if unsuccessfully, to get McNamara to buy more B-52s and fund the B-70 (Kotz, 1988, pp. 72–4; McNaugher, 1989, pp. 56–7; Brown, 1992, pp. 209, 223).

SAC was especially keen on the B-2. This was evident in the position it took during the debate over strategic bomber modernisation which occurred when the Reagan administration came into office in 1981. Air

Force command wanted to rush the B-1B into production and develop
the B-2. SAC preferred to abandon the B-1B and acquire updated ver-
sions of the FB-111 as an interim strategic bomber while the B-2 was
being developed. The FB-111H would clearly have been a far less capable bomber than the B-1B and it was for this reason that SAC preferred it to the B-1B: acquiring the FB-111H, which was really only a
jumped-up tactical bomber, would only strengthen the case for acquiring the B-2, whereas acquiring a highly capable strategic bomber such
as the B-1 would weaken it. SAC had no qualms about defying Air
Force command and arguing its case on Capitol Hill; CINCSAC General Richard Ellis testified before the SASC that skipping the B-1B and
proceeding straight onto the B-2 would be best option (Brown, 1992,
pp. 277–8). On this occasion SAC lost out and Air Force command's
two bomber modernisation plan (i.e. to acquire the B-1 *and* B-2) was
adopted by the administration. While Weinberger was inclined towards
SAC's position, he was under pressure from the Under Secretary of Defence for R&D, Richard DeLauer, and Air Force Secretary Verne Orr,
as well as from Air Force command, to proceed with the acquisition
of both the B-1B and B-2 (Kotz, 1988, pp. 202, 209–10). In addition, as
will be discussed shortly, Reagan had his own self-interests to advance
by backing the two bomber programme.

Notwithstanding the clash with SAC, Air Force command strongly
supported the B-2 as well. This support was bound to grow after the
Air Force had deployed the B-1B in 1986. Indeed, the Air Force was
quite willing to risk a serious row with the Navy in order to drum up
support for the B-2 in the DoD and Congress. In late March 1990, Air
Force Secretary Donald Rice wrote a memorandum to Cheney, which
was subsequently leaked to the press, in which he suggested that the B-
2 was a much more cost-effective system than the A-12, and that if cuts
were necessary they should fall on the Navy plane and not the Air
Force one.[92] In response, Vice Admiral John Nyquist, Assistant Chief
of Naval Operations for Surface Warfare, told the Senate Appropriations Committee that the Navy's new Aegis radar could track stealth
aircraft. Navy officials also suggested that the service had recently put
a satellite in space which could also track stealth aircraft. The Air Force
was quick to dismiss these comments: 'If stealth is no good, how come
the Navy's spending $75 billion on its A-12 stealth attack plane?' one
Air Force officer asked a reporter.[93] Still, this dispute continued to
simmer and emerged again the following year. In May 1991 the Air
Force Association, with service help, distributed a white paper on
Capitol Hill which claimed that: 'Just eight B-2s, operating from the

continental US, can deliver the same daily tonnage of ordnance as an entire carrier air wing'.[94] By knocking the A-12 in order to boost support for the B-2, the Air Force was effectively attacking a Navy core function. The Air Force was willing to do this because it deemed the B-2 to be crucial to its ability to meet one of the service's core functions.

The President's Bomber

The B-2 attracted presidential interest and support throughout its lifetime. The Air Force started the B-2 with Carter in mind. The service needed a new strategic bomber programme that would find favour with Carter after the President had cancelled the B-1 in 1977. Hence the Air Force Deputy Chief for Research and Development, General Thomas Stafford, decided that research into stealth technologies, which at the time was aimed at developing an advanced fighter, should be extended to develop the next generation of penetration bombers (Kotz, 1988, p. 204).

The B-2 did find favour with Carter, partly because it was a totally different system from the B-1, but more specifically because by 1980 the President desperately needed a new bomber. Congress was particularly concerned at the apparent lack of a penetration bomber to replace the ageing B-52s. Air Force reservations about the capabilities of cruise missiles along with reports of improving Soviet air defences prompted Congress into taking action; in July 1980 it approved an amendment to the Defence Authorisation Act requiring the Defence Secretary to start developing a new strategic bomber. The timing could not have been worse for Carter. The collapse of détente left the President in a vulnerable position in the run up to the 1980 presidential elections. Carter's opponents were accusing him of mishandling defence policy and citing the cancellation of the B-1 as an example. Needless to say, the problems surrounding MX basing were adding to the perception of a President who was weak on defence. The B-2 provided the President with a way out. In August 1980 Carter had his Defence Secretary confirm press reports that research was being conducted into building a stealth bomber. The implication was that Carter had wisely chosen to scrap the B-1 for a revolutionary new plane when in fact it was the loss of the B-1 which prompted the Air Force to start research on the stealth bomber in the first place (Brown, 1992, pp. 272–3).

Presidential politics played a lesser, but still significant, role in determining policy on strategic bomber modernisation, if not on the B-2, under the Reagan administration. Some evidence suggests that the Air Force's two bomber modernisation plan was adopted at Reagan's insistence and against Weinberger's advice (Kotz, 1988, p. 215). The strategic need for the B-1B may not have been apparent but Reagan had clear incentives to ensure that it was acquired.

By the time Reagan came to office, the B-1 and B-2 bombers had acquired partisan labels and rival political lobbies: Republicans and the House supported the B-1 while Democrats and the Senate supported the B-2 (Kotz, 1988, p. 205). Since the Senate majority was Republican, Reagan could only improve his standing with Congress by backing the B-1B. Key members of Congress were quick to make the President aware of this fact. The ranking Republican on the HASC, Bill Dickinson, and the Chairman of the SASC, John Tower, both impressed upon Reagan the need for both bombers. Perhaps more importantly, a ranking member of the HDAS, William Chappell, suggested to Reagan that he could deliver the support of 40 Democrats in the House for the President's tax bill in exchange for the B-1B. Lastly, the Republican Majority Leader of the Senate, Howard Baker, called on Reagan to remind the President of the symbolism of the B-1B: to build it was to prove Carter wrong (Kotz, 1988, pp. 213–14). Had Reagan followed Weinberger's and SAC's advice instead of his own political instinct, the B-1B would not have been acquired and the development of the B-2 may have taken a very different course.

Bush's support for the B-2 does not appear to have been motivated by political interests. Once again the JCS made their support for an arms reduction treaty conditional on the acquisition of a weapon. In mid-1989 the Pentagon let it be known that the JCS would not support the Strategic Arms Reduction Treaty (START) unless the B-2 was acquired.[95] In March 1990, CINCSAC General John Chain warned that he would oppose START if the B-2 was cancelled, and the CJCS, General Colin Powell, supported this position (Stockton, 1991, p. 155). However, unlike the MX and SALT II, in this case the military were not warning off the President but certain members of Congress. The President was a strong B-2 supporter and was supportive of the military's tough stance on the issue; in 1990 the Bush administration itself threatened to stall the START talks if Congress killed the B-2 (Stockton, 1991, p. 147), and in 1991 Bush warned that he would veto any defence bill passed by Congress which did not provide 'adequate' funding for the B-2.[96] The military's message to legislators who favoured arms control was clear: 'don't stand in our way and we won't stand in yours.'

However, the tide of opinion in Congress and the administration was turning against the Air Force. As will be discussed in the next chapter, by 1990 most legislators saw the budget deficit to be a far greater threat to national security than the Soviet Union. Finding ways to reduce defence expenditure was more than politically safe, it was considered politically savvy, and those interested in doing so found allies in those legislators who were keen on arms control. Thus, Congress was in no mood to trade an arms control treaty for arms acquisition, especially as the Senate would in all likelihood have ratified START even without the support for the JCS (Stockton, 1991). In late 1991 it was widely reported that Bush was wavering in his support for the B-2.[97] Up to that point the Air Force had been insistent that they needed all 75 stealth bombers. By early January it was evident that Bush would announce in his State of the Union address at the end of the month that he would make do with 20 bombers.[98] Bush did have self-interested reasons for abandoning the B-2 at this stage; there was nothing to be gained by backing a losing policy except perhaps a bad reputation.

The Golden Bird

Little is known about the early stages of the B-2 programme. Originally classified as a black programme, the B-2's very existence was kept secret until it was revealed by Harold Brown in 1980 (after that the B-2 was a special access programme). Even its distinctive flying wing shape was not made public until as late as 1985.[99] The Air Force gave some indication of the B-2's cost in 1986 but other basic declassified programme information on the B-2 was not released until 1990.[100] As with the A-12, therefore, it is impossible to determine when detailed performance requirements were set for the B-2.

The B-2 is also another gold-plated plane. The Air Force was clearly far less bothered about controlling costs and keeping to schedule than with getting the most capability out of the B-2. In 1990 the GAO reported that the B-2 programme was $12 billion over its baseline cost and three years behind schedule.[101] In 1988 the Air Force blamed these cost and schedule increases on a major redesign of the B-2 which was undertaken in 1984: according to the Air Force Chief of Staff, General Larry Welch, this redesign added $1 billion and 'months' to the programme.[102] This still left $11 billion and years of programme time unaccounted for.

What was the purpose of this redesign? It was made necessary by a change made to the B-2's performance requirements just before it entered full-scale production in 1981. Up to this point the B-2 was only required to fly at high altitudes. In 1981 a low altitude penetration capability was added to the programme's performance requirements. In high altitude penetration a bomber relies on defensive avionics,[103] or in this case stealth technologies, to avoid detection. By the late 1970s it was generally accepted that low altitude penetration was more effective because, in addition to radar-jamming or radar-evading technologies, a bomber could take advantage of the difficulty radars have in detecting any objects which are flying very fast and close to the ground. Flying at very high speed a mere few hundred feet above the ground is beyond the capabilities of human piloting: it requires special flight control and terrain-following radar to stop the plane slamming into mountains. Ground-hugging high speed flight is also very hard on the plane itself: the constant sudden changes in altitude as the plane follows terrain features are very stressful on the airframe (Brown, 1992, pp. 296–7). An initial redesign of the bomber did take place then in 1981 before it entered full-scale development, but this redesign failed to take adequate account of the extra weight and stress which the low altitude requirement placed on the B-2's airframe. Thus a second redesign was carried out in 1984 three years after the stealth bomber had entered full-scale development.[104]

Such a major redesign at this stage can be costly in terms of time and money to a programme. This leads to the question of whether adding the low altitude penetration requirement was worth it or even necessary. The whole point about stealth technologies was that they promised to make the stealth bomber undetectable, or at least untrackable. So surely the B-2 could have evaded enemy air defences at any altitude. The Air Force claims to have been worried not about the immediate threat to the B-2 but about what the distant future held. According to General Welch:

> In order to give the [B-2] more future flexibility and to ensure that it would have a useful penetration life as long as we could possibly sustain it, we decided that it would need all-altitude capability. None of us can sit here today and project what kind of defensive capabilities are going to be surfaced [*sic*] over the next 30 years.[105]

This would seem to suggest that it was desirable to give the B-2 as much capability as possible but that is not to say that it was necessary.

Furthermore, the Air Force's experience in developing the B-1B bomber should have made the service aware that adding the low altitude capability was likely to create more trouble than it was worth. It has already been noted that although the Air Force deployed the B-1B in 1986, it spent subsequent years trying to fix problems with the bomber. The B-1B's offensive avionics proved particularly troublesome. The bomber's automatic terrain-following (ATF) system kept malfunctioning: the ATF persistently caused the plane to pitch-up to avoid imaginary mountains, thereby wasting fuel and exposing the B-1B to radar, and to pitch-down as it approached real mountains. These faults in the offensive avionics still had not been ironed by 1988.[106] As a result, and in no small part due to crew concern, low flying exercises had to be restricted for the B-1B until ATF functioning improved in 1989 (Brown, 1992, p. 288).

Adding the low altitude penetration capability to the B-2 programme was classic gold-plating. The B-2 did not *need* to have this capability provided that the stealth technologies worked (if they did not work then there was no point in building a stealth bomber in the first place). Moreover, it should have been pretty obvious to the Air Force that adding this requirement was bound to cause problems for the programme. The fact that the Air Force went ahead anyway suggests that they did not care about cost or timetable overruns.

Buy First, Ask Questions Later

Uncertainty is bound to surround any programme based on revolutionary technologies, and everything about the B-2 was revolutionary: the design, the materials and the manufacturing process. All the more reason, one would think, for not using a concurrent acquisition strategy. Sequential acquisition strategies are far better at handling uncertainty because weapons are rigorously tested before they leave the development stage and enter production. In spite of all this, the B-2 was acquired concurrently. The Air Force awarded Northrop a full-scale development contract in 1981 to produce six development aircraft. In 1987 the B-2 was moved into production start-up and Northrop was awarded a contract to build five production planes. No testing whatsoever had begun at this stage; developmental testing was not due to start until a year later.[107]

Considering that brand new technologies and techniques were used in the construction of the B-2, the programme should have proceeded at a slower rate and allowed for greater schedule slippages. Northrop starting manufacturing the B-2 in January 1986, even though they had not completed the aircraft design, in order to meet the first flight deadline in 1988.[108] As a result, the first three development aircraft required substantial additional manufacturing work after they had been delivered to the Air Force.[109] Since the contractors and the Air Force were more concerned with how long it was taking to build the bombers than with how they were being built, the programme continued to be plagued with manufacturing problems right into the early 1990s. A higher than expected number of manufacturing defects were reported in the first seven planes: for example the third bomber was expected to contain 101,000 defects but ended up containing over 117,000 manufacturing defects. The B-2s were also taking far longer to produce than was expected: plane three took 29 per cent (or 426,000 labour hours) longer to build than was expected. Specifically, these manufacturing problems were caused by constant changes to the engineering drawings and by the development of manufacturing procedures and tools concurrent with actual production, as well as the sheer difficulty of building such demanding planes.[110]

Not surprisingly, the flight test programme did not go as planned either. The first test flight was delayed 19 months while problems with the first stealth bomber were ironed out.[111] After that things went from bad to worse. By 1991 the date for the completion of the flight test programme, including early operational testing, had slipped by three years to August 1996. These delays were caused by test aircraft being delivered to the Air Force late and incomplete, by the first B-2 being taken out of the test programme for retrofitting, and by the periodic repair of cracks discovered in the B-2 airframes.[112] Predictably, delays in the test flight programme were not allowed to affect the rate of B-2 production, which only fell behind schedule because of manufacturing problems.

As a result, the production start-up and full-rate production decisions were based on very little DT&E data and no OT&E data at all. By mid-1991, the Air Force was authorised to order the first ten production aircraft (on top of the six developmental aircraft) even though only 4 per cent (133 hours) of the 3, 600 hour flight test programme had been completed.[113] These tests revealed extremely little about the bomber's actual capabilities. Block I flight tests, which were completed in June 1990, showed that the stealth bomber could take off, fly around at undemanding speeds and altitudes, and land again.[114] The Block II flight tests, which were completed in March 1991, were similarly restrictive. As well as providing further data on the flight worthiness of the bombers, the Block II tests were merely designed to 'partially' measure, and provide 'preliminary' assessments of, the radar signature of the first B-2.[115] Equipped with this flimsy information the DoD were prepared to buy ten stealth bombers. Even more worrying was the rate of production and investment prior to completing early OT&E. In 1985 the DoD planned to invest about $40 billion, and commit itself to acquiring almost 60 per cent of the total B-2 production run, *before* early OT&E had been completed. In 1991, after Cheney's decision the year beforehand to acquire only 70 production bombers instead of 127, the DoD intended to invest more than $55 billion, and commit itself to acquiring just over 70 per cent over the production run, before the completion of early OT&E.[116]

Stealth in Name But Not in Nature

Early developmental testing was able to prove that the B-2 could fly. The stealth bomber's unconventional shape had meant that flight was by no means assured (Brown, 1992, p. 295). However, these tests revealed little about the B-2's supposedly unique ability to evade detection. The fact that the Air Force carried out extremely little and very limited low observability (LO) testing before investing so much into the B-2 programme was a matter of considerable controversy. In a letter to the Chairman of the Research and Development Subcommittee (RDS) of the HASC, Ronald Dellums, former RDS staff director Tony Battista wrote that:

> Contrary to present claims, the B-2 does not render Soviet air defence systems obsolete . . . There are technologies that have been around for over three decades that can detect objects with a cross section advertised by the Air Force [for the B-2] with more than adequate reaction time.[117]

Battista also claimed that the 'Red Team' responsible for examining counterstealth technologies was not pursuing this task aggressively enough. This accusation was confirmed by another congressional staffer who said that the Red Team was 'not interested in finding defects' in the B-2 (Shuger, 1991, p. 18). In his response to Dellums in September, Air Force Secretary Rice wrote that Battista did not know what he was talking about and stated that the Red Team was 'independent of government and contractor programme offices'.[118]

The clear lack of adequate overall early T&E in the B-2 programme has been noted. Thus deficient testing of this critical aspect, that is, the stealthiness, of the B-2 should come as no surprise. As it happens, the B-2 was not exposed to certain types of radar which promised counterstealth capabilities. In December 1990 the DoD Inspector General started investigating charges that B-2 supporters had been actively discouraging research into one such technology called 'ultra wideband' or impulse radar. About the same time, the B-2 programme office turned down a suggestion by a DoD radar specialist that the B-2 be tested against a Customs aircraft, which are able to detect small two-seater planes up to 200 miles away (Shuger, 1990, p. 17). A press report in late 1991 claimed that one of the major B-2 subcontractors, Boeing, were warned by one of their employees that impulse radar could track stealth aircraft. According to the report, Boeing attempted to discourage the employee from pursuing his research and finally fired him when he challenged a Defence Advanced Research Projects Agency report which had dismissed impulse radar. This report also noted that impulse radar was not that new; in 1989 Los Alamos National Laboratory conducted an unclassified study for the Navy which first revealed the counterstealth capabilities of impulse radar.[119] Claims by radar specialists that they can built super-radars are as questionable as claims by the Air Force that they can build super-bombers. However, the fact that the B-2 was not comprehensively tested against a variety of advanced radars, including impulse radar, is suspicious.

Even the limited tests that the Air Force did conduct indicated that all was not right. The GAO gave a carefully worded luke-warm report on the first round of LO testing in late 1990: it noted that the bomber's radar signature was larger than expected but that 'no major redesign of the B-2 should be required' to reduce the signature in line with programme requirements.[120] GAO officials were more blunt in their off-the-record remarks: one told Fred Kaplan that 'In GAO lingo, that means the plane flunked the test.'[121] The second set of LO testing, conducted in July 1991, went even worse. This time the B-2 proved to be far easier to detect than it should have been. The Air Force was quick to point out that the B-2 was never intended to be 'invisible' to radar; enemy radars would not only have to detect the B-2, but track it and guide a AD weapon onto it.[122] They also claimed that tests had shown that the B-2 was more stealthy than the F-117A.[123] Nevertheless, Rice openly admitted that, even after redesigns, the B-2 would only ever be about 80 per cent as stealthy as originally expected.[124]

Rice was quick to state that test failure did not constitute 'a major problem' but Congress saw things differently. Both the SASC and SDAS, traditionally supporters of the B-2 programme, clearly indicated that they were deeply concerned about the test results.[125] If this was a problem for Congress then it was a problem for the Air Force.

Conclusion

Institutional considerations account for the origins of the B-2. The Air Force has always had a strong affinity with strategic bombers, not in the least because they serve two of the service's core functions. This meant that any strategic bomber was bound to receive strong Air Force support. The B-2 was particularly attractive because it incorporated exotic technologies. The B-2's strongest supporter in the service was the powerful SAC. SAC was perfectly willing to take on its parent service, just as the Air Force was willing to start a row with the Navy, in order to promote the B-2.

The stealth bomber also attracted presidential interest and support. The Air Force started the B-2 programme to give Carter a bomber to support after he cancelled the B-1. Carter ended up supporting the B-2 in order to promote his defence credentials in the 1980 presidential elections. Reagan had no political interest in promoting the B-2, but he did have political incentives to back the Air Force's two bomber modernisation plan, which in turn shaped the B-2 programme. Bush was a strong supporter of the B-2. However, his support does not appear to have been based initially on any political calculations.

The development of the B-2 can also be explained in terms of institutional interests. The Air Force developed the B-2 without concern for cost. Stealth technologies, which are extremely expensive to develop, can in themselves be seen as a form of gold-plating. In addition, a low altitude requirement was unnecessarily added to the programme. The bomber was developed concurrently despite the fact that it was obvious that a plane incorporating such revolutionary design and materials ought to proceed in a sequential fashion. Billions of dollars were quickly sunk into the programme before hardly any DT&E and no early OT&E had been conducted. It is quite clear that the Air Force claim that 'the B-2 is in fact the most thoroughly tested aircraft in history' is completely bogus.[126] However, it would also seem that the Air Force had good reason to take their time testing the B-2; they feared that the stealth bomber would not be as stealthy as they had claimed it would be.

Institutional considerations can only partially account for the limited success of the B-2 programme. Bush decided to cancel the programme after 20 bombers had been acquired because he knew that Congress would fund no more than this number. Bush did not contest the issue because no President likes to take on losing battles. While the Air Force officially maintained its support for the B-2 right up to

Bush's decision, in a climate of budget cutbacks, support for the bomber in the service may have been weakened with the disbanding of SAC in July 1991.[127]

CONCLUSION

It is clear from Table 3.1 that institutional issues deeply influence weapons acquisition. This may be no big revelation. Certainly the conclusion that the military services support the acquisition of their own weapons is predictable. But what this chapter has also shown is how institutional considerations affect weapons acquisition, by examining why and how the services influence the acquisition of certain weapons.

Table 3.1. Institutional Issues in Weapons Acquisition

| | Military Services | | President | | |
	Core interest	Manipulated acquisition	Much involvement?	Support?	Institutional issues
A-12	Yes	Yes	N/A	N/A	Origins, development
DIVAD	Marginally	Yes	N/A	N/A	Development, outcome
MX	Yes	Yes	Yes	Carter/Reagan	Origins to outcome
B-2	Yes	Yes	Yes	Carter/Bush	Origins to outcome

Above all else, the services seek to protect and promote their organisational essence by acquiring the means to implement their core functions. In all of the case studies examined, the weapons served one or more of the core functions of their respective services. As a result, the Air Force strongly supported the MX and B-2, as did the Navy the A-12. Army backing for the DIVAD was not so strong. In this case, while the weapon did serve a core Army function, it was not vital to that function. At the same time the Army was developing several weapons which were crucial to its strategy and it was on these weapons that the Army was placing most interest and effort. So, it may be said that the DIVAD was peripheral to the Army's core function.

The services are able to influence weapons acquisition by controlling the detail of programme development. Institutional self-interests lead the services to manipulate the acquisition cycle by engaging in certain acquisition practices, many of which are contrary to DoD policy. Detailed performance requirements are often established early in weapon programmes in order to exaggerate the need for the weapon and facilitate the building of a constituency to support the weapon. Building constituencies of supporters and exaggerating likely programme and weapon performance also leads to gold-plating, where excessive performance requirements are built into, or added to, a programme without concern for programme cost or schedule. The services also like to rush programmes into production because programmes at this stage in the acquisition cycle are rarely cancelled: sunken funds and spent political capital encourage politicians and policymakers to ensure that any weapon that enters production is procured. So weapons tend to be acquired concurrently. Invariably, concurrent programmes enter production before any early OT&E has been conducted, thus the decision to start production is based on wholly inadequate information. Naturally, this suits the services fine; the services prefer to acquire weapons first and fix any problems with them later.

Table 3.2. Manipulating the Acquisition Process

	A-12	DIVAD	MX	B-2
Early detailed performance requirements	Unclear	Yes	No	Unclear
Gold-plating	Yes	Yes	Yes	Yes
Concurrency without early OT&E	Yes	Yes	Yes	Yes

As Table 3.2 shows, these practices are present in almost all of the case studies. It proved most difficult to determine when detailed performance requirements were set. They were established early with DIVAD, and probably also with the A-12. Gold-plating and concurrency without early OT&E were more prevalent: in all the case studies the weapons were gold-plated and developed concurrently without early OT&E.

This chapter has shown that presidential policy on weapons acquisition can also be driven by self-interest. Presidents do not get involved in conventional weapon programmes because the only important ones are the programmes receiving bad press and, from the President's perspective, they are best handled by the Defence Secretary. Presidents do get involved in nuclear weapon programmes because they are expected to, but the level of their involvement depends on congressional, press and public, as well as presidential, interest.

The degree and nature of presidential involvement in a weapon programme will also depend on the likelihood of a successful outcome: if the programme is going to fail the President will want to distance himself from it. On the other hand, if they are already closely identified with the programme then they can be expected to fight to ensure a successful outcome. In short, the President will seek, whenever possible, to be identified with successful programmes. Success is important for reputation and popularity, which in turn help the President to persuade other actors in government to support his policies. It is also possible that a President may support a weapon merely as part of a logrolling bargain in order to drum up support for a different presidential policy. Finally, Presidents may use policy on weapons acquisition in order to promote a particular image of themselves in election campaigns. Moreover, stances which they took in election campaigns may end up restricting their options when they enter, or return to, office.

As Table 3.1 shows, both the MX and B-2 programmes attracted presidential interest and support. Carter professed to have a general dislike of nuclear weapons which may have contributed to his specific dislike of the MX, yet he allowed the MX to enter full-scale development because this was the only way he could get the JCS to back the SALT II Treaty. Carter also supported the B-2 because he needed to promote a pro-defence image of himself for the 1980 presidential election campaign. Whether he liked it or not, Reagan had to get involved in the MX and B-2 programme because they both became prominent defence policy issues in the 1980s. Reagan had attacked Carter's MX MPS in the 1980 election and so this basing programme was cancelled as soon as Reagan came into office. His administration sought solutions to the problem of MX vulnerability based on political and not military calculations. Similarly, his administration backed the Air Force's two bomber modernisation plan even though there was no apparent need for two new strategic bombers. Bush's initial support for the B-2 does not appear to have been based on any political incentives. However, his sudden withdrawal of support may have been due to his realisation that he was unlikely to be able to get Congress to fund more than 20 stealth bombers.

All of the findings on service interest and influence are consistent with the bureaucratic politics model. Service acquisition practice is driven by organisational self-interest, and service ability to influence weapons acquisition is based on their institutional position in the acquisition policy structure. The role of the President is a different matter. The President is unique in terms of the kinds of self-interests he may seek to promote and the nature of his involvement in weapons programmes. No less than six self-interested reasons for presidential involvement in nuclear weapons programmes have been identified in this chapter: responding to public pressure, rescuing a failing programme, being closely identified with a programme, promoting a particular electorial self-image, being constrained by a campaign pledge, and using a programme in a log-rolling deal. Presidents tend to get involved late in programmes, when there are usually few choices facing them, often simply a choice between entering production or cancelling a weapon. Yet, since the President has the final word on this matter, he can have a dramatic impact on a weapon programme. The bureaucratic politics model fails to adequately account for the President's unique political perspective and hierarchical position.

The services are able, through their management of weapons programmes, to determine the pace, cost and shape of weapon programmes. However, they cannot ensure that programmes are successfully acquired. The A-12 was cancelled, and the DIVAD and B-2 were only partially successful, despite the fact that they were all goldplated and had concurrent acquisition strategies. This would suggest that institutional considerations are better at explaining the origins and development of weapon programmes than the outcomes of weapons programmes.

4   Budgetary Issues

Budgetary considerations have obvious appeal in explaining the outcomes of weapon programmes. A specific weapon may be acquired because administration officials and legislators believe it to be good value (or, at least, not bad value). Clearly, the cancellation of weapon programmes may also be explained in terms of budgetary considerations. If a weapon programme is seen to be too expensive then it risks getting cut or cancelled. If defence expenditure is perceived as being too high then weapon programmes may also be cut or cancelled to reduce it. In addition, questions about cost are most likely to be considered towards the later stages of the weapon programme and not the outset. There are two reasons for this, both of which have been dealt with in the previous chapter. First, weapon programmes almost always seem cheaper to start with than they actually turn out to be; there are institutional pressures which lead the services to underestimate the final cost of weapon programmes. Second, weapon programmes swallow up increasing amounts of money as they mature from R&D into production. Explaining the origins of weapons programmes is a different matter. Weapon programmes are rarely, if ever, started because of budgetary issues. It is difficult to imagine that they are ever started for the purpose of simply using up defence dollars. Weapon programmes are never started to reduce the defence budget because the services control weapons acquisition and they have no interest in reducing overall defence expenditure. Weapon programmes may be *promoted* by civilian policymakers, in order to replace more costly service weapons, but only the services are able to truly *start* a new weapon programme, that is, ensure a weapon design enters development.

This is because institutional support is as important (if not more important) than technological know-how in weapons acquisition. There are countless examples of weapons which were belatedly acquired, or never even built, solely because of service disinterest or opposition. According to Matthew Evangelista, the neutron bomb, which was conceived in 1958 and acquired in 1978, 'was not built for twenty years, for lack of a service interested in it' (1988, p. 250). Similarly, the acquisition of cruise missiles was held up not by the pace of technology, nor for lack of a strategic rationale, but because all the services were opposed to them; each service saw the cruise missile as a potential competitor with favoured weapons, namely, strategic bombers for the Air Force, carriers for the Navy and battlefield artillery for the Army (Duncan, 1985, p. 55).

A Secretary of Defence may get a service to acquire a weapon which is already in development. In 1962, when the OSD systems analysts had failed to persuade the Air Force to abandon their own service plane, the F-105, in favour of a Navy plane, the F-4, McNamara settled the issue by simply cancelling the F-105. As a result, 'given the choice of buying the F-4 or perhaps no plane at all, [the Air Force] bought the F-4 and eventually became an enthusiastic supporter of it' (Lynn and Smith, 1982, pp. 56–7).

Defence Secretaries have, on occasion, been able to initiate new weapon programmes with the support of a particular branch or component within a service. McNamara was able to get the Army to develop the 1st Air Cavalry Division with the support of Army aviators (Lynn and Smith, 1982, p. 57) although, according to another account, it was the air aviators who initiated this innovation and the Defence Secretary merely supported their efforts to develop the Air Cavalry Division (Rosen, 1991, pp. 91–2). Service secretaries may also intervene in a similar fashion with similar effect. Navy opposition to the Poseidon programme (a successor SBLM to Polaris), on the grounds that the money would be better spent on conventional weapons, was only overcome when the Navy branch responsible for developing Poseidon, the Special Projects Office, was able to get the Navy Secretary to persuade the CNO that the programme should proceed (Spinardi, 1994, p. 110).

It has also been said that the SASC, SDAS, HASC and HDAS (hereafter referred to as the defence committees) have in recent years attempted to add programmes to the DoD budget. James Lindsay notes that this first started in 1980 and that over the following eight years the defence committees tried to add 36 different programmes to the DoD budgets (1991, pp. 37–8). However, many of these additional programmes are not new weapons but modifications to existing weapons such as the safety modifications for the Titan II ICBM mandated by the SASC in 1982 (Lindsay, 1991, p. 28). Those new weapons that Congress does get the DoD to buy have the support of a service or service branch. For instance, when Cheney cancelled the V-22 Osprey tilt-rotor aircraft, a helicopter-plane hybrid that the Marine Corps were desperately keen to acquire, Congress responded by providing funds for the programme which it forced the DoD to spend.[1] Lindsay offers a clear exception to this. In 1983, as part of a deal to release funding for the MX, the Reagan administration agreed to develop a new single-warhead Small ICBM (SICBM) dubbed the Midgetman (1991, p. 38). The Midgetman was the idea of a bunch of liberal arms control proponents in Congress headed by Senator Al Gore who saw a survivable SICBM as providing a more stable deterrent than the ten-warhead MX which was likely to remain vulnerable; at the time the Air Force was not really interested in developing a SICBM as this might take funds away from the MX. Yet, as Fred Kaplan argues, even the Midgetman benefited from belated interest from some Air Force circles.[2]

I argue, therefore, that budgetary considerations do not provide good reasons for the origins of weapons programmes. This is because such programmes do not always appear so costly to start with. Weapon programmes are never started to reduce overall defence expenditure because such programmes never get off the ground without some service support and the services have no reason to help cut defence spending. However, budgetary considerations can account for the outcomes of weapons programmes.

The impact of budgetary issues on weapons acquisition is not constant: it varies according to the overall budget climate, and from programme to programme. The budget climate refers to the size of the defence budget and amount of defence expenditure as well as the degree of civilian control over both.

This chapter will start by examining the size of the defence budget as well as the level of defence expenditure from 1975 to 1993; the former is the amount of money Congress gives the DoD to spend while the latter refers to the amount of money the DoD spends on a year-by-year basis. This will be used to determine the availability of funding for weapon programmes as well as to gauge support within successive administrations and Congress for expenditure on weapons acquisition.

The degree of civilian control over the defence budget and defence expenditure will be established by examining the executive policy process. Control by executive policymakers is indicated by the degree of centralisation in the DoD resource allocation and acquisition policy structures. This is defined by the amount of formal policy responsibility given to the services: the services have more formal policy responsibility in decentralised than centralised policy structures. As was suggested in the previous chapter, there is a strong correlation between formal policy responsibility and influence over policy; it is because they are responsible for managing weapon programmes that the services are able to shape these programmes. Thus, in centralised DoD policy structures the Secretary of Defence and the OSD offices and directorates are likely to have more influence over policy than the services.[3]

Unfavourable budget climates are ones where the defence budget and defence expenditure are decreasing and/or civilian control of defence expenditure is increasing. This study shows that in such climates budgetary considerations are likely to have a greater impact on weapons acquisition than during favourable budget climates.

Budgetary issues essentially refer to considerations about the cost of the programme, and as such, may come in three forms. Firstly, there are considerations about the basic cost of the weapon. A programme may come to be seen as a budgetary problem if it is so expensive that all other programme considerations, be they strategic or institutional, come to be outweighed by concerns over the weapon's sheer cost. Alternatively, a programme may benefit by appearing to be inexpensive and thus affordable. Secondly, a weapon may be in trouble if it is perceived to be cost-ineffective just as it may gain support by being perceived as cost-effective. In this case, there is general agreement among policymakers that the weapon meets a genuine strategic requirement and what is at issue is whether this requirement can be met by a cheaper method. Judgements about cost-effectiveness may take precise or crude forms. McNamara strove to ensure that weapons acquisition was based on precise judgements about cost-effectiveness (McNaugher, 1989, p. 54). More common, perhaps, is for policymakers to simply compare the cost of weapons without proper consideration of their purpose let alone effectiveness. Thus the common saying that nuclear weapons provide 'more bang for the buck' when it is obvious that any cost-effective comparisons between nuclear and conventional weapons could only be crude in the extreme. Another example of crude cost-effective comparisons can be seen in the case of DIVAD when the weapon was criticised because it would 'cost nearly three times as much as the M-1 tanks it is designed to defend' (Easterbrook, 1982, p. 103); such an argument was not really useful for if DIVAD was able to defend, say, ten tanks then it would have been a worthwhile investment. Thirdly, a weapon may attract opposition if programme costs spiral of out control, that is, if costs increase at such a rate that the final overall programme costs are highly unpredictable but expected to be far greater than originally estimated. Likewise, a programme may gather support if it stays within cost and appears likely to continue to do so.

This chapter will first assess the budget climate under the Carter, Reagan and Bush administrations; the size of defence budget and degree of centralisation in the resource allocation and acquisition policy structures throughout this period will discussed in turn. Then each of

the case studies will be examined to see how the outcomes of these programmes were affected by budgetary considerations.

THE DEFENCE BUDGET AND DEFENCE EXPENDITURE

The size of the defence budget is often measured according to Budget
Authority (BA). According to the DoD, BA is 'the authority to enter
into obligations for payment of Government funds [which are] provided
by Congress in the form of enacted appropriations'. However, more accurate measurement of the defence budget in any fiscal year is provided
by the Total Obligational Authority (TOA). The TOA takes account of
other actions legislated by Congress, such as the transfer of unspent
funds from one account to the next, which do not affect the BA but do affect the direct value of the total DoD programme for a fiscal year.[4]

Table 4.1 US Defence TOA, 1975–93 ($ in billions)

	Then Year dollars	Constant FY 1993 dollars	% real growth
FY 75	86.1	228.3	-3.6
FY 76	95.6	236.3	3.5
FY 77	107.5	244.8	3.6
FY 78	116.1	244.3	-0.2
FY 79	124.7	242.0	-1.0
FY 80	141.9	246.8	2.0
FY 81	175.5	275.8	11.7
FY 82	210.6	307.7	11.6
FY 83	235.4	331.6	7.8
FY 84	255.2	348.6	5.1
FY 85	276.0	361.5	3.7
FY 86	278.1	355.0	-1.8
FY 87	282.5	349.4	-1.6
FY 88	288.5	344.2	-1.5
FY 89	292.1	335.2	-2.6
FY 90	293.8	327.3	-2.4
FY 91	309.1	328.2	0.3
FY 92	286.0	296.6	-9.6
FY 93	271.3	271.3	-8.5

Source: adapted from DoD Comptroller, *Defense Budget Estimates, FY 93*,
pp. 58–9.

The size of the defence budget in a particular fiscal year is not the same
as the level of defence expenditure in that year. Congress will usually

approve enough funds for a programme, or phase of a programme, which may actually take several years to complete: in this case these funds would not be entirely spent until the programme is completed. Thus, defence expenditure in any given fiscal year is measured according to outlays (or obligations for payment), that is, funds which are actually spent in that fiscal year but which may have been appropriated in previous fiscal years. To use an analogy, TOA may be thought of as the DoD's credit card limit and outlays as its cash.

Table 4.2. US Defence Outlays, 1975–93 ($ in billions)

	Then Year dollars	Constant FY 1993 dollars	As % federal outlays
FY 75	84.9	230.1	25.5
FY 76	87.9	222.4	23.6
FY 77	95.5	225.2	23.4
FY 78	103.0	226.4	22.5
FY 79	115.0	234.6	22.8
FY 80	132.8	241.9	22.5
FY 81	156.1	253.9	23.0
FY 82	184.5	273.6	24.5
FY 83	205.0	291.1	25.4
FY 84	220.8	301.7	25.9
FY 85	245.3	320.4	25.9
FY 86	265.6	338.6	26.8
FY 87	274.0	339.6	27.3
FY 88	281.9	338.4	26.5
FY 89	294.8	339.8	25.6
FY 90	289.7	323.5	23.2
FY 91	262.3	278.2	20.4
FY 92	294.6	305.5	19.8
FY 93	278.2	278.2	18.0

Source: adapted from DoD Comptroller, *Defense Budget Estimates, FY 93*, pp. 92–3.

While the TOA may provide some indication of congressional support for defence expenditure, defence outlays provide a better clue to congressional concern about expenditure, since outlays measure what is actually being spent on defence in any fiscal year (White, 1993, p. 190). High defence outlays may worry Congress if the federal budget deficit is high, just as low defence outlays may concern Congress if they perceive the threat from a foreign military power to be great. Thus, the trend in defence outlays from 1975 to 1993 will also be examined in order to establish possible reasons for congressional concern.

As Tables 4.1 and 4.2 show, funds may be measured in Then Year (TY) or constant dollars. TY dollars (also known as current dollars) refer to the amount of dollars in terms of the years when they were actually spent. Constant dollars refer to the amount of dollars which have been adjusted to reflect their value in a specific fiscal year. Generally, it is more useful to have budget figures in constant dollars when making comparisons across several fiscal years because it makes such comparisons easier and more realistic. For instance, in terms of TY dollars, the defence TOA gradually rose between FY 1986 and FY 1991 from $278 billion to $309 billion. When displayed in constant FY 1993 dollars, this gradual rise is revealed to be a gradual fall in real terms from $355 billion to $328 billion (see Table 4.1). Nevertheless, TY dollars may be more useful when trying to gauge congressional support for, and concern about, defence expenditure in any year. This is because TY dollars show the actual value of funds *at the time* when they were appropriated by Congress and spent by the DoD.

The Carter Defence Build-up

The 1970s was not a 'decade of neglect' for US national security. Yet, accusations to this effect, made in the early 1980s by the Republican Party and right-wing defence analysts, stuck (Komer, 1985, p. 70). In fact, as Table 4.1 shows, defence budgets declined under two Republican Presidents, Nixon and Ford, while they grew under Carter. Colin Gray and Jeffrey Barlow accept this point but they still find grounds for criticising Carter. They note that there was considerable real growth in Ford's last defence budget and they argue that Ford's Five Year Defence Plan (FYDP) allowed for far more growth than actually occurred in the annual defence budgets under Carter over the same period. Gray and Barlow conclude that Carter was complacent about the Soviet threat and so 'was neither willing to nor capable of reversing the decade of decline' (1985, p. 61).

Gray and Barlow are probably right to argue that Ford would have spent more on defence than Carter. Indeed, presidential candidate Carter declared in a televised debate with Ford that he intended to cut the defence budget by about $5 to $7 billion (Wells, 1983, p. 643). This was not mere campaign rhetoric: one of the first things Carter did upon assuming office was to 'dismantle' the Ford defence programme by cutting $40 billion from defence over four years.[5] However, Robert Komer offers a more convincing overall assessment of Carter's record in office. He agrees that the Carter defence budgets 'fell short' of what was required but, nevertheless, he argues that 'to deride the Carter effort as the centre-piece of a "decade of neglect" is sheer partisan politics' (1985, p. 75). Komer blames the decline in defence expenditure during the 1970s, which amounted to about 20 per cent in real terms, on the Vietnam War and its aftermath: the war drained resources away from defence programmes; it further encouraged Congress to chip away at the Nixon, Ford and Carter defence budgets; and it greatly contributed to the high inflation the United States experienced throughout this period (which reduced the value of defence dollars).

In his final defence budget for FY 1982, Carter did project significant real growth of 5.3 per cent in the TOA which would finance an acceleration of the defence programme which had been outlined in the FY 1981 defence budget. However, given that it was released in an election year, doubts were expressed about the true purpose of this defence budget; many analysts believed that the FY 1982 budget was designed to build-up Carter's image as being strong on defence rather than to build-up the US military. Carter's performance the year before, when he accepted congressionally mandated increases in defence with reluctance, did much to fuel such beliefs (Wells, 1983, p. 650).

The bottom line is that, during the early Carter years, Congress was only willing to support modest increases in defence budgets. Thus, Carter asked for $116.8 billion for FY 1878 and was given $116.5 billion, and similarly he asked for $126 billion for FY 1979 and got $124.7 billion. However, by 1979 Congress began adding slightly to the President's defence budget: $5 billion to the FY 1980 defence budget submission (Gray and Barlow, 1985, p. 61). Throughout this period Congress were acting very much in line with national opinion polls which showed public support for greater defence spending gradually increasing (Wells, 1983, p. 647; Russett, 1990–1, p. 531).

The Reagan Defence Binge

The Reagan administration appeared to have been taken in by its own campaign rhetoric; its actions demonstrated a strong belief that US defences desperately needed to recover after a decade of neglect and that a window of vulnerability was opening which needed to be slammed shut.[6] Consequently, the incoming administration quickly pushed for increases in defence budgets above the $20 billion real growth already contained in the Carter FY 1981 and FY 1982 budgets: formal budget revisions were submitted to Congress requesting an additional $7 billion (4 per cent) for FY 1981 and $26 billion (13 per cent) for FY 1982

(Wells, 1983, p. 650; Stubbing, 1985, p. 849). This was the beginning of an unprecedented rise in the defence budget, the largest and most sustained in US peacetime history, which was to continued unabated until FY 1986: there was approximately 40 per cent real growth in the annual defence TOA as over $100 billion (or just under FY 93 $86 billion) was added to it during this period (Table 4.1).

As was mentioned earlier, there was strong support for this rapid increase in defence expenditure among public opinion and in Congress when Reagan first came into office. Indeed, Congress appropriated almost 13 per cent more funds for defence in FY 1981 than was requested by the Reagan administration. The following year, Congress only trimmed about 4 per cent off the administration's defence budget submission. However, as Table 4.3 shows, this initial enthusiasm for the defence build-up was short lived. Congressional support for Reagan's defence programme was already beginning to wane by FY 1983; Congress cut 6–7.5 per cent from the administrations defence budget submission each year from FY 1983–5.

Table 4.3. BA Requests by Weinberger and Congressional Responses, FY 1981–9 (TY $ in billions)

	Request	Response	Amount	Difference %
FY 81	158.2	178.4	20.2	12.8
FY 82	222.2	213.8	−8.4	−3.9
FY 83	257.5	239.5	−18.0	−7.5
FY 84	273.4	258.2	−15.2	−5.9
FY 85	305.0	286.8	−18.2	−6.6
FY 86	313.7	281.1	−32.6	−11.6
FY 87	311.6	279.5	−32.1	−11.5
FY 88	303.3	283.2	−20.1	−7.5
FY 89	323.3	290.8	−32.5	−11.2
FY 81–88	2468.2	2311.3	−156.9	−6.9

Source: Kaufmann, 1989, p. 61.

By early 1983 Reagan was being severely criticised for the pace of his defence build-up. In January, six former cabinet secretaries (five of them former treasury secretaries) launched an advertising campaign in national newspapers calling on Reagan to reduce defence spending.[7] Congress was not only concerned about the size of the defence budgets being submitted by the administration. It was also infuriated by Weinberger's uncompromising attitude: the Defence Secretary refused to give any ground on the defence budget and insisted that every cent was needed. In January and February 1983 congressional leaders, among them the Republican majority leader of the Senate, Howard Baker, called on Reagan to slow down the defence build-up and further suggested that Weinberger ought to be removed from his position because of his stubbornness over the defence budget.[8]

Weinberger believed that by standing firm he would able to secure more defence funds than by forging a deal with Congress; NSA Clark shared this viewpoint, while White House Chief of Staff, James Baker, disagreed. The dispute within the White House, and between the executive and legislature over the FY 1984 defence budget request, demonstrated that Reagan backed his Defence Secretary's position but that this position was ill-advised. Senate leaders had called on the President to reduce his defence BA request for FY 1984 from 10 per cent to 8 per cent real growth. The Senate Budget Committee (SBC) Chairman, Pete Domenici, even delayed his committee's vote on the defence BA by a few weeks to allow the administration to strike a deal with Congress. Finally, after intense pressure from Baker, Reagan approved two compromise positions but he made both conditional on Weinberger's agreement which, naturally, was not forthcoming. In the end, the SBC approved a 5 per cent increase in the defence BA when, according to congressional staffers, the committee would have approved a 7 per cent increase had Weinberger be willing to compromise.[9]

Notwithstanding the decline in congressional and public support for the Reagan build-up from 1982 to 1984, defence TOA grew throughout this period. It simply did not grow as fast as it had in the previous two fiscal years (Table 4.1). In 1985 things changed, and defence TOA shrank for the first time in six years.

The Deficit Dominates the Agenda

A new trend was evident in congressional and public opinion from 1985 which was to have a dramatic impact on defence appropriations thereafter: the Soviet Union was viewed with decreasing concern while the growing federal budget was viewed with increasing alarm. If the primary threat to US security came from federal over-expenditure, and not from the Soviet Union, then high defence budgets were no longer desirable; under such circumstances they were part of the problem rather than a solution.

According to Reagan's budget director, David Stockman, the President had repeatedly said that 'Defence is not a budget issue. You spend what you need' (1986, p. 303). By 1984 this attitude was already beginning to wear thin with Congress. With elections looming, Congress had its sights firmly placed on the big election issue: the federal budget deficit. Republicans and Democrats on Capitol Hill were reportedly engaged in a 'bidding war to see who [could] come up with the largest reductions' to the deficit.[10] This concern about the deficit dominated congressional deliberations on defence.[11]

The DoD maintained that the budget deficit was not their fault. Deputy Secretary, Frank Carlucci, echoed Weinberger's views when he stated the year before that 'We are not responsible for the budget deficit', adding that, 'You shouldn't measure defence against social programmes. The starting point is to measure it against the threat.'[12] This argument was not convincing. Reagan's FY 1981 budget produced a structural deficit when it locked in higher spending on defence and social welfare with lowered taxes: when the gap between government expenditures and revenues began to grow, Democrat legislators refused to cut social welfare spending, Republicans in the administration and Congress refused to cut defence spending, and nobody was willing to take responsibility for raising taxes (Peterson and Rom, 1988; Jacobson, 1993). In short, clearly defence expenditure *was* partly responsible for the federal budget deficit. This much was obvious to legislators in 1984 since defence expenditure amounted to almost 26 per cent of all federal outlays in that fiscal year (see Table 4.2).

Defence outlays continued to rise in FY 1986 jumping from $245 billion to $265 billion in TY dollars (or $320 billion to $338 billion in FY 1993 dollars) (see Table 4.2). Congress reacted by cutting defence TOA in real terms, for the first time in six years, for that fiscal year by 1.8 per cent (that is, by FY93 $6.5 billion). As Table 4.1 shows, Congress continued thereafter to reduce defence TOA in real terms by ever-increasing amounts (with the exception of FY 1991 which is accounted for by the Gulf War). By this stage few people believed that too little was being spent on defence (Hartley and Russet, 1992, p. 907). In fact, most people believed that the level of defence expenditure was damaging to the United States: a survey conducted in 1988 (for the American's Talk Security project) found that three in five respondents believed that 'the amount of money spent on defence is hurting our economic well-being' and 86 per cent of respondents thought that the United States may 'seriously damage our economy by spending too much to defend other countries' (Yankelovich and Smoke, 1988, p. 8). Legislators now found that cutting defence was politically acceptable, indeed desirable, where previously it could have been damaging (Stockton, 1991, pp. 158, 163).

Table 4.3 shows that throughout this period Weinberger kept pushing for substantial increases in the defence budget and Congress kept turning him down. The differences between the Secretary's requests and congressional responses were significant from FY 1983 to FY 1985 but for the following four fiscal years they were dramatic (over TY $30 billion or 11 per cent for most of these years) (see Table 6.3). According to Barry Blechman, legislators were simply sick of Weinberger's intransigence and so they simply ignored his budget submissions (1990, p. 36; see also Kaufmann, 1989, p. 62; Smith, 1988, pp. 209–10). Pleas from the President did little to change the minds of legislators. Reagan went on television to rally support for the FY 1987 defence budget submission only to have Aspin declare it 'dead before arrival'.[13]

The defence budget was also squeezed by the passing of the Balanced Budget and Emergency Deficit Control Act in 1985. This Act was better known as Gramm-Rudman-Hollings (GRH), so-called after its three main sponsors in the Senate (although Fritz Hollings, a Democrat Senator played less of a role in developing the bill than his Republican colleagues Phil Gramm and Warren Rudman). GRH was designed to produce a balanced budget in five years by setting annual deficit targets which had to be met. If the budget deficit exceeded these targets by more than $10 billion then sequestration would occur whereby all eligible accounts would be cut by equal amounts in order to trim away the excess expenditure. In this way GRH was supposed to encourage both Congress and the administration to co-operate in reaching the deficit targets because sequestration promised to hit both Democrat social welfare programmes and Republican defence programmes equally. In the end, deficit targets were never reached but sequestration was avoided by both Congress and administration agreeing to fiddle the figures (LeLoup, 1993, p. 45). For example, both sides agreed to place the multi-billion dollar Savings and Loan bailout 'off-budget' in 1989 and so avoided triggering sequestration (Collender, 1992, pp. 286–7). Despite cheating by the administration and Congress, GRH still added to the pressure on Congress to cut defence budgets (LeLoup, 1993, pp. 45–6).

The Soviet Threat Disappears

Just as the deficit problem appeared to grow, the Soviet threat appeared to shrink. From the administration's perspective, US–Soviet relations improved somewhat in 1984 and greatly in 1985, due to Gorbachev's accession to power that year (Cannon, 1991, pp. 739–91; Shultz, 1993, pp. 463–538, 561–607). Subsequent developments were to lead to a rapid easing in tension between the superpowers and leaps forward in arms reduction with near agreement at Rejkjavik in 1986, Gorbachev's visit to Washington and the signing of the Intermediate-range Nuclear Forces (INF) Treaty in 1987, and Reagan's visit to Moscow and Gorbachev's speech to the UN in December 1988 (Shultz, 1993, pp. 751–82, 879–900, 983–1015, 1080–108).

Oddly, Shultz makes little of Gorbachev's speech in his autobiography (1993, pp. 1106–8). This is misleading for the speech was momentous: it promised massive unilateral reductions in the Soviet armed forces (500,000 troops, 10,000 tanks, 8,500 artillery pieces and 800 combat aircraft) and spelt out a new vision for future US–Soviet relations. It had a dramatic impact on opinion in Congress. The size of the concession being offered by Gorbachev was not lost on Nunn as he would later stress on the Senate floor:

> The unilateral Soviet withdrawals from Eastern Europe alone . . . will be greater than the entire US 7th Army and 20 per cent greater than the most ambitious proposal that NATO ever made in the long and disappointing 14-year history of the Mutual and Balanced Force Reduction Talks.[14]

One senior congressional staffer later declared of Gorbachev's speech that, the 'world changed in profound ways that day. We were finally waking up to the changes that were occurring in the Soviet Union.'[15] While the speech caught everybody by surprise, it was in line with expectations; it was seen to confirm the adoption of a defensive Soviet military posture under Gorbachev, which defence analysts had long charted, and which was typified by the doctrine of 'reasonable sufficiency' unveiled by Gorbachev in 1986 (Parrott, 1988; Sestanovich, 1988; Dibb, 1989; Herspring, 1989a; Garthoff, 1990; MccGwire, 1991).

Some analysts and administration policymakers saw Gorbachev's speech more as a sign of hope than a watershed in itself; in this sense the speech was more important for what it revealed about power struggles in the Soviet Union than as a definitive statement of Soviet policy. Western analysts placed the origins of a truly defensive Soviet military posture down to the emergence, and growing influence, of civilian defence specialists (largely from the institutes of the Academy of Sciences) in the Soviet Union (Rice, 1989; Warner, 1989). Indeed Stephen Meyer argued that the development of a new Soviet thinking on security was primarily designed to give Gorbachev the upper hand over the military on defence policy rather than to produce a defensive military doctrine *per se* (1988, pp. 155–6). While Soviet military chiefs were happy to espouse the rhetoric of reasonable sufficiency, they were unable to explain to their counterparts in the US military and to US defence officials what this actually meant in operational practice. From this perspective, Gorbachev's UN speech in 1988 was taken as indicating that, as one Soviet expert in the State Department put it, 'the institute people had won round one of the debate', but only round one mind you; US policymakers still had to be convinced that real and irreversible change was occurring in the Soviet military.[16]

Bush Finally Cuts Defence

Bush was elected on a platform of little or no change, what he called 'status quo plus', but even his administration could not ignore the change being brought in by Gorbachev. According to one State Department official, policy towards the Soviet Union during the first 14 months of the Bush administration was characterised by a combination of caution and optimism; the tendency towards caution, which was evident in the first half of 1989, was replaced by optimism in the autumn of 1989 after the Soviet Union did nothing to prevent the democratic revolutions in Eastern Europe.[17] This approach was, by and large, in line with public opinion at the time. Such was the conclusion of one extensive study on public opinion in 1988: 'The current mood can be characterised as a wary readiness . . . distinctly hopeful yet cautious' (Yankelovich and Smoke, 1988, p. 2).

However, right up to mid-1990, Congress was critical of the pace with which Bush was reacting to events. As late as April 1989 the administration was projecting continuing real increases in the defence TOA. The dramatic developments in Europe during that year led the DoD to finally accept that defence budget would be cut and so Cheney ordered a revision of the FYDP to assume an annual real rate of decline of 2 per cent up to FY 1995.[18] The FY 1991 defence budget submission which was presented to Congress in 1990 was still generally seen to be too large on Capitol Hill. Most legislators perceived a policy vacuum and proposed policies of their own to remedy this situation.[19] The most conspicuous contribution came from Nunn in the form of five speeches which he delivered on the Senate Floor in late March and late April 1990.[20] Congress did not see much need for caution when the conventional threat had collapsed in Europe along with the WTO and deliberate nuclear war became more unimaginable with the end of the Cold War.[21] In contrast, some administration officials still saw some possibility for a resumption of tense relations with the Soviet Union should Gorbachev fall or his reforms fail.[22] The FY 1991 defence budget was in particular trouble because, whereas Cheney had given some assurances to Nunn that the FY 1992 budget submission did take account of the events in 1989, none were forthcoming for the FY 1991 budget submission.[23] The reason for this was simple: the FY 1991 budget submission had not been revised to take account of the democratisation of Eastern Europe and collapse of the WTO because the laborious Planning, Programming and Budgeting System (PPBS) process made such radical revisions all but impossible to complete at short notice and, in any case, no consensus existed within the administration favouring such a revision.[24]

Bush did finally produce a new defence strategy, which had been drafted by a handful of DoD officials and JCS officers, which he unveiled in August 1990 (Stockton, 1993, p. 242). This new strategy re-focused the DoD's effort away from the threat of attack by the Soviet Union, which was now seen as remote, towards regional contingencies.[25] In line with this new strategy, General Powell issued a guidance called the 'Base Force Concept' which instituted a re-design of the US force structure to be completed by FY 1995. Under the Base Force Plan the US force structure was to be cut by 20–25 per cent (up to 1.64 million personnel).[26] The Base Force Plan also envisaged the annual defence budget being reduced by about 20 per cent by FY 1995.[27]

Relations continued to improve with the Soviet Union: in 1990 a Conventional Forces in Europe (CFE) Treaty was signed and in July of the following year the START Treaty was signed in Moscow by Bush and Gorbachev (International Institute for Strategic Studies, 1991, p. 216). Then hard-liners tried to seize power in the Soviet Union. As was argued in Chapter 2, the failure of the August 1991 coup attempt by Soviet hard-line conservatives sealed the fate of the Union they were trying to save, and finally buried the so-called Soviet threat. Since the Gorbachev regime appeared benign, this threat had rested on Soviet nuclear capabilities, which could have been mobilised by some hypothetical future conservative regime to intimidate the West. The failure of the coup demonstrated that a conservative regime would be unable to gain control of an increasingly democratised USSR and, more specifically, that this was in part because the Soviet military would not support it.[28]

The collapse of the Soviet Union merely encouraged DoD planners to look for threats from other countries. The Gulf War provided a convenient backdrop for this exercise. Notwithstanding the obvious, the

DoD was keen to stress to legislators that it had learned from the mistakes of the previous budget submission, and that the FY 1992 defence budget was designed in line with this new set of priorities. Accordingly, the 1992 report to Congress reminded legislators that 'our FY 1992–3 biennial request assumed that regional contingencies, not Soviet military power, would be our main security concern in the future'.[29] Nevertheless, many in Congress believed that the Base Force Plan was simply obsolete with the collapse of the Soviet Union (Adams and Kosiak, 1993, p. 36). Aspin was a particularly harsh critic of the plan and called for a new one (he offered three options labelled A, B and C) which would allow far greater force cuts and a genuine restructuring of the armed forces (Zakheim and Ranney, 1993, pp. 51–3, 72–4). Aspin's favoured option C envisaged $91 billion in cuts to the FY 1993–8 defence programme, saving almost twice as much money as the Base Force Plan.[30]

Even though Bush was slow to revise his defence strategy in line with congressional opinion, the general perception in Washington was that, right from the start of his administration, he was far less interested in defence than Reagan had been. Bush was far more concerned with bringing down the budget deficit, without having to raise new taxes (his main campaign pledge had been 'no new taxes'), than with raising defence funding.[31] So, while the Bush administration and Congress disagreed on the solution, at least both institutions recognised what the major problem was. By this stage both institutions had very good reason to be so concerned about the annual budget deficits; the US Comptroller General told the SASC that the administration was using 'creative book-keeping' to hide the true size of the annual budget deficits which he predicted would result in a national debt of $4.5 trillion by FY 1995. He went on to note that 'A debt of this magnitude would require annual interest payments of over $335 billion and would represent the largest single item in the federal budget.'[32]

Agreeing to recognise the main problem was not enough; the disagreement over how to solve it was to result in a crisis in 1990 when Congress was unable to pass a balanced budget. The crisis was only resolved in a series of budget summits between the two institutions at which Congress was able to force Bush to break his pledge in exchange for their agreement to cut social welfare programmes (Jacobson, 1993, p. 381; LeLoup, 1993, p. 50). This budget crisis revealed the strain which GRH had put on the budget process and executive–legislative relations. It also showed how unrealistic it was to expect the administration and Congress to reduce the deficit when they could barely stop it from growing. Therefore Congress and the administration abandoned this task and replaced GRH with the Budget Enforcement Act (BEA) in 1990.[33] The BEA was the administration and congressional budget compromise put into law and it was designed to require merely that the federal budget be balanced. This was to be done on a 'pay-as-you-go' system, which meant that any increase in government expenditure had to be financed by increasing revenues (that is, taxes) (Collender, 1992; LeLoup, 1993, pp. 53–5). The BEA established separate ceilings for defence, as well as international and domestic, discretionary spending for FY 1991, FY 1992 and FY 1993. It also established ceilings for overall discretionary spending for FY 1994 and FY 1995.[34] Both the Bush administration and Congress operated within the confines of the BEA, unlike the cheating which accompanied GRH, and pressure was maintained to reduce the defence budget (LeLoup, 1993, p. 60). Thus, the Congressional Research Service reported that the administration's projected defence budget submissions for FY 1992 through to FY 1995 were within BEA spending targets.[35]

Conclusion: Funding for Weapons Acquisition

The defence budget is divided up into eleven titles, or accounts, the three main ones being Operations and Maintenance, Procurement, and Research, Development, Testing and Evaluation (RDT&E) – these last two encompass weapons acquisition. Table 4.4 shows that TOA for weapons acquisition rose significantly under Carter between FY 1976 and FY 1980 and dramatically under the first Reagan administration from FY 1981 to FY 1985 (by 166 per cent for procurement and 82 per cent for RDT&E). Congress was keener than Carter on defence budget increases. This keenness began to fade towards the end of the first Reagan administration, and this was to lead to a 30 per cent fall in TOA on weapons procurement from FY 1986 to FY 1990. Although, interestingly enough, TOA on weapons RDT&E continued to rise significantly until FY 1987 and then only fell by 9 per cent between FY 1988 and FY 1990. This anomaly may be explained by the general Congress perception of funds being wasted in the Weinberger DoD on weapons procurement. One former Navy DoD budget official reportedly said that instead of investing the extra acquisition funds wisely, old weapon designs were 'just pulled off the shelf' and as a result 'a lot of crap' weapons got funded (Lehman, 1984, p. 2). A lengthy GAO report in 1982 was less critical but it did find that the DoD had failed to carry through its pledge to cancel marginal weapon programmes and concentrate funds on acquiring priority programmes at more efficient rates.[36] Criticism of weapons research were less evident in the mid-1980s and Congress strongly backed weapons testing; hence funds for RDT&E were not cut.

Table 4.4. DoD TOA by Title, FY 1975–93 (FY 93 $ in billions)

	O&M	Procure	RDT&E
FY 75	65.6	46.3	22.0
FY 76	67.5	52.1	22.5
FY 77	69.0	60.6	23.0
FY 78	69.7	60.6	23.1
FY 79	69.7	57.5	22.7
FY 80	74.2	58.6	22.5
FY 81	80.1	73.1	25.5
FY 82	85.7	92.4	29.2
FY 83	90.6	107.2	32.0
FY 84	94.2	112.9	36.3
FY 85	101.8	118.0	40.1
FY 86	99.1	111.0	42.9
FY 87	100.8	101.9	44.3
FY 88	100.5	97.6	44.2
FY 89	100.5	90.8	43.0
FY 90	99.1	89.5	40.4
FY 91	114.8	74.3	37.1
FY 92	96.8	63.5	39.6
FY 93	86.5	56.2	38.8

Source: adapted from DoD Comptroller, *Defense Budget Estimates, FY 93*, pp. 52–3.

What did this all mean for weapons acquisition? Funding increased for procurement from the mid-1970s onwards; as Table 4.4 shows, there was only a slight increase in TOA for RDT&E during this period. Funding shot up for weapons RDT&E and procurement under the first Reagan administration. This led to plenty of programmes being started or continuing to be funded and none getting cut. From 1985 onwards these funds began to dry up as Congress became increasingly preoccupied with the budget deficit and the Soviet threat began to recede. By late 1990, even the Bush administration accepted the need for massive cuts in the defence budget. Since programmes get far more costly as they approach production and procurement, weapons near or at this stage would have faced increasing funding difficulties, particularly in the late 1980s and early 1990s. On the other hand, since R&D is far cheaper than procurement, and R&D received proportionality more funds than procurement during this period, those programmes which were starting out in the late 1980s and early 1990s would not have found life so difficult.

DOD POLICY STRUCTURES

Budgetary decisions which affect weapons acquisition are made in two parallel policy structures, namely, the PPBS and the DSARC/DAB. The DSARC/DAB was discussed in the previous chapter. The PPBS is the DoD's resource allocation policy structure. It was established by McNamara in 1961 and, like the DSARC, its basic features have remained the same since then (Art, 1990, p. 28). The PPBS was intended to ensure that programming and budgeting was preceded by planning and that budgeting took a long-term perspective.[37] This section will examine the amount of control exercised by civilian policymakers in the OSD versus the amount of autonomy given to the services in these two policy structures under Brown, Weinberger, Carlucci and Cheney. Each Defence Secretary, upon taking office, instigated management reviews which then led to reforms of the PPBS and DSARC\DAB. However, the most dramatic and widespread reforms of the DoD were initiated by Congress in 1986; indeed, the Cheney reforms were really a continuation of this process.

Brown Keeps a Tight Reign

Brown was explicit in stating that the purpose of his 'management innovation' was to centralise responsibility for defence policymaking. Specifically, his reforms were intended to 'increase top-level management attention to policy development, resource management and programme evaluation matters' and to 'separate those staff elements that are consumers or users of a resource from those that develop or acquire resources'.[38] This meant in practice giving more say on weapons acquisition to civilians in the OSD.

To this end two new OSD offices were created, those of Under Secretary of Defence for Policy (USD(P)) and Under Secretary of Defence for Research and Engineering (USD(R&E)). The USD(P) drew up the basic document, called the Consolidated Guidance (CG), which provided guidance on national defence policy and fiscal guidelines to the services. Therefore, the USD(P) influenced weapons acquisition in so far as he was responsible for ensuring that service programmes adhered to DoD policy.[39] However, the services paid scant attention to the CG and so the actual influence of the USD(P) on service programmes was not all that great (Puritano, 1985, p. 364; Art, 1990, p. 50).

The USD(R&E) was tasked with being the Defence Secretary's 'principal advisor for all research and engineering matters, including major weapon systems acquisition'.[40] But the powers and purpose of the first USD(R&E), William Perry, were more impressive on paper than in practice. Perry noted in his report to Congress that he had been appointed the Defence Acquisition Executive, and thus permanent Chairman of the DSARC. He also stated his main objective as being 'to apply *a broad and comprehensive management approach to all major system programme activities*, with emphasis on developing and producing military capabilities effectively and at the lowest possible cost'.[41] Yet, despite all this big talk, Perry's office ended up focusing on only specific aspects of weapons acquisition. According to Walter Slocombe, a former deputy USD(P) under Brown, the 'chief function' of the USD(R&E) was the promotion of 'innovation and setting technological priorities' in weapons acquisition (1990, p. 95). Slocombe's perception is reinforced by a comparison of Perry's annual reports to Congress in 1978 and 1979. Whereas in the early report Perry mostly discussed broad acquisition policy and practices (as well as his office's role in both), his report the following year focused exclusively on technological issues.[42]

The most significant reform of the PPBS undertaken by Brown was the creation of the Defence Resources Board (DRB). The board was effectively a committee of the OSD heads.[43] The DRB served to oversee the service's programme and budget submissions and to advise the Secretary of Defence on resource allocation in the DoD. Overall, while the Under Secretaries of Defence and systems analysts individually exercised limited influence over weapons acquisition, collectively they represented the philosophy of the Brown Pentagon, which was one of centralised civilian control of DoD activities. In fact, things were so centralised under Brown that it appears that, as much as possible, he wanted to have direct control over everything in the DoD. To this end, the USD(P) and the USD(R&E) fulfilled their primary function which was to help the Defence Secretary run his department as he saw fit. Brown made explicit reference to this state of affairs in his annual report to Congress in 1981 when he stated that his reform of the PPBS 'provided for the early and continuous involvement of the President and Secretary of Defence' in this policy structure.[44] When Brown talked about increasing 'top-level management attention' to DoD policy and programming he meant the very top! However, Brown was far more interested in how money was spent in the DoD than how weapons were acquired. Thus, he was more attentive to, and successful at, reforming the PPBS policy structure (by creating the DRB) than the DSARC.

Weinberger Devolves Power to the Services

Slocombe argues that under Weinberger the DoD was organised according to what he calls the 'Delegation Model' wherein the Defence Secretary 'undertak[es] some minimal intervention to protect against excessive parochialism' but his 'principal programme role . . . is public and congressional advocate' (1990, p. 93). Similarly, David Stockman derided Weinberger for knowing little about defence and acting merely as a salesman (1986, p. 303). Such views placed Weinberger in poor light, particularly in contrast with Brown who was a defence expert and an interventionist Defence Secretary. Were they fair? According to Nicholas Lehman, Weinberger started off critically examining service programmes, but at the same time the Defence Secretary was concentrating on securing defence budgets large enough to implement his defence programme. Lehman argues that Weinberger became increasingly preoccupied with this second task thereby neglecting his management responsibilities (1984, pp. 2, 16). Lehmans account is convincing. It would explain Kotz's depiction of Weinberger, upon entering office, critically examining the Air Force's B-1B bomber programme on grounds of strategic need, performance and affordability (1988, pp. 203–4, 207–9). It also marries with Weinberger's own account of his purpose in the DoD: 'to concentrate on major policy decisions and goals and to secure the resources needed to achieve them' (1990, p. 45).

On 2 March 1981, a team of OSD officials, Joint Staff and service officers, led by ASD Comptroller, Vincent Puritano, was instructed by Weinberger to conduct a 30-day review of the PPBS and DSARC.[45] On the recommendations of this review team, Weinberger expanded the membership and responsibilities of the DRB. The Defence Secretary told Congress that the membership of the board had been increased 'to include the service secretaries and, when appropriate, the CINCs of the unified and specified commands.[46] Furthermore, according to Puritano, the 'service chiefs became, in effect, *defacto* members of the DRB, and [were] invited to all meetings where major policy issues [were] discussed' (1985, p. 367). Puritano also noted that the DRB was made responsible for the 'total management of the revised

PPBS' (1985, p. 367) and as such, according to another former OSD official, it was 'clearly the major DoD decisionmaking body' (Odeen, 1985, p. 379). For Robert Komer, former USD(P) under Brown, this was a most unwelcome development: 'The DRB has become . . . a court of last resort . . . in which the services not only submit the programmes, but sit in judgement on them' (1985, pp. 218–19).

This, then, was the real state of affairs which Weinberger only ever hinted at: power was devolved to the services. Puritano notes that OSD officials were told to 'concentrate on broad central policy guidance rather than the detailed programme guidance of previous years' (1985, p. 366). This was, of course, a pointless actively for the services simply ignored policy guidance. Under Weinberger, the instrument for ensuring that service programmes met broad policy guidance was the DRB, but since the services were effectively on this board, they were well placed to ensure that their programmes were well received. In this sense, the services were given a free reign over weapons acquisition.

Congress Takes the Lead

Major initiatives by the administration and Congress to restructure the DOD were completed in 1986. The Blue Ribbon Commission on Defence Management, chaired by a former Deputy Secretary of Defence, David Packard, submitted its final report to President Reagan on 30 June 1986. Acting on earlier drafts of the Packard Commission report, the President had in fact implemented most of the Commission's final recommendations, in National Security Decision Document (NSDD) 219, two months beforehand.[47] The Goldwater-Nichols Defence Reorganisation Act was also passed by Congress in September of that same year. This act was co-sponsored by Barry Goldwater, the outgoing Republican Chairman of the SASC, and Bill Nichols, then ranking Republican member of the Investigations Subcommittee (IS) of the HASC.[48] This two initiatives were complementary. Indeed the SASC waited until after the Packard Commission had delivered its final report before drafting the Senate's Defence Reorganisation Bill so as to ensure the enactment of relevant Commission recommendations.[49] Nevertheless, the reform effort was led by the Senate and House armed services committees; Weinberger followed the service chiefs in openly opposing the reforms and Reagan was merely following the prevailing tide of opinion in Washington when he reluctantly jumped aboard the reforms bandwagon.[50]

These reforms grew out of growing public concern over two distinctive issues and, as such, were designed for two purposes. The first issue was highlighted in numerous public reports in the early 1980s of 'waste, fraud and abuse' in defence acquisitions. This problem was to be remedied by strengthening civilian control over acquisitions and management in the DoD.[51] Concern was also raised in the media and Congress about the adverse effects of interservice rivalry on the planning and execution of military operations, not to mention the quality of military advice to the National Command Authorities. Both operations and advice were to be improved by reducing the influence of the services over both by providing more authority and resources to CJCS.[52]

The most significant changes, from the perspective of this study, occurred in the acquisition policy structure. First of all, the position of USD(A) (or 'acquisition czar') was created. The USD(A) is the third most senior official in the DoD in the area of acquisition policy, being outranked only by the Secretary and Deputy Secretary of Defence.[53] This last act mandated the USD(A) to 'direct' all aspects of defence acquisition, previously the responsibility of the services.[54] The services were still intended to have a major input in acquisition policy, co-operating with the USD(A) through their acquisition executives and with service secretaries sitting on the Defence Acquisition Board which is chaired by the USD(A).

The second major change occurred in the services' own acquisition structures. Two basic changes were required of the services, namely to simplify these structures and to strengthen civilian control over them. Policymaking and direction in each service comes from the Chief of Staff's office and from the service secretary's office. Traditionally, most expertise and responsibility on acquisition matters resided in the staff offices as opposed to the secretariats: specifically, the Army and Air Force both had deputy chiefs of staff for research, development and acquisition who had overall responsibility for acquisition, while in the Navy, as a result of reforms in the early 1980s, responsibility for acquisition was split between eight warfare offices.[55] Implementation of acquisition policy was largely controlled by the 'supply' or 'buying commands' in each service: the Army Material Command, Air Force Systems and Logistics Commands, and the Navy Material Command up to 1985 when it was split up into three separate commands (Naval Sea Systems, Air Systems, and Space and Naval Warfare).[56] The Packard Commission recommended that a civilian Service Acquisition Executive (SAE), comparable to the USD(A), should be established in each service. This appointee should be equivalent to service under secretaries and should have full-time responsibility, under the USD(A)'s guidance, for service acquisition programmes. Each SAE should, in turn, appoint a number of Programme Executive Officers (PEOs) who would each be responsible for a number of acquisition programmes. The managers of these programmes should report directly and exclusively to their PEOs who would report to the SAE. Thus, the Commission sought to establish a clear acquisition structure which strengthened civilian control within the services and the overall position of the USD(A) over service acquisition programmes.[57]

The Services Resist the Reform Process

Predictably, the reforms of the services' acquisition structures did not go as intended by the Packard Commission. The GAO found that each service responded to Commission's findings differently but all did so in an unsatisfactory manner: each service did create a new acquisition structure but these were either superimposed on existing acquisition structures or made dependent on existing structures for the implementation of management decisions. Needless to say, this state of affairs made life hectic for programme managers who found themselves under competing pressures from the new and existing structures. In each service responsibility and resources for acquisition policy and oversight were transferred from the staffs to the secretariats but this simply involved transferring military personnel from the staff offices to the secretariats; there was little change in the ratio of service officers to civilians in policymaking positions. In addition, the GAO found that the Army and Navy secretariats still had to rely on military commands and staff offices for access to information on specific programmes.[58]

The first two acquisition czars also had little success 'directing' weapons acquisition primarily because they were not given the authority to do so. One month after entering office, the first USD(A), Richard Godwin, sent a draft charter for his position to Weinberger for approval. In this draft charter he proposed that the SAEs report directly to the USD(A) and that the USD(A) direct the service secretaries on all acquisition matters. Naturally the service secretaries strongly objected to this draft charter and so far more restrictive responsibilities and limited authority was given to the USD(A) in DoD Directive 5134.1 issued by the Deputy Secretary in February 1987. It provided for SEAs to report to their service secretaries, and not to the USD(A). More importantly, the USD(A) was denied the authority to direct the services on acquisition matters in a key paragraph in the directive:

> Where agreement on acquisition matters cannot be reached between the USD(A) and the Secretaries of the Military Departments, the matter shall be presented jointly to the Secretary/Deputy Secretary of Defence for resolution.[59]

This directive was condemned by the chairman and ranking minority leader of the HASC. The two men noted that, in effect, this directive was 'gutting the intent of the law' because '[i]t says the service secretaries can effectively veto any decision by the acquisition czar and buck anything and everything they don't like upstairs'.[60] As a result of such fierce reaction from the HASC the offending paragraph was removed. However, the GAO noted that 'the second USD(A) stated in January 1989 that the practice of circumventing or appealing the USD(A)'s direction was still in effect'.[61] Godwin also discovered that he had little influence on the DRB. Thus, services were given the opportunity to reverse unfavourable decisions made on the DAB, which was chaired by Godwin, by securing funds for programmes on the DRB, which was chaired by Deputy Secretary William Taft. In effect, the services were provided with yet another way to appeal over Godwin's head.[62]

Considering how the cards were stacked against him, it was no wonder that Godwin resigned in September 1987 after being in the post for only a year: he declared that he was leaving because 'resistance was so strong that I did not think that the job was doable'.[63] Robert Costello was appointed as Godwin's successor on 18 December 1987. He assured the SASC that he did have sufficient authority on acquisition matters and that he would be able to work closely with the new Secretary of Defence, Frank Carlucci.[64] Costello did, nevertheless, request a statement from the Deputy Secretary outlining his authority and responsibilities. In response, he received a memorandum in which the Deputy Secretary clearly stated that Costello had the authority to direct the services on acquisition matters and to issue acquisition policy guidance. However, the appropriate changes were not made to existing directives to reflect this position and so some ambiguity remained. In the end, Costello did not even try to exert his authority but instead he relied upon consensus building and informal relationships to get things done. Arguably, Costello adopted such an approach out of choice rather than necessity. He clearly stated in his confirmation hearings before the SASC his intention to work to achieve a consensus for change.

He also stressed that consensus building did not come from weak leadership but rather 'consensus takes very strong leadership'.[65]

The limitations of Costello's consensus approach were demonstrated in the case of the B-2. Costello tried in vain to have the B-2 programme cancelled but was stopped from doing so by Carlucci. Costello argued that the stealth bomber was not needed, was too costly, and that the programme was being poorly managed by the contractors.[66] Overall, while Costello was satisfied that he had made some progress in directing weapons acquisition, he still felt there was much more room for improvement; specifically he argued that the informal arrangements under which he had been working ought to be formalised (Lindenfelser, 1990, p. 244).

Genuine Reform Under Cheney

Bush promised to ensure that the 1986 defence reforms were properly and completely implemented. To this end, in his first address to Congress, he directed his Defence Secretary to conduct a review of defence management. In his subsequent *Defense Management Report to the President (DMR)*, in July 1989, Cheney found that the reforms had lagged behind the Packard Commission's findings and he set out a plan to bring them back in line. Three years later the DoD reported that service acquisition structures had been clarified and streamlined, effectively by abolishing the old structures and keeping the new ones, that each service had established an acquisition corps, and that a Defence Acquisition University had even been set up. [67]

Cheney also stated in his *DMR* that the USD(A) would be given the authority to direct the services on all acquisition matters and sole authority to issue guidance on acquisition policy. The GAO found that, under Cheney, the USD(A) was indeed 'provided [with] the authority and support needed to supervise DoD's acquisition system as envisioned by the Packard Commission'. This was done by Cheney issuing an amended charter for the USD(A) in August 1989 which substantially increased the authority and responsibilities of the USD(A) beyond those contained in the original 1987 charter. This amended charter explicitly gives the USD(A) the authority to direct the services on acquisition matters. It also strengthens the USD(A) control over the acquisition cycle by giving the USD(A) the authority to establish the exit criteria that programmes must reach to progress from one Milestone to the next and to reach decisions on Milestone reviews by the DAB.[68]

The USD(A) appointed by Cheney in August 1989, John Betti, used the office's increased powers cautiously. Like Costello, Betti believed that the services accepted his authority, but he also felt that reform of the acquisition system should be evolutionary rather than revolutionary and that it was best not to force unwanted changes on the services. It would seem that he placed too much trust in the services. Betti ended up resigning after just 16 months in office because the Pentagon's Inspector General, Susan Crawford, found him partly responsible for delays in revealing the troubled status of the A-12 programme. Crawford concluded that Betti 'failed to exercise a necessary degree of scepticism' towards assurances from the Navy and the contractors.[69]

Even though the experiences of the first few acquisition czars were discouraging, the overall prospect for the congressional-led reform process started under Weinberger's tenure, and continued under Cheney, appears good. Authority and responsibility have shifted from the service secretaries to the USD(A), and within the services themselves from the staff offices to the secretariats. Simple, clear acquisition structures, running from programme managers to PEOs to SAEs to the USD(A), were finally established thereby enabling the USD(A) to oversee and direct weapon programmes.

Conclusion

For much of the 1970s and 1980s the services had it pretty easy when it came to weapons acquisition. Brown was more interested in controlling how defence funds were spent than in overseeing weapons development. As a result, the services had far more formal responsibility and informal influence over weapons acquisition than OSD officials: the services were able to ignore policy direction from the USD(P) and the USD(R&E) ended up confining his activities to simply promoting technological innovation. Nevertheless, because of Brown's interest in the area, the services had far less success influencing defence budgeting than weapons acquisition. Weinberger gave the services an even freer rein: not only were OSD officials instructed to leave programming to the services, but the services were also given a far greater say over the funding decisions. Thus, the services were in good positions to control weapons acquisition.

Things got tougher for the services from the mid-1980s onwards. Congress, with the reluctant support of the President, was able to force Weinberger to accept reform of the acquisition policy structure. Nevertheless, the services were able to resist these reforms under Weinberger and Carlucci until Cheney finally forced them to toe the line. Throughout this period the services continued to have the formal access to the PPBS structure which they had gained under Weinberger but they were less able to translate this into influence. The budget crisis meant that programmes were going to have to be cut; the only questions being which programmes ought to be cut and by how much. These decisions, while made within the PPBS, were to be influenced by the deliberations of the DAB and, in particular, the opinions of the USD(A).

A-12 AVENGER[70]

The Navy was never going to present the A-12 as an inexpensive bomber; weapons based on state-of-the-art technology do not come cheap. Certainly, if it was possible to do so convincingly, the Navy would have sold the A-12 on these merits. In 1985 Navy Secretary Lehman pushed the F-14 Tomcat as a bargain by announcing that he had managed to reduce its unit price by almost $4 million (to $20 million) over the previous three years by introducing competition between the plane's contractors.[71] But for the A-12, the only issue was whether or not cost was going to undermine support for the programme.

Costs Appear to Be Out of Control

Initially, budgetary considerations caused no problems for the A-12 programme. This was because the Navy refused to tell Congress how much the bomber was going to cost. As was noted in the previous chapter, the A-12 was a special access programme and so only the members of the four defence committees were briefed on some aspects of the programme on a need-to-know basis. Much more limited information was only made more widely known to legislators when the A-12 entered full-scale development in 1988. Even so, projected cost figures for the A-12 were not given to Congress until 1990.[72]

When the Navy did finally release figures for the programme it was revealed that the A-12 was going to be hugely expensive. According to projections made in December 1989, the 'total' programme costs for 858 A-12s was $74.3 billion which put the unit cost of the bomber at $86.6 million. Moreover, this figure did not even reflect the true total programme costs as the Navy had not included operation and support (O&S) costs: this practice was common in order to make programmes appear less expensive, in this case by $28.7 billion (in FY 1990 dollars).

Congress did not receive these figures until 25 April 1990, which was one day before Cheney announced that as a result of his Major Aircraft Review, only 620 A-12s were to be acquired. That meant that the first figures which were released on the A-12 were obsolete almost as soon as Congress received them. More importantly, legislators could hardly complain about the programme costs when it was obvious that they would be significantly reduced after Cheney's announcement. In June 1990 the DoD drew up new cost projections based on the smaller requirement for 620 A-12s. These new figures showed that the projected total programme costs had been reduced to about $57 billion but at the same time the unit costs had risen to over $100 million. This was hardly surprising as buying fewer bombers is not very cost-effective: the total R&D costs are spread out over less planes; and production is often stretched out in order to keep factories going rather than the cheaper option of merely shortening production. Amazingly, the June 1990 estimates were not sent to Congress until 29 October 1990. By this stage both the House and Senate had passed the Defence Appropriation Bill (on 25 and 26 October respectively) and had adjourned on 28 October.[73] So, once again, the DoD had blatantly timed the release of cost projections in order to limit any potential damage to the programme. In addition, the defence committees were likely to have been distracted by the crisis triggered by Iraq's invasion of Kuwait in August 1990. Indeed, congressional hearings were held throughout late November and early December on US responses to the crisis (Woodward, 1991 pp. 326, 331–2, 341–3, 345).

This explains why the A-12 did not receive much flak from Congress for its sheer cost. It must also have been difficult for legislators, or even administration officials, to judge the cost-effectiveness of the A-12. As was noted in the previous chapter, bickering did break out in 1990 between the Navy and Air Force over the comparative effectiveness of their respective stealth bombers. Moreover, in December of that year, the DoD Inspector General started investigating charges that B-2 supporters were suppressing research into anti-stealth radar technologies. However, real doubts about the effectiveness of stealth warplanes did not surface until after the A-12 programme had been terminated in 1991 when it was revealed that the B-2 would not, and the F-117A probably did not, work as well as had been previously thought.

However, when it came to the issue of controlling programme costs, the A-12 did not get away so easily. According to Cheney the A-12 programme was cancelled because its costs appeared to be spiralling out of control: the Defence Secretary's reason for killing off the A-12 was that 'no one can tell me exactly how much money it will cost to keep [it] going' (Morrison, 1991, p. 30). Cheney also indicated extreme concern about the schedule slippages in his mid-December memorandum to Navy Secretary Garrett.[74]

General Dynamics and McDonald Douglas were awarded a 'fixed-price incentive contract' in 1988 to fully develop the A-12 within a target price of $4.4 billion and a ceiling price of $4.8 billion. Under the terms of the contract, if the programme exceeded the target price then the government and contractors were to split any additional costs up to $400 million 60/40 between them. However, any costs above the ceiling price were to be met by solely by the contractors. Based on the rosy report from his Major Aircraft Review, Cheney told the SASC in late April 1990 that full-scale development would be completed on time and within cost. However, one month later the A-12 Programme Office were officially reporting that the contract ceiling price would be exceeded. On 1 June the contractors advised the Navy that the programme was behind schedule, over-budget and that they were unable to absorb the additional development costs. More significantly, at a Milestone review meeting of the A-12 programme in early December 1990, the DAB were informed that the A-12 Programme Office estimated the total cost for completing full-scale development had risen to $7.5 billion. At the time, the contractors were claiming that the total development cost would be $5.4 billion. The Programme Office estimate, which was accepted by OSD analysts, showed that the full-scale development costs for the A-12 had exceeded the contract ceiling price by $2.7 billion. Thus, Cheney had good reason to be concerned about costs spiralling out of control; the A-12 was hugely over-budget even before it had entered production.[75]

A Bailout is Ruled Out

Cheney's decision to cancel the A-12 programme reportedly took everybody by surprise (Morrison, 1991, p. 30). In the past, the DoD could be expected to restructure the programme, bailout the contractors, and acquire the weapon later on and at greater cost. But, in this case, the Defence Secretary rejected the Navy's plan to do so, declaring that 'I do not believe a bailout is in the national interest.'[76] The budget climate in 1991 gave Cheney little choice. Unlike his predecessor, Cheney was looking at ways to save money rather than to spend it. In real terms defence TOA had been declining for six years and was set to continue doing so (see Table 4.1, p. 126). Defence outlays were also beginning to decline in real terms (Table 4.2, p. 127). TOA for defence procurement had fallen dramatically in FY 1990 to $89.5 billion from its high of $118 billion in FY 1985 (these figures are in FY 1993 dollars) (see Table 4.4, p. 139). Throughout 1990 the Bush administration was criticised by Congress for not reacting quickly enough to Gorbachev's peace initiatives and the democratic revolutions in Eastern Europe. Cheney's FY 1991 defence budget was under heavy fire from legislatures, as was Bush's 1990 'Base Force Concept', for not making large enough cuts to the force structure and defence budget. Under these circumstances, Cheney would have found it difficult to bailout the A-12 programme even if he wanted to. Broader national security issues, namely the end of the Cold War and the Gulf War, may have occupied legislators in 1989 and 1990. However, Cheney could be sure that it would not have been long before legislators got around to reviewing the A-12 programme and, given the continuing budget deficit problem, they would doubtless have found it ripe for cancellation. So, even if Cheney had wanted to save the A-12, he was unlikely to be able to do so for long.

As it happens, Cheney had two reasons to cancel the A-12 programme in order to make an example out of it. First, Cheney may have wanted to show DoD officials, service officers and legislators alike, that he would not tolerate weapons surviving not on merit but through duplicity and manipulation of the acquisition process. The Defence Secretary must have been embarrassed by the failure of the DAB process to identify the A-12 as a programme in difficulty despite the fact that he had just implemented reforms to this process (in line with the Packard Commission recommendations) which were supposed to enable it to pick up just this sort of problem. The fact that USD(A) Betti had been given the authority and resources to direct the services and acquisition matters and yet still allowed himself to be fooled by false assurances from the Navy was particularly galling. Cheney must have been especially embarrassed as the problems with the A-12 came to light just one month after he had assured Congress that it was a fault-free programme. Second, Cheney may have been sending a message to defence contractors that they could no longer expect to be bailed out should they get into trouble. Thus, the government argued that the A-12 contract had been terminated for default because General Dynamics and McDonald Douglas contract team were unable to develop and produce the A-12 within budget and on time. The contract team argued that the contract had been terminated for convenience (which would place the blame on the government's shoulders) and that, in any case, the inflexible 'fixed-price' contract was not appropriate for a weapon based on leading edge technologies, such as the A-12, which was bound to encounter difficulties in development and production. This dispute ended up with the government asking for the return of $1.35 billion of the $2.7 billion they paid to the contract team, and with the team suing the government for $1.4 billion.[77]

In conclusion, the A-12 was cancelled not because it cost too much or was cost-ineffective, but because its costs appeared to be spiralling out of control. In previous times, such a situation was more likely to be resolved with the programme being restructured rather than cancelled. However, the budget climate in 1990–1 gave Cheney every reason to kill the plane and no reason to save it.

SGT YORK DIVAD

The DIVAD programme was not terminated for reasons of cost, cost-effectiveness or cost controllability. As was discussed in Chapter 2, DIVAD was cancelled because it was unable to fulfil its mission requirement. Institutional issues explain why it took five years to terminate the flawed programme enabling the Army to acquire 64 DIVADs.

Cost Is Not an Issue

The total costs for the DIVAD programme were estimated in 1985 to have been $4.8 billion for 614 units.[78] That may appear to be a lot of money but compared to other conventional weapon programmes it was not. It was noted above that the A-12 was originally expected to cost well over ten times this amount ($57 billion) for almost the same number of units (620 planes). The Navy was not alone in funding such hugely expensive programmes: the Army planned to spend $66 billion acquiring 4,500 new helicopters under its Light Helicopter Family (LHX) programme.[79]

Even more revealing is the programme which replaced DIVAD. In 1985, after the DIVAD fiasco, the Army Secretary instructed the Army Chief of Staff to set up a study group to examine what had gone wrong and to recommend what ought to be done next. This group concluded that DIVAD was doomed to fail since no single weapon was able to meet all the necessary mission requirements. Consequently, they suggested that the replacement programme, which they called the Forward Area Air Defence System (FAADS), be composed of no fewer than *five* anti-aircraft weapons. FAADS was adopted by the Army and approved by the DAB in 1986 even though its total cost was initially estimated at over $9 billion. Army officials even admitted to one congressional subcommittee that the eventual price tag for FAADS may be as high as $22 billion. By 1990 costs had indeed risen but only to about $11 billion; but that was still well over twice as much as that for DIVAD.[80] So it would appear that, as far as the Army was concerned, DIVAD had not got into trouble with the administration or Congress because of its sheer cost. Why else would they seek approval for a programme which was expected to cost at least twice as much, and why else would they be willing to suggest that FAADS may even cost twice as much again?

As was discussed in Chapter 2, the CBO reckoned that DIVAD was not cost-effective. The hilly terrain in the European theatre limited the total area for which each SHORAD weapon was able to provide air defence cover. According to CBO calculations (based on an average 50 kilometre front for each heavy US division), the Army needed to acquire 1,200 new SHORAD units in order to provide adequate air defence cover for frontline formations. Instead the Army intended to buy half this number of DIVADs. The CBO concluded that, at about $6.4 million each, DIVAD was simply too expensive to be acquired in necessary numbers.[81] But cost- ineffectiveness never became an issue for DIVAD. Indeed it is striking that, in the TWS Hearing on the DIVAD in October 1984, Senators were far more concerned about whether DIVAD would work than how much it would cost. The subcommittee were even told by ASD James Wade that the Office of PA&E were against allowing DIVAD to proceed into production on the grounds that it was not cost-effective. Wade also noted that this objection, which had been raised at the DAB review of Milestone 3 of the DIVAD programme, had been subsequently overruled by Deputy Defence Secretary Frank Carlucci. This information did not elicit any questions from subcommittee members as to the basis for the Deputy Secretary's decision or the cost-effectiveness of the weapon; the Senators simply continued to ask about the timing of developmental and operational tests.[82] For the DoD and Congress, the debate surrounding DIVAD centred on its effectiveness and not its cost-effectiveness.

When it came to cost control, on balance, DIVAD received more praise than criticism. The Army had negotiated a fixed-price development contract with Ford in 1981 that also included three fixed-price production options to commence in 1982 and to be exercised at one year intervals for 50, 96 and 130 (subsequently reduced to 117) DIVADs respectively.[83] The Defence Contract Audit Agency criticised the

Army for negotiating 'an excessively costly contract [with Ford] for the initial production of DIVAD'. In his testimony before the TWS, the DoD Inspector General, Joseph Sherick, defended this conclusion but he also noted that the Army disputed that most of these 'excessive costs' were in fact so.[84] The *New York Times* also reported that Sherick had chided the Army for failing to notice that Ford had been forwarding subcontractor bills which were not 'fair or reasonable'.[85] Sherick's criticisms appeared to have fallen on deaf ears. Indeed one subcommittee member, Senator Bob Wilson, who heaped praise on the contracts on two separate occasions during the hearing, even went so far as to say that the DoD and Army 'have prudently negotiated what has to be considered among the best procurement contracts within recent memory'.[86] However, Wilson's sincerity on this point may be questioned given that the Ford plant which produced DIVAD was based in his state, California. Nevertheless, the other subcommittee members appeared content to accept Wade's assurances that the contracts were good.

As was noted in the previous chapter, the Army actually sold DIVAD as a programme which made savings. The service admitted that the choice of a concurrent acquisition strategy entailed certain development risks (risks which they mistakenly believed would be contained by building the weapon from mature components) but such risks were justified on the grounds that concurrency would save money by reducing development time.[87] The DIVAD programme manager told a HASC subcommittee that '[t]his innovative strategy we believe will save taxpayers hundreds of millions of dollars'.[88] In late 1984 the Army told a SASC subcommittee (the TWS) that this approach had indeed paid off: concurrency was credited with knocking about five years off the normal development time and saving $1 billion.[89] The GAO reported in 1986 that, at termination, DIVAD appeared to be over schedule but *not* over-budget: 'The Sergeant York program's acquisition strategy contained elements which succeeded in controlling costs, but it would not have achieved the desired deployment date.'[90] The GAO suggested that the use of mature components was probably less important in controlling costs (given the trouble they eventually caused) than the use of a fixed-price development contract and fixed-price production options. However, the GAO was less optimistic about the Army's chances of negotiating an equally favourable full production contract with Ford. This concern was not shared by the TWS and Senators did not question the Army's ability to cut a good deal with Ford.[91]

The Myth of the Sacrificial Lamb

The budget climate explains why cost was not an issue for DIVAD. The development contract was awarded and production options were exercised during a period of staggering growth (real and otherwise) in defence TOA and defence outlays, that is, from FY 1981 to FY 1984 (see Tables 4.1 and 4.2). TOA for defence procurement almost doubled over these four years, from $73 billion to $113 billion, while TOA for defence R&D shot up from $25.5 billion to $36 billion (all figures in FY 1993 dollars) (see Table 4.4). Since the DoD was simply awash with money in the early 1980s, a programme only costing $5 billion must have seemed cheap!

The decentralisation of the DoD acquisition and resource allocation policy structures in the early to mid-1980s accounts for the inattention within the administration to the cost-effectiveness of DIVAD. In general, Weinberger was far more interested in service opinions on weapons acquisition than those of his own OSD analysts. PA&E objections to the cost-effectiveness of DIVAD were brushed aside by the Deputy Defence Secretary. This also explains how the Army were able to get away with fooling DAB meetings as to DIVAD's progress for so long.

According to some accounts DIVAD was cancelled for budgetary reasons. It is argued that once DIVAD's problems became public, Weinberger cancelled DIVAD in order to shore up support in Congress for the his defence budget submissions.[92] As one senior congressional aide said at the time: 'Killing the DIVAD was vital to saving any fig leaf of Weinberger's viability on the Hill.'[93] Or was it? Weinberger initially suggested to Congress that funds for DIVAD be withheld in 1984 when TOA for defence procurement was set to rise for the following fiscal year.[94] Admittedly, when Weinberger decided to cancel the programme in mid-1985, TOA for defence procurement and defence in general were set to fall the following fiscal year for the first time in his tenure as Defence Secretary (see Tables 4.2 and 4.4). But it would be wrong to conclude that Weinberger was cowed by Congress's tougher line on the defence budget. This may possibly explain his decision to cancel DIVAD but it still would not explain why he voluntarily halted the programme in 1984. Furthermore, as was discussed previously, Weinberger routinely fought budget battles with Congress, when it was clear beforehand he would lose and when compromise would clearly have been more advantageous to him. So why should he act any differently over DIVAD? The whole idea that Weinberger gave up a weapon programme to save his image on Capitol Hill is not convincing. A more plausible explanation is that Weinberger's attention was drawn to DIVAD by the numerous adverse national press reports and, because he had taken a personal interest in the weapon, he was able to by-pass the usual institutional considerations supporting the programme and cancel it once he was convinced it was useless.

Overall, budgetary issues only explain the outcome of the programme in so far as OSD criticisms of DIVAD were ignored during the favourable budget climate in the early 1980s. A shift in this climate led to direct intervention by the Defence Secretary by which time the Army had already partially acquired the weapon.

MX PEACEKEEPER

This study has argued that the MX was acquired out of strategic and institutional considerations. Despite the fact that it promised to be a hugely expensive programme, budgetary considerations had little impact on the programme. This was partly because the strategic implications of MX deployment were so great that they overshadowed any questions about cost. But it was also due to the budget climate which was favourable for weapons acquisition when the MX entered full-scale development and production in the early to mid-1980s.

Money Doesn't Matter for MX

The Air Force made no secret of the fact that the MX was going to cost a lot of money: when it entered full-scale development in September 1979 the Air Force estimated that it would cost $51 billion to acquire 200 operational MXs, deploy them in MPS, and to buy over 100 MXs for testing and evaluation. The GAO also reported that, using Air Force figures as a baseline, at least another $8 billion would be needed to cover life-cycle O&S costs up to 1999.[95] One year later, the MX Programme Office revised its estimates for the total MX life-cycle costs (including O&S), in order to take into account some restructuring of the programme and increasing inflation rates, up by about $10 billion to $70 billion.[96]

Nobody seemed bothered by this cost. Carter was opposed to the MX but he reluctantly allowed it to enter full-scale production after the DoD produced some evidence to support their window of vulnerability thesis and after the JCS made their support for SALT II conditional on the purchase of MX. Reagan's advisors appeared more concerned about the political costs of MX than its financial costs. In any case, Reagan believed that his defence build-up should not be constrained by budgetary considerations. Moreover, he had made MX the centrepiece of his Strategic Modernisation Plan and so was prepared to go to great lengths to ensure its success.

Congress was also unconcerned about the cost of MX. Congressional debate on MX throughout the early 1980s focused almost exclusively on strategic considerations: the main issues were MX survivability and the missile's impact on crisis stability and arms control (Holland and Hoover, 1985, pp. 151–85; Hampson, 1989, pp. 135–45; Lindsay, 1991, pp. 64–7). Indeed Congress forced Reagan to abandon the plan to replace MPS with interim silo basing even though the administration had sold the latter as a cheaper option: interim silo basing was priced at about $28 billion compared to almost $40 billion for MPS (Holland and Hoover, 1985, p. 219). Liberals in Congress saw MX as an anathema because of its nuclear warfighting capabilities and so would have opposed it regardless of its cost. Moderates in Congress agreed to secure the release of funds for the MX programme in the mid-1980s in exchange for pledges from Reagan to take arms control more seriously and to honour legislation requiring the DoD to develop the Midgetman.[97] Funds were withheld for the MX only when it became clear that the Reagan administration was continuing to stonewall in arms control talks, and was planning to either abandon the Midgetman or pervert the original purpose of the SICBM by placing multiple warheads on it.[98] It was because of these broken promises, and not concerns about cost, that Congress adopted (in the FY 1985 Defence Authorisation Bill) Nunn and Aspin's proposal to limit the number of deployed MXs to 50 missiles (Smith, 1988, pp. 758–9; Lindsay, 1981, pp. 68–9).

In terms of cost-effectiveness, the MX did face rival nuclear weapon programmes from within its own service and the Navy. SAC and the Air Force were trying to acquire two new strategic bombers and were ordered by Congress to acquire Midgetman at the same time as MX. The MX compared favourably to the B-1B programme which according to 1981 estimates would cost $20.5 billion for 100 bombers;[99] thus B-1Bs were expected to cost over $20 million each whereas MXs would each only cost $16 million. No official figures were released in the early 1980s for the B-2 programme. On the other hand, the Navy's big nuclear weapon programme, Trident II, seemed to be far better value. The DoD estimated in 1982 that it would cost $51.7 billion to acquire 740 D-5 SLBMs and 7 Trident II submarines; that is, almost the same amount as the MX programme but for over twice as many ballistic missiles.[100] But when life-cycle O&S costs were included Trident II cost $155 billion, as against only $70 billion for the MX, and as such it would have been the most expensive weapon programme in US history.[101]

The problem in making all these cost-effectiveness comparisons was that not only did costs have to be compared but also effectiveness. So, while strategic bombers were portrayed as offering unique capabilities, and while SAC clearly favoured them, most policymakers believed that ICBMs offered greater military capabilities. The debate over the Trident II versus the MX was not so clear cut. Traditionally, because of their accuracy and warhead yield, ICBMs had been seen as offering greater hard target capabilities than SLBMs. This study has argued that SAC and DoD officials were generally far more impressed by nuclear weapons capability than concerned about their survivability; thus the fact that SLBMs were survivable was not considered as big a deal as perhaps it should have been. Traditionally, the Navy did not even try to compete with the Air Force on the same terms but rather choose to stress the importance of city-counter targets which Polaris could hit, while the Air Force's ICBMs covered the dominant sets of targets in the SIOP (Spinardi, 1994, p. 34). As was noted earlier, this deliberate attempt by the Navy to differentiate between the purpose of SLBMs and ICBMs was motivated by the desire to avoid a direct confrontation with the Air Force which the Navy felt it might well lose. It was also noted that with the acquisition of Trident II came a greater willingness by the Navy to take on the Air Force, as this new SLBM offered about the same hard target capabilities as the MX and had the additional advantage of being survivable (Wit, 1982, p. 168; Slocombe, 1985; Cote, 1991; Spinardi, 1994, p. 151). In addition, Trident II enjoyed more widespread support in Congress because it was seen as a weapon which enhanced (rather than undermined) crisis stability and because the programme was proceeding smoothly.[102] Thus, in 1983, CNO Admiral Watkins was happy to tell Congress: 'By 1991, we believe you could have four to five D-5 equipped *Trident* submarines, which is more than the equivalent of an MX field in terms of hard target capability' (cited in Spinardi, 1994, p. 151). This study has argued that for many administration policymakers, the MX was needed not for its targeting capabilities but in order to demonstrate US resolve. So while comparisons were made in terms of cost-effectiveness with Trident II, the value of such comparisons are limited because they do not address the real purpose of the MX as it was perceived in the 1980s.

Meaningful comparisons could be made with the Midgetman. It was never intended to be traded away but it was supposed to demonstrate US resolve to maintain its ICBM fleet. Although here the MX stood on firmer ground. Support for Midgetman waned in Congress throughout 1986 and 1987 after DoD officials and senior Air Force officers repeatedly pointed out that MX was better value for money.[103] By 1985 the overall MX programme costs had shrunk from the 1981 figure of $70 billion to $21.6 billion because of the decision to only acquire 100 missiles and to base the first 50 of them in existing silos. At the same time, the acquisition of 500 Midgetmen was expected to cost anywhere between $43 billion and $49 billion.[104] The Reagan administration's decision to cancel Midgetman in October 1988 was reaffirmed by Cheney in April 1989 on the grounds that it would only cost $5.4 billion to deploy 50 ten-warhead MXs in Rail Garrison whereas it would cost $23.55 billion to deploy 500 single-warhead Midgetmen on trucks.[105]

Measuring cost control in the MX programme would also have been problematic. The programme was in a flux for so much of the time that it proved extremely difficult to predict its overall costs with any degree of confidence. The Air Force could legitimately point out that costs may increase through no fault of their own if, say, the basing mode was changed or if Congress held up funds for the programme for political reasons. In 1980 the GAO gave six reasons, mostly to do with uncertainty surrounding the eventual basing and actual size of the MX fleet, for why the estimated costs for the MX programme may end up being far greater.[106] A year later the GAO gave six *new* reasons for why costs could increase dramatically.[107] In the end, the original estimates were indeed totally inaccurate: not because of a massive increase in cost but rather due to a huge decrease in cost from $70 billion in 1981 to around $21 billion in 1985. By 1985 the MX programme was far less ambitious, and so while total programme costs had declined, unit programme costs (that is, the cost of each missile) could have increased. As it happens the GAO reported at the time: 'To date, no major deviations to cost, schedule, or performance milestones are evident.'[108] In any case, even if unit costs had risen dramatically, they would not have appeared out of control because of the dramatic fall in the overall programme cost.

Defence Before the Deficit

The fact that considerations about cost mattered so little to the MX programme can be partly explained in terms of the budget climate in the late 1970s and early 1980s. In FY 1979, when the MX entered full-scale development, defence TOA had shrunk by 1 per cent and TOA for defence RDT&E was pretty stable. There was only a slight increase of 2 per cent in defence TOA the following year, but thereafter defence TOA increased massively for five years running under the Reagan administration as did TOA for defence RDT&E and procurement (see Tables 4.1 and 4.4). It was during this time of plenty in defence funding that MX entered production. Specifically, between FY 1983 and FY 1986 (when defence TOA first started to gradually decline), almost all of the R&D funds ($6.1 billion out of $6.6 billion) and half the procurement funds ($6.4 billion out of $14 billion) were appropriated for the MX programme.[109] So just when the MX programme needed money the most there was plenty of it to go around.

However, the MX programme was unusual in terms of civilian intervention at the time. The budget climate was favourable in the early to mid-1980s not only because of the high defence budgets and levels of defence expenditure, but also because the acquisition and PPBS policy structures were decentralised under Weinberger. This meant that the services were usually able to acquire weapons without too much interference from civilians in the DoD. This did not apply in the case of MX. Decisions on the MX programme were routinely taken in the White House and on the floors of the two congressional chambers. Why was this so?

It has been suggested that, in general, nuclear weapons received far greater attention from senior administration policymakers and legislators than conventional weapons: the argument goes that such attention is given because of the impact nuclear weapons are perceived to have on US foreign policy and world survival and, in turn, on domestic political debate (Lindsay, 1991, pp. 129–30; see also Holland and Hoover, 1985, pp. 29–31). This study has argued that, because of the above perceptions, Presidents are frequently forced to intervene in nuclear weapons programmes, and that such interventions are likely to be motivated as well as constrained by the desire to avoid high political costs. The MX was a deeply troubled programme and for this reason it occupied much presidential time and attention.

Equally, it attracted the attention of legislators. Congressional debate focused mostly on the strategic implications of MX deployment, rather than the cost, and most of the action took place on the chamber floors. The four defence committees proved unable to determine funding for the MX programme; amendments were repeatedly adopted by both chambers to reduce funding for MX below the level proposed by the defence committees. In 1982 the four defence committees supported interim silo basing for MX but failed to convince the rest of Congress to support the President's plan, and again, in 1985, they favoured funding the acquisition of all 100 MXs when Congress would only fund 50 (Lindsay, 1991, p. 51). Against this, it was noted earlier that Aspin was behind the rescue package (that is, the Scrowcroft Commission) which bailed MX out of trouble in Congress in 1983, and it was Aspin and Nunn who ended up proposing that the number of MXs be capped at 50 in 1985. As with the MX programme as a whole, the decision to limit MX deployment to 50 missiles was taken for strategic reasons, that is, because Congress was not convinced of the need for any more.

B-2 STEALTH BOMBER

The fact that the B-2 programme was only partially successful can be explained in terms of budgetary issues: Congress felt that the plane could not be afforded. Had the B-2 entered full-scale production in a more favourable budget climate, far more stealth bombers would probably have been bought.

Congress Was Shocked by the Stealth Bomber's Cost

When the Air Force declassified the B-2 budget in June 1989 a storm of protest erupted in Congress over the plane's cost. The Air Force estimated that it would cost $70.2 billion to acquire 132 stealth bombers; by 1989 the service had already spent $23 billion of this and it expected to spend around $8 billion annually on the B-2 programme up to the mid-1990s.[110] Legislators expressed shock not only at the overall programme cost but also at the fact that this cost had been hidden from them for so long. One HASC member sarcastically suggested to senior Air Force officials at a hearing on the B-2 that it was a 'stealth' bomber because 'it can somehow dip into our congressional budget and fly away with $23 billion before anyone knows where we're going'.[111]

As was noted previously, the existence of the B-2 was first made public in 1980 but it was still classified as a special access programme and so little else was revealed about the plane. People guessed that the bomber had a weird shape, used exotic technologies, and would probably be expensive, but that was about all they knew.[112] The Air Force released a report on the B-2's cost in 1986 in order to placate legislators who were complaining about being kept in the dark about the stealth bomber and so were advocating, in the absence of any reassuring data, the acquisition of more B-1Bs than the administration wanted.[113] However, this report revealed very little about the plane: one congressional supporter of the B-2 described the report as 'less than a page long, highly classified, [and lacking] any substantial information' (Mayer, 1991, p. 23). In May 1988 the *Washington Post* reported that the Air Force Chief of Staff, General Larry Welch, revealed not only the cost of the B-2 programme but also that programme costs had shot up from an earlier estimate of $36.6 billion in 1986 to about $43 billion (both figures in FY 1981 dollars).[114] So why did uproar over the cost of the B-2 only occur in Congress after the declassification of the programme budget in mid-1989 and not before?

A second puzzle exists, in that despite its special access classification, members of the four defence committees should have been kept apprised of the programme costs, so why did they not complain at an earlier date? The Air Force argued in a 'B-2 Information Package' sent to legislators in March 1989 that the service had been keeping the defence committees informed. The B-2's prime contractor, Northrop, also issued a fact sheet in which it was claimed that over 170 legislators and staffers had made about 420 visits to the B-2 production plant. It could be that some defence committee members were faking it: they may have been aware of how costly the B-2 would be, done nothing about it, and then pretended to be surprised when the rest of Congress reacted with fury after the costs became public. Cheney suggested as much when he rebuked HASC members for what he considered to be unwarranted surprise.[115]

But were the defence committee members really being hypocritical? It seems more likely that while the Air Force was supposed to keep the four defence committee informed on the B-2 programme, in practice the service failed to do so. The case of the A-12 showed that the DoD did not honour its obligation to keep Congress informed in a full and timely fashion but, rather, manipulated the release of programme information to suit its own organisational goals. Even when it comes to unclassified programmes, congressional agencies routinely found that the DoD did not fully meet its reporting requirements. Since 1969 the primary way the DoD has informed Congress on the cost, schedule and performance of weapon programmes has been through Selected Acquisition Reports (SARs) on each major acquisition programme.[116] However, congressional agencies have repeatedly found these SARs inadequate.[117] In 1982 the HASC Special Panel on Defence Procurement Procedures complained that the 'SAR system does not provide timely and complete information'.[118] In separate reports in 1984 and 1989 the GAO also reached the same conclusion, especially with regard to the realism of DoD cost estimates. The title of the earlier report says it all: *DoD Needs to Provide More Credible Weapon Systems Cost Estimates to the Congress.*[119]

If the DoD was not being honest about programmes open to public scrutiny, why should it be any more honest regarding programmes about which it was obliged to say little? Special access classifications gave the DoD many more opportunities to avoid keeping legislators informed. Some defence committee members, Aspin included, were content that the system of legislative oversight of special access programmes 'has worked reasonably well'.[120] However, only the chairs and ranking minority members had access to all special access programme information; other committee members and a few staffers were given information on a 'need-to-know' basis and it was the DoD, and not the committee chairs and ranking minority members, that decided who needed to know what.[121] So Aspin and some other senior defence committee members may have thought that they were being told enough about special access programmes but they could not rely on their staffers to verify these beliefs. Judging by past DoD behaviour, most defence committee members had good grounds for suspecting that they were not being given accurate and timely information on special access programmes. In addition, they would not have found out much more about the B-2 from Northrop. One report also suggests that members of Congress, and DoD officials for that matter, would have learnt little from their visits to the B-2 plant: apparently Northrop put much effort into choreographing such visits so as to fool outsiders into believing that the programme was proceeding smoothly and apace.[122] It comes as no surprise that one defence committee member should complain that B-2 briefings were a 'song and dance by the military. They presented it very quickly, and we were in a very difficult position to question all their numbers.'[123] The actual cost of the B-2 probably only dawned on the defence committee members from 1986 onwards and this probably accounts for Aspin's claim that, although 'nobody else [in Congress] knew what was going on', members of his committee did raise concerns with the DoD about the cost of the B-2.[124] This still does not explain why the defence committees, and rest of Congress, reacted fiercely when the B-2 budget was declassified but not the year before when the Air Force admitted how much the B-2 would cost. This question will be dealt with shortly.

It ought to be noted that the B-2 was not only in trouble because of its sheer cost, but also because it was increasingly seen as cost-ineffective and, as with the A-12, its costs were perceived to be spiralling out of control. According to Michael Brown, because strategic bombers were commonly believed to offer unique capabilities, the cost-effectiveness issue was not really raised in the debate surrounding the B-2 (1989, p. 6.). Chapter 2 examined the strategic need for these so-called unique capabilities and reached the same conclusion as Brown: 'the B-2 is a strikingly cost-ineffective system' (1990, p. 130; see also 1989). Even a cursory glance at the B-2 programme cost ought to have suggested that the Air Force would want to come up with very good reasons for paying so much money for so few planes.

What did emerge in the B-2 debate was the fact that the Air Force estimates did not give a true account of the real B-2 cost; service estimates on the B-2 cost did not include O&S costs. This was a problem common to many other programmes (such as the A-12) and was yet another inadequacy in DoD reporting to Congress. In 1990 the GAO criticised the DoD for its failure to 'routinely provide Congress with complete [O&S] cost estimates for most [strategic weapon programmes]' even though Congress had specifically directed it to do so.[125] When O&S costs were added, by one estimate, the B-2 would have been the most expensive weapon programme in US history. A 1990 report by the Union of Concerned Scientists concluded that the total programme (including O&S) costs of the B-2 were greater than any other nuclear weapon programme: $155 billion compared to $121 billion for Trident II, $89.9 billion for B-1B, $55 billion for B-52 (armed with ACMs), $48.8 billion for Midgetman, and $19.4 billion for MX Rail Garrison.[126] This was a lot to pay for only 132 bombers (at least the Trident II programme promised well over 700 SLBMs). As a result of Cheney's Major Aircraft Review the B-2 programme requirement was reduced from 132 to 75 bombers. This lowered the overall programme cost but not by that much. The Air Force estimated the overall cost of 75 B-2s to be $61.1 billion where previously it had been estimated at $70.2 billion for 132 bombers.[127] Yet again, the Air Force figures did not include O&S costs. When such costs were taken into account, GAO estimated that it would cost $84 billion to acquire and operate 75 B-2s through to 2020.[128] Brown put the real cost of the programme as high as $106 billion (1990, pp. 144–9). It was small wonder that legislators began to question the cost-effectiveness of the B-2 programme. One B-2 critic, Representative Les AuCoin, argued that $19 billion could be saved and the bomber fleet modernised by scrapping the B-2 and buying instead converted Boeing 747s armed with cruise missiles.[129]

Originally, the Air Force maintained that the B-2 would be a cost-effective bomber in that the Soviets would have to spend far greater amounts of money to defend against stealth bombers than the United States would spend acquiring them.[130] In 1989 the head of Air Force Systems Command (AFSC), General Bernard Randolph, claimed that: 'The B-2 will render useless some $200 billion the Soviets have invested in spectacular air defenses.'[131] About the same time, as more details were emerging about the B-2 and the public debate was shifting from the B-2's capability to its cost, the Air Force and DoD also adopted a new tack. Two arguments were used to gloss over the huge programme costs and suggest that it would be far more cost-effective to complete the B-2 programme and acquire all 75 bombers rather than terminate the programme prematurely. First, the Air Force argued that with so much already invested in the programme, it would be more cost-effective to complete the programme than abandon it. Hence, the service drew attention to the 'cost-to-complete': by 1990 $26.7 billion had already been spent on the B-2 programme and another $8.7 billion had been appropriated for the first 15 bombers; the Air Force argued that the remaining 60 B-2s could be built for only $36.1 billion.[132] This was hardly a bargain but still the Air Force had a point. Buying more bombers would have given greater returns on the money invested in developing the B-2: whether or not this was worth over $36 billion was a different matter. Second, both Air Force Secretary Donald Rice and Deputy Defence Secretary Donald Atwood maintained that attention ought to be solely focused on the 'flyaway cost' (that is, the purchase price which excludes non-recurring costs like R&D and tooling) of the stealth bomber.[133] Rice basically argued that there was no point in focusing on programme costs, which included non-recurring costs, because the money had been already spent: 'Since more than forty percent of the total [B-2] programme cost has already been expended, making decisions on the basis of total programme cost is of limited value' (Rice, 1990, p. 122). Again, the Air Force had a point: programmes based on pioneering new technologies and manufacturing techniques will inevitably have very high non-recurring costs which, in the case of the B-2, were a third of the programme cost.[134] According to Rice's figures, the 'flyaway cost' of each B-2 was $417 million which compared nicely to the programme cost of $752 million per plane (Rice, 1990, p. 123). Nevertheless, the Air Force was trying to have it both ways by first saying that previous programme expenditure should be considered and then saying that it ought to be ignored. Clearly both 'cost-to-complete' and 'flyway cost' figures were being used to present the B-2 in the best possible light.

After 1989 the B-2 was going to need all the help it could get. In 1987 it was reported that the B-2 costs had soared although few details were given.[135] As was noted earlier, one year later General Welch told *Washington Post* reporters that costs had risen from the 1986 estimate of over $36 billion to nearly $43 billion (both figures in FY 1981 dollars). In 1990 more precise figures emerged on the spiralling costs of the B-2: B-2 programme costs grew in real terms by 12 per cent from $32.7 billion in 1981 to $36.6 billion in 1986, and increased again by 20 per cent to $43.8 billion in mid-1989 (all figures in FY 1981 dollars).[136] In 1989 and 1990 members of the HASC, in particular Les Aspin, criticised the spiralling costs of the B-2 programme.[137] In a speech on the House floor Aspin noted that in March of 1990 the DoD had estimated that it would cost over $75 billion to buy 132 B-2s and a few months later, after Cheney's Major Aircraft Review, the DoD was saying that it would still cost almost $63 billion to acquire 75 stealth bombers. Aspin noted that this was '$4.6 billion more than 132 planes were supposed to cost as recently as 1986. And the $840 million per plane price tag is almost double the cost per plane that the Air Force gave us in 1986.'[138]

In 1992 the rate of cost growth had taken on almost comical proportions. By this stage the DoD had abandoned its efforts to get 75 stealth bombers and was simply concentrating on persuading Congress to provide funds for 20 B-2s. In 1992 Secretary Rice told Congress that the estimated cost for 15 B-2s had escalated to $41.8 billion from previous estimates of $33.3 billion in 1989 and $35.4 billion in mid-1990; incredibly, the Air Force was unable to provide a clear explanation for this cost growth.[139] By 1989 Congress realised that the B-2 was a hugely expensive programme which was cost-ineffective and had runaway cost increases. But this information was available at least as early as 1988; so why the year delay?

Bucks Are Needed More than Bombers

In addition to it serving no real strategic need, there were plenty of budgetary reasons for scrapping the B-2: it was extremely expensive; it was not worth such great cost; and its costs were growing at an alarming rate. This being the case, why did the successive administrations support the weapon to the end and why did Congress even bother funding 20 stealth bombers? This study has argued that the Carter supported the B-2 for institutional reasons: he needed the bomber to prop up his sagging defence image with the electorate. Institutional considerations also explain why the B-2 enjoyed such support within the Air Force: it was a pet programme of the most influential branch within the service, that is, the SAC. The decentralised structure of the Weinberger DoD meant that under the Reagan administration the Air Force was in a good position to ensure the survival of its favoured programmes. Hence the Air Force was able to justify the massive B-2 budget using flimsy strategic rationales; OSD officials were not given the chance to vet this programme. As was shown in the case of DIVAD, Deputy Secretary Carlucci shared Weinberger's sympathy for service views. So little changed when Carlucci succeeded Weinberger in 1988: as was noted earlier USD(A) Costello's proposal to cancel the B-2 programme was overruled by Carlucci. The DoD became much more centralised under Cheney as he forced through radical reforms to the DoD and service acquisition policy structures. This did not affect the B-2 programme, however. This may have been because Bush had institutional reasons for supporting completion of the B-2 programme, which he did until it was obvious that Congress would not fund more than 20 bombers. A more likely reason, though, is that the Bush administration really believed that more bombers ought to be bought as this would give greater returns on the funds already sunk into the programme: Cheney told Congress that the administration wanted to proceed with the B-2 programme in order to 'gain the payoff on the enormous investment' in the stealth bomber (Brown, 1992, p. 302).

The timing of congressional opposition to the B-2 programme can be explained in terms of the budget climate. The perception of the Soviet threat changed dramatically between 1988 and 1989. This study has argued that Gorbachev's speech before the UN in December 1988 had a far greater impression on opinion in Congress than the administration. Administration officials simply took it as a welcome development whereas legislators and staffers saw it as a watershed signalling the end of the Soviet threat. By mid-1989 even administration officials had to admit that the changes occurring in the Soviet Union were momentous, a perception reinforced by Soviet acceptance of the democratic revolutions in Eastern Europe in late 1989. Coupled with this declining concern about the Soviet threat was growing alarm among legislators, policymakers and the public over the budget deficit. To make matters worse, the Savings and Loan bailout was proving to be extremely costly; so much so, in fact, that both Congress and administration treated it as an 'off budget' item in 1989 in order to avoid triggering sequestration under GRH. One year later GRH was replaced by the BEA after both institutions agreed to abandon efforts to reduce the deficit and concentrate instead on capping it. In short, in 1989 all eyes were on the deficit and ways to control it. Congress was highly critical of the pace with which the Bush administration was reacting to developments in Europe; in particular, legislators felt that more savings could be made by cutting defence expenditures. The B-2 was a prime target for such cuts in 1989. Thus CINCSAC General Chain complained that legislators were focusing exclusively on cost considerations. Another Senator observed that 'the merits of the programme have been lost a long time ago in the frenzy of defence budget cutting' (Stockton, 1991, p. 162). Even many Republicans in Congress who had traditionally been strong supporters of weapons acquisition were attacking the B-2 (Stockton, 1991, p. 161): one declared that '[n]obody's pushed harder for the Cheney defence budget than I, but America cannot afford the B-2'.[140] It is this shift after December 1988 in the perception of the Soviet threat and the deficit problem which explains why the B-2 got so much flak in 1989 and not before. Had the Air Force declassified the B-2 budget in 1988 it may not have received the same amount of unwanted media and congressional attention. General Welch's comments that year on the stealth bomber's cost and cost growth in the programme appear to have resulted in comparatively little (bad) press: the *Washington Post* article on this story was curiously entitled 'Stealth Called Nuclear Deterrent' and was printed on page ten of the paper.[141] Perhaps this explains why Aspin wrongly told the House floor in 1990 that '[u]p until last year, almost everything about the B-2 programme was highly classified, including its costs'; he must have missed the *Post*.[142]

We have an explanation for why Congress reacted so furiously in 1989 to the B-2's costs and not in 1988. But why did it fund 20 bombers? For a start, the Air Force used a concurrent acquisition strategy which meant that the B-2 entered initial production in 1987 only six years into full-scale development, so by 1990 the DoD already had contracts with Northrop for the first 16 planes.[143] The real question then is why did Congress fund the last four bombers? The answer lies in the role the four defence committees played in determining funding levels. The SASC and SDAS advocated continued funding of the B-2 programme and were able to rally support in 1989 and 1990 against 'B-2 Termination Bills' sponsored by Democratic Senators Alan Cranson and Patrick Leahy.[144] In 1989 Aspin also rejected a similar proposal from two prominent liberal members of his own committee.[145] But in 1990 Aspin decided that no more than 16 bombers ought to be bought: the full House voted in favour of the HASC's recommendation to halt production at 16 planes; Nunn was able to get the House to drop this position in conference.[146] Once again, in 1991, the HASC rejected a request for $3.2 billion from the administration for four more bombers while the SASC authorised these funds.[147] The HDAS reluctantly supported the HASC while the SDAS approved these funds but required another vote by Congress in 1992 before they could be released. At the authorisation conference it was agreed that $1 billion would be put aside for B-2 procurement in 1992 but this money would not be made available until 1993 and its release would be subject to a House vote of approval.[148] Since the House had voted two years in a row to terminate B-2 production it was expected that they would do so again in 1992.[149] However, in 1992 all four defence committees agreed to provide $2.7 billion for the acquisition of the last four bombers.[150]

The four defence committees have traditionally been more conservative than the rest of Congress. The continued support of the SASC and SDAS for the B-2 programme can be understood in these terms. The fact that these committees were able to get the Senate to support their position demonstrates the limited constraints congressional macrobudgeting placed on their ability to micromanage the defence budget. In the past, the HASC and HDAS were also more conservative that the rest of the House but from the mid-1980s they were put under increasing pressure by the House Democratic Caucus to adopt a more liberal line (Blechman, 1990, p. 38; Lindsay, 1991, pp. 58–60; Deering, 1994, pp. 166–7). In addition, throughout the 1980s and early 1990s the liberal membership of the HASC became larger and more assertive (this was related to Causus pressure on the HASC, in that it was partially due to the House leadership appointing more liberals to the committee).[151]

The reason why Congress funded the last four B-2s was that the bombers had very strong backers in the Senate defence committees. The House defence committees would have been under tremendous pressure from the House Democratic Causus to delete these funds. The fact that the eventual 'compromise' was to buy the additional planes anyway suggests that the sympathies of many (if not most) HASC and HDAS members may have been closer to those of their Senate counterparts than their colleagues in the House. The fact that Aspin switched from initially being in favour of the additional bombers in 1989 to opposing them in 1990 may be explained by looking at his position in Congress at the time. Surprisingly, in 1989 Aspin attempted to rally support for Cheney's defence budget submission in the House. Since the House was already looking for a peace dividend Aspin suffered an embarrassing defeat. According to Christopher Deering '[b]y all accounts, that event really did mark a turnaround'; Aspin restructured the HASC, courted the House Democratic Caucus, and realigned his committee's line with that of the Caucus (1994, p. 166).

In conclusion, the partial success of the B-2 can be explained in part in terms of the budget climate. Congress was truly shocked by the cost of the planes. In addition, despite Air Force arguments to the opposite effect, the B-2 was commonly perceived as being highly cost-ineffective. To make matters worse for the plane, its costs were growing at an alarming rate, especially towards the end of the programme. In the early 1980s these cost considerations were not a problem for the B-2 because the Air Force did not release this information and Congress was more worried about the Soviet threat than the budget deficit. However, in 1989 the B-2 budget was declassified and the Soviet threat was seen to disappear overnight. Then cost was a consideration and for the B-2 a major programme problem. The 20 bombers were bought because the programme had already entered production start-up and it had strong backers in the administration and Senate who were able to keep the programme going a little longer in the face of wider congressional opposition.

CONCLUSION

This chapter has shown that budgetary issues do matter to weapons acquisition in that they can affect the outcomes of weapon programmes (see Table 4.5). Budgetary issues boil down to considerations about cost. These cost considerations come in three forms: concern about the sheer cost of a weapon; concern about a weapon's cost-effectiveness; and concern over the amount of cost control over a weapon programme. Cost considerations explain the cancellation of the A-12 but not DIVAD. The fact that the A-12 was a hugely expensive programme and not very cost-effective was largely ignored by policymakers and legislators; however, its spiralling costs were not and this led it to its cancellation by Cheney. DIVAD was a cheap weapon by comparison which was seen to be cost-effective (even though it was not) and which was praised for its cost control. Cost considerations cannot account for the successful acquisition of the MX but they can explain why the B-2 programme was only a partial success. The strategic issues surrounding the MX programme overshadowed cost considerations; the programme did not suffer because of its expected huge cost nor did it benefit by being perceived to be cost-effective nor because of its declining costs. On the other hand, concerns about its massive and spiralling costs and cost-ineffectiveness led to the premature termination of the B-2 programme.

Table 4.5. Budgetary Issues in Weapons Acquisition

Weapon programme	Sheer cost	Cost-effectiveness	Cost control	Cost considerations
A-12	Ignored	Ignored	Very bad	*Costs out of control*
DIVAD	Good	OK	Good	*Cost not an issue*
MX	Ignored	OK	Good	*Cost not an issue*
B-2	Very bad	Bad	Very bad	*Far too costly*

While some weapon programmes may receive praise for being affordable, cost-effective or within budget, none really benefit from it. In none of the case studies were the weapons acquired for these reasons. For the most part, budgetary considerations are probably negative rather than positive; if present, they are more likely to create problems for the programmes rather than opportunities. Thus DIVAD was cancelled despite the fact that it was relatively inexpensive, seen to be cost-effective and within budget.[152]

Under certain conditions, cost considerations are more likely to have a greater impact on the outcomes of weapon programmes. These conditions, which are collectively referred to as the budget climate, are the size of the defence budget and defence expenditure, and the degree of centralisation in the DoD acquisition and resource allocation policy structures. Each of these conditions indicates the level of concern about cost considerations and the likelihood that this concern will affect weapon programmes. Take the case of an unfavourable budget climate. Decreasing defence budgets indicate a reluctance in Congress and/or the administration to spend money on weapons acquisition. Increasing centralisation indicates a shift in influence over weapons acquisition away from the services which are unconcerned about cost towards OSD officials who are more likely to be looking for good deals. The state of DoD policy structures also reveals much about the attitude of the Secretary of Defence and of Congress towards the role of the services; centralising policy structures indicates a declining trust of the services.

Table 4.6 The Budget Climate, 1977–92

Period	DoD budget	Policy structures	Budget climate
Brown	Increasing	Mixed	Favourable
Weinberger 1981–5	Increasing	Decentralised	Favourable
Wein/Carlucci 1986–7	Decreasing	Decentralised	Unfavourable
Cheney	Decreasing	Centralised	Unfavourable

The defence budget rose up to the mid-1980s and fell thereafter. The DoD policy structures experienced varying degrees of centralisation during this period, from partial centralisation under Brown, to total decentralisation under Weinberger, to full centralisation under Cheney. This meant the budget climate switched from being increasing favourable for weapon acquisition in the late 1970s to mid-1980s, to being increasingly unfavourable since then (see Table 4.6).

Table 4.7 The Budget Climate and Weapons Acquisition

Weapon programme	DoD Budget	Policy structures	Budget climate
A-12	Decreasing	Centralisation	Unfavourable
DIVAD	Increasing	Decentralising	Favourable
MX	Increasing	Decentralising	Favourable
B-2	Mixed	Mixed	Mixed

The budget climate can explain why similar cost considerations have different impacts on the outcomes of weapon programmes (see Table 4.7). Both stealth planes were viewed as rotten deals yet one was partially acquired while the other was terminated outright. This is because for the first eight years of its existence, the budget climate was favourable for the B-2 programme: during this time the defence budget was increasing and Weinberger had devolved power to the services. The budget climate began to get worse from 1986 onwards, that is, shortly after the A-12 programme started. By the time the Air Force and Navy got around to revealing details about the costs of their respective stealth programmes the budget climate had become distinctly unfavourable: by 1989–90 Congress was slashing the defence budget and Cheney had centralised power in the OSD. The Air Force got 20 planes because the B-2 programme had entered production start-up by 1989. The Navy got nothing because the A-12 was still in development in 1990. The budget climate also explains why cost considerations were irrelevant to the DIVAD and MX programmes: neither benefited from their good records on these counts. In the early to mid-1980s, when the MX entered full-scale production and DIVAD entered production start-up, the budget climate was favourable which meant that policy-makers and legislators were not too bothered about cost considerations and the services had greater say over weapons acquisition.

5 Weapons Without a Cause

Anybody who quotes me as saying things are good needs their bolts tightened

DoD Inspector General, Joseph Sherick[1]

This book has not provided an answer to the question why does the United States acquire certain weapons and not others? The answer is not straightforward but rather differs from programme to programme. However, this book has provided a framework for addressing this question. The strategic, institutional and budgetary issues surrounding each weapon must be examined in order to explain why it is acquired, partially acquired or not acquired. Strategic issues refer to the strategic rationale(s) for a weapon, institutional issues are the organisational and presidential politics surrounding its acquisition, and budgetary issues have to do with its cost. The validity of this model has been demonstrated in this study by an examination of four case studies of weapon programmes. As the next section discusses, in none of the cases examined can strategic, institutional or budgetary issues alone explain the origins, development and outcome of a programme; these conclusions are laid out in Table 5.1. In addition to developing a causal model, this book also makes some general observations about weapons acquisition in United States, in particular how strategic, institutional and budgetary issues interact (that is, their causal patterns) to produce particular programme outcomes. The overall findings of this study have important policy implications which will be discussed in the final section of this chapter.

Table 5.1. Study Findings

Programme stages	*A-12*	*DIVAD*	*B-2*	*MX*
Origins	Institutional	Strategic	Institutional	Strategic Institutional
Development	Institutional	Institutional	Institutional	Institutional
Outcome	Budgetary	Strategic Institutional	Institutional Budgetary	Strategic Institutional
Programme outcome	*Failure*	*Partial success*	*Partial success*	*Success*

EXPLAINING THE CASE STUDIES

The Navy needed a new naval bomber but not the A-12, which was developed to serve excessively demanding mission requirements, based on the Navy's suicidal forward strategy, which the plane was unable to meet anyway. Institutional considerations explain why the A-12 programme was started and how it was developed. The Navy wanted its own stealth bomber to serve a core organisational function, and, in order to improve the plane's prospects, the service gold-plated it and developed it concurrently without early OT&E. Budgetary issues explain the cancellation of the A-12; Cheney terminated the programme because its costs were spiralling way out of control. ·

DIVAD was started for strategic reasons but the programme was unable to adapt when the threat changed from bombers to helicopters. This was, in part, because the Army chose to develop a fancy AD gun when a simpler system would have been more cost-effective. Strategic considerations account for the programme's premature termination in that Weinberger finally cancelled it when he discovered how useless it was. At the same time, institutional issues explain why the weapon was still partially acquired; by developing the weapon concurrently, the Army were able to rush it into production and acquire 64 units before the programme got the chop.

As with the A-12, the B-2 was started for institutional reasons. The strategic rationale for the bomber kept shifting and was never really convincing. At one stage, it was claimed that the B-2's primary mission would be to hunt down mobile targets even though it would have been unable to do this. Later, the Air Force claimed that the bomber was needed to cover VHTs even though the service could fulfil this mission requirement by other, more cost-effective means. Since the B-2 was a black programme for most of it life, it clearly was not started to demonstrate US resolve or gain leverage in arms talks with the Soviets. The B-2 was developed because the Air Force, and SAC in particular, were organisationally disposed towards manned penetration bombers. Accordingly, the plane was gold-plated and developed concurrently without early OT&E. The Air Force also appears to have started the B-2 in order to court the support of President Carter after he cancelled the B-1. Carter ended up giving that support in order to beef-up his pro-defence credentials for his (unsuccessful) 1980 re-election bid. The B-2 programme was prematurely ended after Congress refused to fund any more bombers once the programme's cost, cost-effectiveness, and cost control became widely know on Captiol Hill. As with DIVAD, it was still partially acquired because the Air Force managed to get 16 units by developing the bomber concurrently. In addition, the pro-defence SASC and HASC also agreed to fund an additional four planes.

Strategic issues do, just about, account for the origins and outcome of the MX programme. SAC wanted a new ICBM to give added target coverage in the SIOP and Congress was persuaded that a survivable ICBM was needed. But these programme requirements did not reflect genuine mission requirements: there was already far too much overkill in the SIOP and US ICBMs did not need to be survivable as, unbeknown to Congress, SAC intended to launch their ICBMs on warning of a Soviet attack, that is, before Soviet warheads hit America. While the MX was clearly not acquired simply to be negotiated away, policymakers did genuinely believe that the United States needed a new large ICBM in order to demonstrate its resolve to enemies and allies alike. Institutional issues also explain the origins and outcome of the MX, and its development. The missile served a core Air Force function, programme requirements were established early-on, the missile was gold-plated, developed concurrently, and entered production without being tested properly. The MX also benefited from presidential support. Carter allowed it to enter full-scale development in order to ensure that the JCS did not oppose ratification of the SALT II Treaty in the Senate. In addition, the MX came to be closely identified with Reagan thus giving the President a stake in the programme's success.

WHAT THIS STUDY REVEALS ABOUT US WEAPONS ACQUISITION

The most alarming revelation from this book is how little influence strategy considerations have on weapon programmes. You would expect it to at least have some impact on most, if not all, of the programmes. This book uncovered two cases of weapons which lacked a strategic rationale, the DIVAD and B-2, and yet were partly acquired. Furthermore, strategic considerations were irrelevant to the failure of the A-12; it should not have reached full-scale development in the first place. Only one weapon served a strategic purpose, namely the MX. In this case, the weapon was successfully acquired thus suggesting that favourable strategic considerations, when present, may have a great impact on a programme outcome. It is all the more striking in this case given that the strategic rationale for the MX, while genuine, was so weak. However, this finding is not conclusive. Not only is the MX a poor example of a weapon acquired for strategic reasons, but also the MX acquisition was undoubtedly aided by the fact that it never became a budgetary issue.

This study has found that strategic issues matter so little largely because institutional issues matter so much in weapons acquisition. Of the three types of issues, institutional ones are clearly the most pervasive: a glance at Table 5.1 reveals as much. Institutional considerations explain, or partially explain, programme origins and outcomes in three cases, and the development of all four weapons. This is quite understandable. It has been argued that service support is needed just to get a weapon programme off the ground. Not surprisingly, those weapons which serve the core functions of services are the ones most likely to get started and to enjoy strongest service support. It is difficult for politicians and civilian policymakers, who are only in office for a few years, to regulate weapons acquisition because of the immense complexity and length of the process. The services, by their very size and nature, are able to use the long timescale and knowledge burden to their advantage. Thus, the services have traditionally been able to develop weapons as they see fit and usually to suit their organisational ends. This can lead to the services acquiring the weapons they want rather than the weapons they need; hence, the Navy has an plenty of aircraft carriers but a shortfall of minesweepers. It also leads them to contradict stated DoD policy and engage in inefficient acquisition practices – the early establishment of detailed performance requirements, gold-plating, and concurrency without early OT&E – which are designed to maximise the weapon's chances of being acquired. As a result, a weapon may be started for strategic reasons but end up being unable to serve these purposes; just as a child may be spoiled by its upbringing, so a weapon can be ruined by being brought up all wrong. DIVAD is a case in point. The Army built it around an expensive radar system which had problems detecting anything near the ground, especially hovering helicopters. A simpler, functional AD gun would have stood greater chances of adapting when the requirement changed from shooting down planes to shooting down helicopters. Institutional considerations led the Army to opt for a fancy gun in order to deflect criticisms of the weapon from those preferring a missile-based system.

However, it is also shown in this book that the services do not always get what they want. Institutional considerations have far less influence over the outcome of weapon programmes than over their origins and development. This is because weapons become far more costly as they enter production and so they are more likely to attract the attention of politicians and civilian policymakers. Hence, it is budgetary issues which determine the impact of institutional issues over programme outcomes. If cost considerations matter, either because the budget climate is unfavourable and/or because the weapon is costly, cost-ineffective or wildly overbudget, then institutional considerations will not. Even though the Navy desperately wanted the A-12 and the Air Force was equally enthralled by the B-2, budgetary considerations led to the former being cancelled and latter being terminated prematurely.

A final observation that ought to be made is how the acquisition of nuclear weapons differs from that of conventional weapons. First, nuclear weapon programmes attract far more political attention than conventional ones. In this regard, institutional issues concern more than just bureaucracies. Presidents also have self-interests which they may promote by supporting or attacking a nuclear weapon programme. In addition, Presidents can have a dramatic impact on nuclear weapon programmes by taking the decision of whether to let them enter production. The bureaucratic politics model as developed by Graham Allison and Morton Halperin fails to take such presidential self-interests and power into account. Second, nuclear weapons may be acquired for international political purposes alone; although evidence was only found to support the symbolic requirement and not the bargaining chip rationale. Conventional weapons may also serve international political purposes, say to reassure an ally, but this is a function of its military effectiveness; if it is seen to be ineffective then it will not reassure anybody. But as the case of the MX suggests, nuclear weapons can be acquired despite serving no useful military requirement and being of doubtful military effectiveness.

POLICY IMPLICATIONS: WASTE IN WEAPONS ACQUISITION

'Weapons without a cause' refers to the conclusion of this study: there ought to be very good reasons for spending billions of dollars on weapons development and acquisition yet, all too often, such reasons are lacking. This book shows the weapons acquisition process to be ineffective and hugely inefficient. Weapons are started and/or developed without strategic reasons. Hence, the Air Force gets the stealth bomber which it wants but does not need and the Army fails to get the SHORAD system which it did not want but needed desperately. The weapons acquisition process also appears to be incredibly wasteful.

Even if the A-12, DIVAD and B-2 were the only major weapon programmes without a genuine strategic purpose to reach full-scale development in the 1980s, which is unlikely, this still means that almost $50 billion was wasted on weapons that were not needed.[2]

It's Macro-Wastage that Matters

It was noted in Chapter 4 that in the mid-1980s the media and Congress became scandalised by fraud and financial mismanagement in the DoD, and that this eventually became one of the driving forces behind the 1986 acquisition reforms. The sheer amount of media and congressional attention that such scandals attracted was staggering; this is evident by the coverage given to scandals in 1985 involving two of the leading US defence contractors, General Dynamics and General Electric, who eventually admitted to overcharging the DoD and using bribes to win contracts.[3] It was also reported that at the time DoD Inspector General Sherrick was investigating charges of fraud against all of the top ten US defence contractors.[4] Another report claimed that 45 of the top 100 contractors were under criminal investigation by the DoD Inspector General.[5]

Was all this attention warranted? Some 'waste, fraud and mismanagement' is probably inevitable since so many defence contracts are being dealt with. Furthermore, it is feasible that all these scandals indicated that the system was able to root out abuses instead of being a system which was out of control: Weinberger was supposed to have told legislators 'you have heard about the $400 hammer. You may not have heard that there was only one hammer involved, and we identified the overcharge. We also got a refund for it.'[6] Even if Weinberger is wrong, in terms of cost, this form of waste, which may be called micro-wastage, was not the worst kind existing in the DoD acquisition process. Far more money was being wasted developing weapons without a strategic rationale or developing weapons badly so that they were unable to meet genuine strategic needs; this may be called macro-wastage. In 1985 one congressional team investigating billing irregularities found that seven defence contractors had collectively overcharged the DoD by $110 million.[7] This seems like a lot of money but compare it to the $2.7 billion and $45 billion wasted on the A-12 and B-2 respectively. Similarly, General Dynamics got into trouble a second time in late 1985 when it was accused of overcharging the DoD by $3.2 million for the full-scale development of its DIVAD prototype.[8] This was peanuts compared to the $1.8 billion wasted because the Army placed institutional considerations above strategic ones and developed the wrong AD gun for the job.

Some macro-wastage is inevitable in weapons acquisition. The whole process takes place in an uncertain technical and strategic environment. Weapons have to be developed before they can be tested to see if they work. Moreover, the requirement for them may change while they are being developed. Thus money is bound to be wasted developing weapons that end up not working or lose their strategic purpose. But this book has shown that institutional considerations have encouraged far more macro-wastage than is acceptable both by developing unnecessary weapons and by developing weapons in a excessively expensive manner.

Why the Services Are So Wasteful

The blame for macro-wastage lies with institutionally motivated service behaviour in weapons acquisition: that is, starting unnecessary programmes and establishing early detailed performance requirement, gold-plating, and concurrency without early OT&E. This is not to say that such motivations are venal; they are, quite simply, organisational self-interests which in this case do not serve national interests.

But is such service behaviour rational? Thomas Hammond suggested to me that it may be that 'what each service is doing is responding rationally, in a variety of quite-possibly-desirable ways, to the political environment it faces'. Hammond's argument goes like this:

> The problem facing a service is that . . . the fate of its weapons systems lies in the hands of its civilian overseers within the [DoD], in the hands of the President, and in the hands of Congress. From the viewpoint of the service, it is relatively infrequent that all three of these sources of authority – *these multiple veto points* – line up in support of the acquisition programme that the service thinks is best. Since the President and Congress, especially, always have other uses for the public's money that is more popular politically, if a service were to never recommend production of a weapon until all the operational tests have been complete, the weapons have been adjusted and improved, etc., the service might well find that *nothing* it needs will ever be approved. Hence strategies such as concurrency, early lockin of contracts, lack of operational testing, etc., however irrational technologically, are rational responses to this kind of political environment.[9]

Hammond is quite right to draw attention to how the services perceive their environment and respond to these perceptions. However, his argument that service behaviour in weapons development may be rational is not convincing. Why else would the services persist in this behaviour even when it ceases to benefit them? Establishing early detailed performance requirements and gold-plating ruined the DIVAD and made the A-12 and B-2 far more costly to build. Concurrency did little to help the DIVAD and the B-2 and nothing for the A-12. Yet DIVAD got into serious trouble the same year (that is, 1984) the A-12 was started and the B-2 was redesigned for a second time. Why did the Navy and Air Force not learn from the Army's experience? Furthermore, Chapter 4 showed that from 1986 onwards the budget climate got far worse for weapons acquisition and so cost considerations became increasingly significant. Yet both services continued to pursue these extremely expensive programmes as before. Furthermore, Hammond's argument only deals with service behaviour in weapons development: it does not handle institutional motivations for the origins of weapon programmes, that is, what makes the services 'think' certain weapons are better than others? Macro-wastage occurs not only by developing weapons inappropriately but also by developing inappropriate weapons.

If service choice and service behaviour are puzzling then the answers to both lie in the way organisations define their interests. In Chapter 3 the services were shown to be 'complex political communities' containing sub-units, or branches, and it was argued that service interests were defined by the service doctrine which was the product of an ideological struggle within the organisation itself. Notwithstanding the strength of service cohesion, plenty of examples have been presented in this study of branches within services pursuing their own interests in weapons acquisition regardless of broader service interests: the missile advocates in the Army were glad to undermine the DIVAD programme; SAC testified against the Air Force's and administration's two bomber programme in Congress; the SSPO gained the Navy Secretary's support for a replacement for SLBM for Polaris against the wishes of the Navy hierarchy. This shows that institutional politics occurs not only between organisations but also within them. Moreover, the manner in which organisations define their interests and pursue them is not only characterised by political struggle but also functional limitations. Individuals and groups within organisations, and organisations themselves, only have a limited capacity to follow what the organisation should be doing and is doing at any moment in time. Indeed, the sociology of science and technology approach, while having the feel of the bureaucratic politics approach, focuses explicitly on the role of social networks, comprised of small groups of people within and across organisations, in shaping weapons acquisition (Spinardi, 1989, 1994; MacKenzie, 1990) As a result organisations do not define their interests precisely: organisational 'interests' may be seen as loose frameworks in which may be slotted the more precise interests of the dominant subunits within an organisation. This is even true of hierarchical, highly disciplined and highly socialised organisations such as the military services: notice that service core interests refer to general military functions which encompass many specific military requirements, such as conventional land warfare in the Army's case.

Even if service interests are no more than collections of various group interests, could these groups not be striving to promote service behaviour which they believe to be in the national interests? Quite possible so, but even then such groups would face two barriers to such an endeavour, namely the cognitive limitations of their own members, and the possibility that other groups will be led by their own cognitive limitations to promote different or competing notions of the national interest. Cognitive limitations refer to the intellectual shortcomings and emotional interference which make it difficult for people to perceive their environment, learn lessons and construct appropriate responses (Jervis, 1976). Lynn Eden argues that a social constructivist approach, which combines organisational theory with the sociology of technology and science, is best able to explain the process whereby organisations accumulate, lose and use knowledge:

> [This is] one in which actors are not seen as simply reading an unambiguous environment and then acting rationally in their best interests, but rather they are squinting into the dark, telling themselves stories about what the world is like, and then acting on the basis of what they think is 'out there', while at the same time competing with others who have different notions (1992, p. 5).

So organisational learning, which is central to how organisations define their interests, proceeds via guesswork and group politics.

We have two explanations then for why institutional considerations produce macro-wastage. Group politics, and not rational choice, determine which interests a service pursues and how it pursues them: it is the most acceptable and not the 'best' interests which get adopted and promoted. In addition, cognitive limitations make it difficult for subunits to react appropriately to changes in their environment. These two explanations account for the services' inability to evolve in line with changes in the strategic and budgetary environments. Hence, the Navy and Air Force kept their preferences for large deck carriers and strategic penetration bombers respectively long after changes in the military environment reduced the cost-effectiveness of such weapons. The naval aviation community and SAC undoubtedly believed otherwise and were able to use their institutional positions to maintain the value of these weapons within their own services. It also explains why the services continued to be neglectful of costs in weapons development when previous experience and the budget climate indicated that everybody else was becoming more concerned about costs. The services (as collections of groups with cognitive limitations) did not see perceive the rising importance of budgetary considerations.

Will the Services Ever Wise Up?

How much hope is there that the services may wise up? On the one hand, group politics and cognitive limitations may lead the services to learn the wrong lessons. The services may intensify their current patterns of behaviour in the acquisition process: early establishment of detailed performance requirements, gold-plating and concurrency may become more pronounced instead of less. However, there are two grounds for hope.

First, there are very strong incentives for the services to change their ways. Some of the literature on organisational behaviour (particular military organisations) draws attention to two things which inhibit organisational learning, namely bias interpretation of events and the lack of incentives for change (Levitt and March, 1988; Rosen 1989; Sagan 1993; Avant 1994). For instance, in his work on the US military and nuclear accidents, Scott Sagan noted that both conditions created severe problems for organisational learning about the causes and chances of nuclear accidents. The history of previous accidents or near accidents was constructed to suit Air Force goals and not to aid organisational learning; the Air Force, which sought more flexible control over larger numbers of nuclear weapons, had strong self-interests in downplaying or even ignoring the occurrence of nuclear accidents and close calls (Sagan, 1993, pp. 256–8). This used to be the case in weapons acquisition as well: it was in the services' interests to exaggerate the need and capabilities and underestimate the costs of their weapon programmes. Now things are very different. The budget climate is sure to remain very unfavourable for weapons acquisition for some time to come: in particular, defence TOA is set to continuing declining at least until 1997 (Kaufmann, 1992; Korb, 1992; Zakhiem and Ranney, 1993; Adams and Kosiak, 1993). This means that budgetary considerations will continue to dominate institutional ones in determining the outcomes of weapon programmes. Indeed, weapons programmes are being cancelled on an unprecedented scale in order to bring defence expenditure down: the DoD has moved from terminating current generation weapon programmes (that is, weapons already in full-scale production) in FY 1991 and FY 1992 to terminating next generation weapon programmes (weapons about to enter, or already in, production start-up) in FY 1993 and FY 1994.[10] Recently it has been reported that the DoD is even considering 'cancelling or delaying virtually every new weapons system in development'.[11] Before the 1990s it was very rare for a weapon programme to be cancelled once it had made it past full-scale development: now it is commonplace. In this new tougher budget climate the services have very strong incentives to reduce the cost of their weapons, make them as cost-effective as possible and to keep them within budget. This will be made easier for them if they produce honest estimates about the costs of weapons: this way acquisition officials and contractors know that they are working within a real programme budget which is rigid instead of a fictitious budget which is sure to be breached; if the estimated programme budget is based on real figures it also means that the programme will not automatically go overbudget.

Second, change is occurring within the services themselves which may result in more responsible service choices and behaviour in weapons acquisition. This study has suggested that the key to ensuring that weapon programmes meet cost considerations is greater civilian oversight over the process. For the moment this conclusion remains valid. However, it is possible that, in the future, the services will treat cost considerations as being in their own interest. This is not the same as saying (as above) that they will adopt such considerations in order to avoid heavy sanctions; rather, that they will come to see the value of cost considerations. This might happen as follows. Each service could develop an acquisition corps which would then develop its own sub-unit identity like the other branches within the services. Officers who specialise in weapons acquisition, as in other branches, would be assigned to this acquisition corps for their entire military careers, perhaps with brief rotations in other branches. These acquisition corps would be different from the old supply and buying commands in that they would have far greater control over weapons acquisition and they would be staffed by a permanent body of officers who would be trained to develop weapons efficiently and promoted according to their ability to do so. Rosen has argued that 'peacetime innovation has been possible when senior military officers with traditional credentials, reacting to . . . a structural change in the security environment, have acted to create a new promotion pathway for junior officers practicing a new way of war' (1991, p. 251). The same may be said of a structural change in the political environment providing incentives for the services to nurture a new way of weapons acquisition. Such change is actually occurring in the services and in the DoD as a whole. In response to the 1991 Defence Acquisition Work Force Improvement Act four acquisition corps were established, one in each of the services and one for the OSD and other defence agencies. According to the DoD: 'The acquisition corps provides a structured career path for military and civilian personnel who choose acquisition as their speciality, and it will ensure that only individuals with the proper management experience and education are placed in critical acquisition positions.' To ensure proper training and career promotion, the Office of the Director, Acquisition Education, Training, and Career Development was established in the Office of the USD(A); similar positions were also established in each of the services, and a Defence Acquisition University was set up.[12] In time, these acquisition corps ought to be able to assert their group self-interests, which are to ensure that the weapons acquisition process is effective and efficient, within their respective services. The recent history of US weapons acquisition is gloomy indeed but the future looks a bit brighter; the harsher budget climate and new service acquisition structures could well lead to less macro-wastage in weapons acquisition.

Notes

Journal Abbreviations

AFJI	*Armed Forces Journal International*
AW & ST	*Aviation Weekly and Space Technology*
IHT	*International Herald Tribune*
JDW	*Jane's Defence Weekly*
NYT	*New York Times*

1 Explaining Weapons Acquisition

1. DoD, *Directive 5000.1* (Washington, DC: DoD, 23 February 1991), p. 2.
2. These seven programmes are the Minuteman III follow-on to the Minuteman, Poseidon follow-on to Polaris, C-141A follow-on to C-130, C-5A follow-on to C-141A, F-15 follow-on to F-4, F-111 follow-on to B-58, and B-1 delayed follow-on to B-70 (Kurth, 1989, pp. 25-6).
3. Gordon Adams, *The Politics of Defence Contracting: The Iron Triangle* cited in Smith, 1988, pp. 236, 1016.
4. Michael Brown cites eleven authors to show that 'it is no exaggeration to say that this line of thinking constitutes the conventional wisdom on the subject in the arms control and scientific communities' (Brown, 1992, p. 11).
5. James Kurth sets out to cut through what considered to be a 'thicket of theories' surrounding US military policy (1989). He examined five competing explanations (strategic, technocratic, bureaucratic, democratic and economic) for four different types of weapons acquisition (innovative, renovative, redistributive and quantitative). While Kurth makes some interesting observations, ironically, his arguments are hidden in the complex framework of his own study. Furthermore, he does not test these competing explanations but rather he simply demonstrates them. To test them would require more research and a far more lengthy study.
6. For a debate on the purpose and performance of the Patriots in the Gulf War, see Theodore A. Postal, 'Lessons of the Gulf War Experience With Patriot', *International Security*, 16/3, 1991-2, pp. 119-71; Robert M. Stein, 'Patriot ATBM Experience in the Gulf War', Raytheon pamphlet, 1992; Postal and Stein, 'Correspondence', *International Security*, 17/1, 1992, pp. 119-240.
7. Snyder, 1988, p. 169. In an earlier study on the problems of meeting the demands of rigour in basic research with the richness of historical detail and relevance of policy applicability in Soviet studies, Snyder points to the structured, focused comparison method as demonstrating that a research strategy can be developed to balance these three seemingly competing demands (1984-5, pp. 89-108).
8. In addition, given that they have not been used in war since 1945, measuring the 'battlefield success' of nuclear weapons would be (mercifully) impossible.

9. Gen. Kelly Burke, Air Force Deputy Chief for Research and Development, 'Peacekeeper (MX) History and Current Status' (1984) [David Dunn's Private Files]; US General Accounting Office (GAO) Report to the Chairman of the House Armed Services Committee (HASC), *ICBM Modernization: Availability Problems and Flight Test Delay in Peacekeeper Programme*, GAO/NSIAD-98-105 (Washington, DC: USGAO, March 1989), pp. 2, 11.

10. GAO Report to the Chairman of the HASC, *Navy A-12: Cost and Requirements*, GAO/NSIAD-91-98 (Washington, DC: USGAO, 31 December 1990), pp. 1–4.

11. Kotz, 1988, pp. 204, 215; GAO Report to the Chairman of the HASC, *Strategic Bombers: B-2 Programme Status and Currrent Issues*, GAO/NSIAD-90-120 (Washington, DC: USGAO, 22 February 1990), p. 2; Melissa Healy, 'The Plug is Pulled on the B-2 Bomber', *International Herald Tribune* (9 January 1992).

12. GAO Report to the Chairman of the Senate Governmental Affairs Committee, *Sergeant York*, GAO/NSIAD-86-89 (Washington, DC: USGAO, 30 May 1986), pp. 1–3.

2 Strategic Issues

1. 'Honing the Defenses With Updates', *Aviation & Space Technology* (2 December 1985), p. 116.

2. GAO, Report to the Chairman of the House Armed Services Committee, *Navy A-12: Cost and Requirements*, GAO/NSIAD-91-98 (Washington, DC: USGAO, December 1990), pp. 1, 15.

3. John Mearsheimer discerns four offensive missions in the Maritime Strategy, the fourth being offensive sea control, that is, controlling the seas by destroying the Soviet Navy (1986, p. 17). However, as far as the Navy were concerned, 'power projection in reality refers to the mission of offensive sea control' of which 'the CVBG is the cornerstone'. Seapower and Strategic and Critical Materials Subcommittee (SSCMS) of the House Armed Services Committee (HASC), *Hearings on the 600 Ship Navy and the Maritime Strategy*, 99th Congress, 2nd session (1985), p. 133. For an official description of the Maritime Strategy, see Admiral James D. Watkins, 'The Maritime Strategy', *US Naval Institute Proceedings* (January, 1986), pp. 3–17.

4. These criticisms were made by Mearsheimer (1986) and Robert Komer (1982). For a reply, see Brooks, 1986, pp. 76–87.

5. Posen, 1982, pp. 28–54; Michael Gordon, 'Officials Say Navy Might Attack Soviet A-Arms in Nonnuclear War', *NYT* (7 January 1986), p. 1; Frank Taylor 'US Navy Plans "Could Start Nuclear War"', *Daily Telegraph* (9 January 1986).

6. Statement by Rear Admiral Eugene J. Carroll, Jr, USN (Ret.), before the SSCMS of the HASC, 6 September 1985, p. 255.

7. Of the 77 Soviet SSBNs, 39 were based in four facilities on the Kola Peninsula (International Institute for Strategic Studies, 1986, pp. 36, 41).

8. Carroll, Statement before SSCMS, p. 259.
9. Bernard E. Trainor, 'Lehman's Sea-War Strategy Is Alive, But For How Long?', *NYT* (23 March 1987).
10. DoD, *Soviet Military Power 1988* (Washington, DC: USGPO, 1988), p. 130.
11. In a previous article I argued that the development of the A-12 could be explained in terms of strategic issues. However, I also argued that if it could be shown (as it has been suggested in this book and in greater detail in my Ph.D. theis) that the forward strategy 'more closely reflected the Navy's budget than military concerns', then this would 'undermine the military requirement for the A-12' (Farrell, 1993, p. 124).
12. 'The Face that Launched 600 Ships', *The Economist* (28 February 1987); Alex Brummer, 'US Navy Chief Quits', *Guardian* (13 February 1987); Trainor, 'Lehman's Sea-War Strategy is Alive'.
13. John Barry, 'The Navy Sails on Rough Seas', *Newsweek* (28 May 1987).
14. Richard Lessner, 'Quick Strike'; 'Navy Secretary's Wartime Strategy Is Contested Legacy', *Arizona Republic* (29 March 1987); Norman Polmar and Scott C. Truver, 'The Maritime Strategy', *Air Force Magazine* (November 1987), pp. 70–9.
15. Ronald O'Rourke, Congressional Research Service (CRS) Report for Congress, *Navy Carrier-Based Fighter and Attack Aircraft in the FY1992 Budget: Issues for Congress*, (Washington, DC: CRS-The Library of Congress, March 1991), p. 11.
16. Daniel, 1993, p. 9.
17. Bert H. Cooper, Jr, *CRS Issue Brief, AX Aircraft Program: Issues and Options* (Washington, DC: CRS-The Library of Congress, November 1991), p. 2.
18. Cooper, *AX Aircraft Program*, p. 4.
19. Towell, 'Cheney Pulls Plug . . .', p. 85.
20. Richard Lardner, 'Controversy Looms Over Jagged-Edge of Air Force's B-2 Stealth Bomber', *Inside the Pentagon* (2 March 1990), p. 1; Mark Thompson, 'Stealth: It Can Fly But It Can't Hide, Navy Says', *Norfolk Virginian-Pilot* (18 May 1990), p. 1; Fred Kaplan, 'B-2 Bomber Fails Tests of Radar Evasion', *Boston Globe* (22 May 1991), p. 3; Melissa Healy, 'AF: Fixed-Up B-2 Would Rate an 8', *Los Angeles Times* (14 September 1991), p. 1; Richard Stevenson, 'Stealth Bomber's Tests Point to Flaws in Ability to Duck Enemy Radar', *IHT* (13 September 1991); Tony Capaccio, 'Lawmakers Warn: B-2 Snags Are Not Insignificant', *Defense Week*, p. 1; Bill Richards, 'Boeing Knew B-2 Detectable By Secret Radar, Expert Says', *Seatle Post-Intelligencer* (3 October 1991), p. 1.
21. Andy Ireland, 'The Real "Stealth" Is in the Tactics of the Planes' Backers', *Christian Science Monitor* (7 January 1992), p. 19.
22. Ireland, 'The Real "Stealth" ', p. 19.
23. Francis Tusa, 'Radar-Makers Scrambling to Unmask Stealth', *AFJI* (August 1991), p. 31; Henry van Loon, 'Stealth Detection at 250 Miles Is Aim of New Dutch Radar Effort', *AFJI* (October 1991), p. 32.
24. Infra-red missiles have problems targeting approaching aircraft because it is from this angle that the heat emissions from the aircraft's engines are least pronounced.
25. Statement of Brig. General James P. Maloney (USA), Deputy Director of Combat Support Systems, Office of Deputy Chief of Staff for Research,

Development and Acquisition and Chairman, Army Air Defence Special
Planning Group, Procurement and Military Nuclear Systems Subcommittee (PMNSS) of the HASC, *Hearings on Military Posture and HR 6495*, pt.2,
96th Congress, 2nd session (1980), pp. 731–2, 738; Tactical Warfare Subcommittee (TWS) of the SASC, *Hearings on the Oversight on the Division Air Defence Gun System (DIVAD)*, 98 Congress, 2nd session (1984), pp. 32–3;
Congressional Budget Office (CBO) Report, *Army Air Defence for Forward
Areas: Strategies and Costs* (Washington, DC: US Government Printing
Office [GPO], June 1986), pp. 10, 21–3.

26. CBO Report, *Army Air Defense*, p. 2.
27. Fighter bombers are dual use aircraft, able to serve ground attack and air
    superiority roles. In this study, unless otherwise specificed, fighter bombers
    will also be taken to mean ground attack aircraft which are designed to
    also serve as air superiority fighters.
28. Statement of Col. Charles C. Adsit (USA), DIVAD Program Manager, be-
    fore the PMNSS of the HASC, p. 803.
29. According to official NATO figures in 1984, the Warsaw Pact had 2,250
    fighter bombers while NATO had 1,960. DoD, *Soviet Military Power 1985*,
    4th edn (Washington, DC: USGPO, April, 1985), p. 88.
30. Close air support (CAS) missions are when tactical airpower is used in di-
    rect support of ground operations.
31. Col. Adsit, Statement to PMNSS, p. 803.
32. DoD, *Soviet Military Power 1985*, p. 64.
33. CBO Report, *Army Air Defense*, p. 2.
34. CBO report, *Army Air Defense*, pp. 6–9, 12.
35. George C. Wilson, 'Divad Air-Defense Gun Scrapped by Pentagon', *IHT*
    (28 August 1985). Weinberger was quoted as saying: 'What went wrong was
    that the [DIVAD] system did not develop the capabilities that we require,
    and those capabilities depend upon the growing nature of the Soviet threat;
    specifically, the ability of the helicopter to sit off and stand off and deliver
    very effective fire against combat troops'.
36. Col. Adsit, Statement to PMNSS, pp. 802, 4–5; TWS, *Oversight on the
    DIVAD*, p. 8.
37. TWS, *Oversight on the DIVAD*, p. 10; 'Weinberger Shoots Down Sgt. York',
    Flight International (7 September 1985).
38. TWS, *Oversight on the DIVAD*, p. 24.
39. CBO Report, *Army Air Defense*, p. 9.
40. Interview with senior staff member of the SASC (Washington, DC: May
    1990).
41. Robert R. Ropelewski, 'Operational Evaluation, Growth in Threat Contri-
    bute to Cancelation', *Aviation Week and Space Technology* (*AW&ST*) (2
    September 1985), p. 27.
42. US Army, Field Manual 100–5, *Operations* (Washington, DC: Headquar-
    ters, Department of the Army, August 1982), Chapter 2. See also Wass de
    Czege, 1984, pp. 101–19 (Wass de Czege was one of the main authors of Air-
    Land Battle Doctrine); Michael R. Gordon, 'The Army's "AirLand Battle"
    Doctrine Worries Allies, Upsets the Air Force', *National Journal* (18 June
    1983), pp. 1274–77; Drew Middleton, 'Army Moves to a Strategy Stressing

Offense', *NYT* (15 April 1984), p. 6; Hanne, 1983, pp. 135–40; Sinnreich, 1984, p. 51.

43. Col. Adsit, Statement to PMNSS, p. 803; see also TWS, *Oversight of the DI-VAD*, p. 33.
44. Interview (Washington, DC: May, 1990).
45. CBO Report, *Army Air Defense*, pp. 16–17.
46. CBO Report, *Army Air Defense*, pp. 17–18.
47. TWS, *Oversight on the DIVAD*, p. 58.
48. See testimonies of James P. Wade, Assistant Secretary of Defence (Development and Support), and Brig. General Michael D. Hall, Deputy Director for Operational, Test and Evaluation, before the TWS, *Oversight on the DI-VAD*, pp. 11–27.
49. TWS, *Oversight on the DIVAD*, pp. 11–20, 34–41.
50. GAO Report to the Senate Governmental Affairs Committee, *Sergeant York: Concerns About the Army's Accelerated Acquisition Strategy*, GAO/NSIAD-86-89 (Washington, DC: USGAO, 30 May 1986), pp. 28–32.
51. Declaratory policy shifted from assured destruction in the 1950s, to no cities counterforce then to a countercity MAD in the 1960s, to limited nuclear options (LNO) and counter-recovery in the 1970s, and finally to countervailing in the 1980s (Sagan, 1989, pp. 10–13).
52. This is indicated in a GAO report on the nuclear targeting process which presented the development of the SIOP as proceeding according to the following four steps.

    (1) Presidential direction for the employment of nuclear weapons is provided to the Secretary of Defence through a National Security Directive or Memorandum, which defines national security objectives and sets policy guidance concerning the deployment of U.S. nuclear weapons.
    (2) The Secretary of Defence issues the Policy Guidance for the Employment of Nuclear Weapons (or Nuclear Weapons Employment Plan [NU-WEP]), which establishes the planning assumptions, attack options and targeting objectives.
    (3) The Chairman of the Joint Chiefs of Staff develops more detailed guidance for preparation of the SIOP based on guidance from the President and Secretary of Defense. The Chairman's guidance is incorporated in Annex C (Nuclear) of the Joint Strategic Capabilities Plan.
    (4) The Chairman's guidance is used by the Joint Strategic Target Planning Staff (JSTPS) in developing the SIOP.

    GAO Fact Sheet for Congressional Requesters, *Strategic Weapons: Nuclear Weapons Targeting Process*, GAO/NSIAD-91-319FS (Washington DC: USGAO, September 1991), p. 1.
53. James R. Schlesinger, Secretary of Defence, *Annual Report to the Congress, Fiscal Year 1975*, reproduced in Bobbit, *et al.*, 1989, p. 376.
54. Hearing Before the Senate Foreign Relations Committee (SFRC), *Nuclear War Strategy*, 96th Congress, 2nd session (Washington DC: USGPO, February 1981), p. 8.
55. Harold Brown, Secretary of Defence, *Annual Report to the Congress, Fiscal Year 1981* (Washington DC: USGPO, 29 January 1980), pp. 66–7; SFRC,

Nuclear War Strategy, pp. 29–30; Sagan, 1989, pp. 48–50; Sloss and Millot, 1984, pp. 24–5.

56. Harold Brown, Secretary of Defense, *Annual Report to the Congress, Fiscal Year 1982* (Washington DC: USGPO, 19 January 1981), p. 39.

57. Ball and Toth, 1990, p. 68; Scheer, 1982, pp. 11–12; Casper Weinberger, Secretary of Defence, *Annual Report to the Congress, Fiscal Year 1983* (Washington DC: USGPO, 8 February 1982), p. 18.

58. Brown, *Annual Report, FY81*, p. 78.

59. SFRC, *Nuclear War Strategy*, p. 29.

60. The GAO noted that 'estimates ranged up to 180 days'. Comptroller General of the United States, GAO Report to the Congress, *Countervailing Strategy Demands Revision Of Strategic Force Acquisition Plans*, MASAD-81-35 (Washington DC: USGAO, August 1981), p. 15.

61. Brown, *Annual Report, FY81*, pp. 67, 82–3; SFRC, *Nuclear War Strategy*, pp. 21, 31. Brown stated the following about the countervailing strategy.

    – It does not even assume, or assert, that a nuclear war could remain limited. I have made clear my view that such a prospect is highly unlikely . . .
    – It does not assume that a nuclear war will in fact be protracted over many weeks or even months. It does however, take into account evidence of Soviet thinking along those lines . . .

    Brown, *Annual Report, FY82*, p. 42.

62. GAO, *Strategic Weapons*, pp. 13, 16.

63. Institute for Defence Analyses (IDA), Research and Engineering Support Division, *The Strat-X Report, Vol. 1*, Report R-122 (Arlington, Virgina: IDA, August, 1967).

64. General Kelly Burke, Air Force Deputy Chief for Research and Development, 'Peacekeeper (MX) History and Current Status' (1984) [David Dunn's Private Files], p. 1.

65. William J. Perry, *The FY 1979 Department of Defence Programme For Research, Development and Acquisition* (Washington, DC: USGPO, February 1978), p. 3.

66. In his report to Congress in 1979 Brown stated that 'the Soviets are now estimated to be introducing new missiles with more warheads and improving the accuracy of their warheads, more rapidly than we had expected a year ago'. Harold Brown, Secretary of Defence, *Annual Report to the Congress, Fiscal Year 1979* (Washington, DC: USGPO, 25 January 1979), p. 116. However, Perry told the SASC that with regard to the National Intelligence Estimate, 'in terms of [Soviet] RV growth, it is really not substantially different than we saw a year ago. In terms of guidance systems, they have shifted from the original figure of a year ago down to this new line . . . That has a profound effect of moving the accuracy of Soviet ICBM'. Senate Armed Services Committee (SASC), *Department of Defence Authorization For Approprations For Fiscal Year 1979* (Washington, DC: USGPO, February 1979), pp. 301–2.

67. Throw-weight refers to the total weight of what a missile can carry over a certain distance. In the case of a MIRVed missile, this not only includes the warhead (or payload), but also the 'bus' which dispenses the warheads over their targets, the guidance mechanism on the bus, and other possible

items such as penetration aids (e.g. decoys). Thus, as Strobe Talbott puts it, 'throw-weight includes a number of components that do not actually arrive, much less blow up, at the target' (1984, p. 215).

68. CBO, Issue Paper For FY 1979, *Planning U.S. Strategic Nuclear Forces for the 1980s* (Washington, DC: USGPO, June 1978), pp. 7–8; William J. Perry, *The FY 1980 Department of Defence Programme For Research, Development and Acquisition* (Washington, DC: DoD, February 1979), p. 3; GAO Report, *Countervailing Strategy Demands Revision Of Strategic Force Acquisition Plans*, p. 3.
69. SASC, *Defense Authorization FY79*, p. 303.
70. Brown, *Annual Report, FY81*, p. 86.
71. Brown, *Annual Report, FY81*, p. 69. In his previous report to Congress Brown offered a counter-argument to this point, that is, that the US 'could be viewed as playing to [its] strengths in SLBMs and cruise missiles'. His conclusion suggests the way his thinking was going. 'My own judgement lies between these alternatives, but closer to the former view.' Brown, *Annual Report, FY80*, p. 118.
72. Betts, 1987, p. 190. Indeed, until recently, it was generally believed that the Soviets had not even reacted in kind to the three US global nuclear alerts; it now appears that they did do so but they kept quiet about it (Blair, 1993, pp. 22–3).
73. Nobody was talking about this at the time because the issue was, in essence, such a delicate one, i.e. US willingness to launch a first strike against the Soviet Union. Betts argues that hawks and doves avoided discussing the problems raised by extended deterrence because they did not want to scare off their moderate supporters of each position by arguing repsectively for US first use or abandoning extended deterrence. In short, everybody saw the advantage of simply ignoring the whole issue (1987, p. 191).
74. Brown, *Annual Report, FY81*, p. 88.
75. SFRC, *Nuclear War Strategy*, p. 13.
76. Pre-launch survivablity refers to the ability of a nuclear weapon to survive a Soviet attack against its base (airfield, port, or silo). Post-launch survivability refers to its ability to penetrate hostile airspace and attack its assigned target(s).
77. Brown, *Annual Report, FY82*, p. 50.
78. Brown, *Annual Report, FY81*, p. 128.
79. CBO Backround Paper, *Retaliatory Issues for the U.S. Strategic Nuclear Forces* (Washington, DC: USGPO, June 1978), p. 10.
80. Chayes, 1987, p. 155. While a certain bias surely colours this assessment, for Chayes is basically saying that she was responsible whereas her predecessor was not, her comments with regard to the Ford administration appear to be mostly fair.
81. Comptroller General of the United States, GAO Report to the Congress, *The MX Weapon System: Issues and Challenges*, NASAD-81-1 (Washington, DC: USGAO, February 1981), p. 9.
82. Burke, 'The Peacekeeper', pp. 8–9; Scoville, 1981, pp. 108–9.
83. 'The Scrowcroft Commission Report', pp. 485–7, 499; Elizabeth Drew, 'A Political Journal', *New Yorker* (20 June 1983), pp. 39–75; Cimbala, 1988.

84. Statement of General John W.Vessey, Chairman of the Joint Chiefs of Staff, before the Senate Defence Appropriations Subcommittee (7 March 1985), p. 5.

85. Elizabeth Drew, 'A Political Journal', *New Yorker* (20 June 1983), pp. 39–75; Les Aspin, 'The MX Bargain', *Bulletin of Atomic Scientists* (November 1983), pp. 52–4.

86. Wilson, 1985; Daivd C. Morrison, 'Missile Gridlock', *National Journal* (7 June 1986), pp. 1366–70.

87. Under the Rail Garrison system MXs were to be deployed on rail cars, stored in military compounds during peacetime, and dispersed through the civilian rail network during war. GAO Report to Congressional Requesters, *ICBM Modernization: Status of Peacekeeper Rail Garrison System*, GAO/NSIAD-89-64 (Washington, DC: USGAO, 12 January 1986).

88. GAO Report, *Countervailing Strategy Demands Revision Of Strategic Force Acquisition Plans*, pp. 13–19; Statement by Vessey to SADS, p. 5.

89. GAO Report, *Countervailing Strategy Demands Revision Of Strategic Force Acquisition Plans*, p. 32.

90. Brown, *Annual Report FY81*, p. 90.

91. Blair, 1993, p. 169. Although it is interesting to note that in 1984 Pentagon lawyers were arguing that the President had the right to launch a nuclear first strike without consulting Congress beforehand. 'US Says It Reserves Right to Launch Nuclear First Strike Without Consulting Congress', *Radio Free Europe*, transcript, 8 September 1984; Charles Mohr, 'President's Power and Nuclear First Use', *IHT* (September 1984).

92. Casper W. Weinberger, Secretary of Defense, *Annual Report to the Congress, Fiscal Year 1987* (Washington, DC: USGPO, 5 February 1986), p. 38.

93. *The Scrowcroft Report*, p. 498; Hearing Before the SFRC, *President's Commission on Strategic Forces*, First Session on the Arms Control and Foreign Policy Implications of the Scrowcroft Commission Report (US Washington, DC: GPO, 11 May 1983), pp. 3, 11.

94. Deputy Air Force Chief of Staff for Reserch, Development and Acquisition, Lt. General Lawrence Skantze, argued that the MX was needed to counter the perception of Soviet superiority which had been created by the alarm over the improved accuracy of Soviet ICBMs. Michael Gordon, 'CIA Downgrades Estimate of Soviet SS-19 Saying Missile Too Inaccurate for First Strike', *National Journal* (20 July 1985), p. 1693.

95. The President of the United States, *Report to the Congress on Continuing the Acquisition of the Peacekeeper (MX) Missile* (Washington, DC: GPO, 4 March 1985); Paul Nitze, *Testimony to Senate Appropriations Panel* (US Information Service, 11 March 1985), p. 3.

96. SFRC, *President's Commission on Strategic Forces*, p. 12.

97. SFRC, *President's Commission on Strategic Forces*, p. 3.

98. Reginald Dale, 'Reagan Presses case for MX as Arms Talks Near', *Financial Times* (5 March 1985); Nitze, *Testimony*, pp. 1, 3–4.

99. 'US Arms Plan: Keep Talking, Keep Building', *US News and World Report* (2 February 1985); 'MX Fails as Missile or Lever', *IHT* (15 March 1985).

100. TASS, English transcript, LD222224, 18:30 GMT (Moscow: 22 March 1985).

101. George Shultz, Secretary of State, *The Importance of the Peacekeeper Missile*, Current Policy No.662 (Washington, DC: US State Dept., 26 February 1985), pp. 1–2; 'Shultz, Weinberger Ask Congress to Support MX', *IHT (27 February 1985)*.
102. The B-52H was the latest updated version of the B-52.
103. The Organisation of the Joint Chiefs of Staff, *United States Military Posture For FY 1987* (Washington, DC: USGPO, 1986), p. 23.
104. 'US Defence Efforts – Exploding Myths', *Defense News*, 3/9 (1988).
105. 'B-1 Bomber: Overweight and Underprotected', *The Economist* (8 November 1986), p. 44; Frank Morring, 'Fat, Leaky B-1B Ready to Fly Despite its Flaws', *Washington Times* (5 December 1986), p. 5; 'U.S. Refuses Payments For B-1B, Citing Defects', *IHT* (5 December 1986); Bruce van Voorst, 'The Pentagon's Flying Edsel', *Time* (19 January 1987), p. 23.
106. 'Chain on the B-1B', *Air Force Magazine* (July 1987), p. 66.
107. GAO Report to the Chairman of the SASC, *Strategic Bombers: B-1B Cost and Performance Remain Uncertain*, GAO/NSIAD-89-55 (Washington, DC: USGAO, 1989), p. 9.
108. Elizabeth A. Palmer, 'The B-1 Stayed at Home', *Congressional Quarterly* (9 March 1991), p. 618.
109. Personal interview with Michael Brown (London, March 1992); GAO Report to Congressional Committees, *Strategic Bombers: Updated Status of the B-1B Recovery Programme*, GAO/NSIAD-91-189 (Washington, DC: USGAO, May 1991), p. 2.
110. Pat Towell, 'Breakthrough Senate SDI Pact Presages Conference Flight', *Congressional Quarterly* (3 August 1991), p. 2184.
111. GAO Report to the Chairmen of the SASC and HASC, *Strategic Missiles: Uncertainties Persist in the ACM Programme*, GAO/NSIAD-91-35 (Washington, DC: USGAO, November 1990).
112. DoD, *Soviet Military Power 1985*, p. 30; DoD, *Soviet Military Power 1987*, p. 26.
113. DoD, *Soviet Military Power 1987*, pp. 30–1.
114. 'Stealth Bomber', *The Federation of American Scientists Public Interest Report* (Washington, DC: FAS, October 1988), pp. 7–8.
115. Dick Cheney, Secretary of Defence, *Annual Report to the Congress, 1992* (Washington, DC: USGPO, February 1992), p. 7.
116. Patrick E. Tyler, 'Pentagon Imagines New Enemies To Fight in Post-Cold War Era', *NYT* (17 February 1992), p. 1.
117. Patrick E. Tyler, 'Top Officials Thrash the No Rivals Plan', *IHT* (12 March 1992).
118. Patrick E. Tyler 'Pentagon Drops Goal of Blocking New Superpowers', *NYT* (24 May 1992), p. 1. More recently, in an important symbolic gesture it was agreed at the Moscow summit in January 1994 that the United States and Russia would no longer target nuclear weapons at each other as of May that year (IISS, 1994, 258).
119. Brown, *Annual Report, FY82*, p. 51.
120. David C. Morrison, 'Getting Together', *National Journal* (19 July 1986), p. 1805.
121. Glenn W. Goodman, Jr, 'B-2 Bomber's Conventional Capabilities Brought to the Fore', *AFJI* (June 1991), p. 11.

122. 'The Might and the Myth of the B-52', *Newsweek* (18 February 1991), pp. 26–8.
123. The difficulty of such a mission was highlighted by the allies' inability to knock out all of Iraqi's mobile Scuds during the Gulf War.

3 Institutional Issues

1. It is possible for an organisation not to seek survival, but simply to fulfil a mandate, the successful implementation of which will result in the termination of that organisation.
2. I have been informed on the nature of service branches through discussions with an acquaintance who is a serving US Army officer (Kiel, Germany: July 1988; West Point Military Academy, NY: July 1990) and through an interview with another US Army officer (Washington, DC: May 1990). See also Rosen (1991, p. 19), Allard (1990, p. 19) and Halperin (1974, pp. 28–35).
3. Kotz, 1988, p. 180–4. According to Kotz, Air Force officials, the Air Force Secretary and the Director of R&D hid the funds for the B-1 development programme under misleading titles in the annual DoD R&D budget (1988, p. 184). Michael Brown argues that the Air Force were able to keep the B-1 programme going by securing funds to build four B-1 prototypes, ostensibly to gather technical information from the cancelled programme, which were then used to maintain Rockwell's B-1 production line (1992, pp. 269–70).
4. Indeed once in office, Presidents need to demonstrate a very different set of skills than those that got them there in the first place: campaigning is about 'image making' and 'the politics of personality' whereas governing is about 'decision making' and 'the politics of coalition building' (Smith, 1988, p. 950; see also Rose, 1991, pp. 144–5).
5. Since the President disliked reading memos, Clark apparently used DoD and CIA documentaries to educate Reagan on national security issues (Cannon, 1991, pp. 156–7).
6. Smith, 1988, pp. 960–6. However, there is some evidence to suggest that when presidential candidates actually do make reasonably specific promises about domestic policy, they will attempt to keep most of these promises (Fishel, 1985).
7. Tidal W. McCoy, ' "Full Strike" – The Myths and Reality of AirLand Battle', *AFJI* (June 1984), p. 83.
8. DoD, *Directive, No. 5000.1* (Washington, DC: DoD, 23 February 1991), pp. 1.2–1.3; DoD, *Instruction, No. 5000.2* (Washington, DC: DoD, 23 February 1991), p. 2.5.
9. Chapter 1 noted that major defence acquisition programmes are distinguished from normal acquisition programmes by their cost. Thus according to a recent DoD directive a major defence acquisition programme is one which it is estimated will cost more than $200 million to research and develop or more than $1billion to procure. DoD, *5000.1*, p. 2. These figures were set by the DoD in 1986, previously they had been set at half these respective amounts. GAO Report to the Chairman of the Senate Governmental Affairs Committee (SGAC), *Acquisition: Status of Defence Acquisition Improvement Programme's 33 Initiatives*, GAO/NSIAD-86-

178BR (Washington, DC: USGAO, 23 September 1986), p. 39 (all figures in fiscal year 1980 dollars).

10. Casper Weinberger, Secretary of Defence, *Annual Report to the Congress, Fiscal Year 1983* (Washington, DC: USGPO, 8 February 1982), p. 134; Mayer, 1991, pp. 60–1.

11. DoD, *5000.2*, pp. 3.7, 3.20–3.21, 5.D.2–5.D.3, 8.2, 8.4–8.5, 8.8 and sections 4.D and 11.B.

12. Harold Brown, Secretary of Defence, *Annual Report to the Congress, Fiscal Year 1981* (Washington, DC: USGPO, 29 January 1980), pp. 313–14; Weinberger, *Annual Report, FY83*, pp. 131–41; Casper W. Weinberger, Secretary of Defense, *Annual Report to the Congress, Fiscal Year 1987* (Washington, DC: USGPO, 5 February 1986), pp. 103–6, 298–9; Frank C. Carlucci, Secretary of Defense, *Biennial Report to the Congress, Fiscal Years 1988–1989* (Washington, DC: USGPO, 11 February 1988), pp. 134–5.

13. William J. Perry, Under Secretary of Defence for Research and Development, *The Fiscal Year 1980 Department of Defence Programme For Research, Development, and Acquisition* (Washington, DC: USGPO, February 1979), pp. 6–7.

14. GAO Report to the Congress, *Effectiveness of US Forces Can be Increased Through Improved Weapon Design*, GAO/PSAD-81-17 (Washington, DC: USGAO, 29 January 1981), p. 10.

15. William J. Perry, Under Secretary of Defence for Research and Engineering, *The Fiscal Year 1979 Department of Defence Programme for Research, Development, and Acquisition* (Washington, DC: USGPO, February 1978), pp. 2–8; Statement by Ruth M. Davis, Deputy Under Secretary of Defence for Research and Advanced Technology, before the Research and Development Subcommittee of the HASC (Washington, DC: USGPO, 20 March 1978), pp. 1–10.

16. See, for example, *Discriminate Deterrence*, The Report of the Commission On Integrated Long-Term Strategy (Washington, DC: USGPO, January 1988).

17. Malcolm R. Currie, Director of Defence Research and Engineering, *The Fiscal Year 1977 Department of Defence Programme of Research, Development, Test and Evaluation* (Washington, DC: USGPO, 3 February 1976), pp. 4–10; Perry, *FY 1980 DoD Programme*, pp. 1–8; Weinberger, *Annual Report, FY87* (Washington, DC: USGPO, 5 February 1986), pp. 61–3.

18. DoD, *5000.2*, pp. 8.4–8.5; GAO Report to the Chairman of the SGAC, *Production of Some Major Weapon Systems Began With Only Limited Operational and Evaluation Results*, GAO/NSIAD-85-68 (Washington, DC: USGAO, 19 June 1985), pp. 3, 4.

19. GAO Report to Congressional Requesters, *Testing Oversight: Operational Test and Evaluation Oversight Improving But More is Needed*, GAO/ NSIAD-87-108BR (Washington, DC: USGAO, 18 March 1987), pp. 4–5.

20. DoD, *5000.2*, pp. 8.2, 8.4; GAO Report to the Secretary of Defense, *Weapons Testing: DoD Needs to Plan and Conduct More Timely Operational Tests and Evaluation*, GAO/NSIAD-90-107 (Washington, DC: USGAO, 17 May 1990), p. 3.

21. GAO Report to the Chairman of the HASC, *Test and Evaluation: The Director, Operational Test and Evaluation's Role in Test Resources*, GAO/NSIAD-9-128 (Washington, DC: USGAO, 27 August 1990), pp. 1–2.

22. CBO Study, *Concurrent Weapons Development and Production* (Washington, DC: USCBO, August 1988), p. 38.
23. GAO, *Production of Some Major Weapon Systems*, p. 1.
24. CBO, *Concurrent Weapons Development and Production*, pp. 4–5.
25. GAO Report to the Chairman of the SSCMS of the HASC, *Navy Weapons Testing: Defence Policy on Early Operational Testing*, GAO/NSIAD-89-98 (Washington, DC: USGAO, 8 May 1989), p. 3.
26. GAO, *Navy Weapons Testing*, p. 9.
27. GAO, *Production of Some Major Weapon Systems*, p. ii.
28. GAO, *Weapons Testing*, p. 2.
29. GAO, *Weapons Testing*, p. 3.
30. GAO Report to the Secretary of the Army, *The Army Needs More Comprehensive Evaluations to Make Effective Use of Its Weapons System Testing*, GAO/NSIAD-84-40 (Washington, DC: USGAO, 24 February 1984), p. 14; see also GAO Testimony, *DoD Test and Evaluation*, GAO/T-PEMD-89-4 (Washington, DC: USGAO, 4 May 1989), pp. 3–4
31. GAO, *The Army Needs More Comprehensive Evaluations*, p. 4.
32. Hessman, 1984; Wright, 1984, p. 44; 'Honing the Defenses with Upgrades', *AW&SI* (2 December 1985), p. 116; Weinberger, *Annual Report, FY87*, p. 197; Hugh Lucas, 'US Navy Plans to Reconfigure Carrier Wing', *JDW* (24 January 1987); The Royal United Services Institute (RUSI), *Crisis in the Gulf: Transition to War? Aide Memoire III* (London: January 1991), p. 3.; GAO Report to the Chairman of the HASC, *Navy A- 12: Cost and Requirements*, GAO/NSIAD-91-98 (Washington, DC: USGAO, 31 December 1990), p. 6.
33. On the B-2 see Chapter 2. On the ATF see: Warwick, 1986; Coniglio, 1990; 'Air Force Requests Proposals for Advanced Tactical Figther', *AW&ST* (14 October 1985), pp. 24–5; Nicholas Kristof, 'Who Will Build the Super-Fighter?', *IHT* (22–3 February 1986), pp. 1, 13; GAO Report, *Aircraft Development: Reasons for Recent Cost Growth in the Advanced Tactical Fighter Programme*, GAO/NSIAD-91-138 (Washington, DC: USGAO, 1 February 1991).
34. Caleb Baker, 'Is Navy Bailing Out?', *Air Force Times* (28 November 1988), p. 26; GAO Report to the Chairman of the HASC, *Aircraft Development: Navy's Participation in the Air Force's Advanced Tactical Fighter Programme*, GAO/NSIAD-90-54, (Washington, DC: USGAO, March 1990).
35. David C. Morrison, 'Getting Together', *National Journal* (19 July 1986), p. 1805. A 'special access programme' is one for which access controls have been established 'beyond those normally required for access to Confidential, Secret and To Secret information'. Such programmes are commonly and inaccurately categorised by commentators as 'black programmes'; according to the DoD a black programme is one 'whose very existence and purpose may in and of itself be classified'. Therefore, all black programmes may also be described as special access programmes but the same does not apply in reverse. Alice C. Maroni, CRS Issue Brief, *Special Access Programmes and the Defence Budget: Understanding the 'Black Budget'* (Washington, DC: the Library of Congress, 24 October 1989), pp. 3–5.
36. GAO, *Navy A-12: Cost and Requirements*, p. 18.
37. Ed Offley, 'Navy Plans "Stealth" Jets For Whidbey', *Seatle Post-Intelligencer* (30 December 1989), p. 1.

38. Adam Goodman, 'Retiring Pace Defends Embattled A-12 Project', *St. Louis Post-Dispatch* (16 December 1990), p. 1.
39. David S. Steigman, 'Navy's Stealth Bomber Has Multi-Mission Punch', *Navy Times* (8 October 1990), p. 24.
40. GAO Report to the Chairman of the House Government Operations Committee (HGOC), *Naval Aviation: Status of Navy A-12 Contract and Material at Termination*, GAO/NSIAD-91-261 (Washington, DC: USGAO, 24 July 1991), pp. 1, 7–8.
41. GAO Testimony before the Investigations Subcommittee of the HASC, *A-12 Default Termination Issues*, GAO/T-NSIAD-91-14 (Washington, DC: US-GAO, 9 April 1991), p. 9; GAO Testimong before the Legislation and National Security Subcommittee of the House Committee on Government Operations, *Information on the A-12 Default Termination*, GAO/T-NSIAD-91-15 (Washington, DC: 11 April 1991), p. 9.
42. GAO, *Naval Aviation: Status of Navy A-12 Contract and Material at Termination*, p. 3.
43. GAO, *Naval Aviation: Status of Navy A-12 Contract and Material Termination*, pp. 1, 9; GAO, *Information on the A-12 Default Termination*, pp. 2, 5
44. GAO Report, *Naval Aviation: Navy A-12 Aircraft Funding Status*, GAO/NSIAD-91-171 (22 March 1991); GAO, *Navy A-12: Cost and Requirements*, p. 5.
45. Benjamin F. Schemmer, 'First DIVAD Gun Rolls Out with Army's "Total Support and Commitment"', *AFJI* (October 1983), p. 26.
46. Bill Keller, 'Demise of Sgt. York Gun: Model Weapon Turns to Dud', *NYT* (2 December 1985).
47. Tactical Warfare Subcommittee (TWS) of the SASC, *Hearings on the Oversight on the Division Air Defence Gun System (DIVAD)*, 98th Congress, 2nd session (1984), p. 29.
48. TWS, *Oversight on the DIVAD*, p. 41; GAO Report to the SGAC, *Sergeant York: Concerns About the Army's Accelerated Acquisition Strategy*, GAO/NSIAD-86-89 (Washington, DC: 30 May 1986), p. 22.
49. TWS, *Oversight on the DIVAD*, pp. 40–1.
50. TWS, *Oversight on the DIVAD*, p. 38.
51. TWS, *Oversight of the DIVAD*, pp. 32–3.
52. Interview, Kiel, Germany: July, 1988.
53. GAO Testimony before the SGAC (Washington, DC: 28 September 1984), p. 6.
54. Keller, 'Demise of the Sgt. York Gun'.
55. TWS, *Oversight on the DIVAD*, p. 29.
56. Interview (Washington, DC: May 1990).
57. Statement of Col. Charles C. Adsit, DIVAD Programme Manager, before the Procurement and Military Nuclear Systems Sucommittee (PMNSS) of the HASC, pp. 803–5; TWS, *Oversight of the DIVAD*, pp. 23–4.
58. GAO, *Sergeant York*, pp. 5, 23.
59. TWS, *Oversight of the DIVAD*, pp. 33–4.
60. GAO, *Sergeant York*, pp. 1–2.
61. Jay R. Scully, 'The Army Defends Its DIVAD Acqusition', *Chicago Tribune* (28 September 1984).
62. GAO, *Sergeant York*, p. 2.
63. TWS, *Oversight of the DIVAD*, pp. 12–13, 21, 31, 34–6.

64. GAO Report to the Secretary of the Army, *The Army Needs More Comprehensive Evaluations to Make Use of Its Weapon Systems Testing*, GAO/NSIAD-84-40 (Washington, DC: USGAO, 24 February 1984), p. 4.

65. TWS, *Oversight of the DIVAD*, pp. 39–40, 51.

66. GAO, *Sergeant York*, p. 17.

67. Indeed, a group of experts convened by the Army Chief of Staff in late 1985 to discuss what ought to replace the cancelled DIVAD programme concluded that 'no single weapon system could provide adequate forward area air defense'. GAO Report to the Senate and House Defence Appropriations Subcommittees, *Major Acquisition Programmes: Selected Aspects of the Army's Forward Area Air Defence System*, GAO/NSIAD-90-191 (Washington, DC: 25 June 1990), p. 12.

68. TWS, *Oversight of the DIVAD*, p. 21.

69. General Kelly Burke, Air Force Deputy Chief for Research and Development, 'Peacekeeper (MX): History and Current Status' (1985) [David Dunn's private files], p. 5.

70. GAO Report to the Congress, *The MX Weapon System: A Programme With Cost and Schedule Uncertainties*, GAO/PSAD-80-29 (Washington, DC: USGAO, 29 February 1980), p. 6; Burke, 'Peacekeeper', p. 9.

71. Holland and Hoover, 1985, pp. 95–108; Chayes, 1987, pp. 158–9; GAO, *The MX Weapon System: A Programme With Cost and Schedule Uncertainities*, pp. 13–5; GAO, *The MX Weapon System: Issues and Challenges*, pp. 27–8, 30–1.

72. *The President's Report on Continuing the Acquisition of the Peacekeeper (MX) Missile* (Washington, DC: The White House, 4 March 1985), pp. 11–15; Burke, 'Peacekeeper', pp. 13–14.

73. Bruce Smith, 'Governors Ask Delay in MX Deployment', *AW&ST* (5 March 1984), pp. 55, 58.

74. Warren Stobe, 'White House Approves Plan to Base MX Missiles on Rails', *Washington Times* (19 December 1986), pp. 1, 4; GAO Report to Congressional Requesters, *ICBM Modernization: Status of the Peacekeeper Rail Garrison Missile System*, GAO/NSIAD-89-64 (Washington, DC: USGAO, 12 January 1989).

75. For example, Bill Keller, 'Reagan, Rejecting Any Compromise, Starts Lobbying Hard for MX Missile', *IHT* (28 February 1985), pp. 1, 2; Hedrick Smith, 'Reagan's Victory on MX Is Setback for Democrats', *IHT* (28 March 1985).

76. 'The MX in the Real World', *IHT* (March 1985).

77. William Perry, Under Secretary of Defence for Research and Development, testimony before the SASC, *Department of Defence Authorization for Appropriations for Fiscal Year 1979* (Washington, DC: USGPO, 1 February 1979), pp. 299, 307.

78. Holland and Hoover, 1985, p. 130; see also, General Richard Ellis, CINCSAC, testimony before the SASC, *DoD Authorization for FY 1979*, p. 381.

79. GAO, *The MX Weapon System: Issues and Challenges*, p. 7.

80. GAO, *The MX Weapon System: A Programme With Cost and Schedule Uncertainties*, p. 22.

81. GAO, *The MX Weapon System: Issues and Challenges*, pp. 7–8.

82. GAO Report to the Congress, *Status of the Intercontinental Ballistic Missile Modernization Programme*, GAO/NSIAD-85-78 (Washington, DC: US-GAO, 8 July 1985), p. 16; GAO Report to the Chairman of the HASC, *ICBM Modernization: Availability Problems and Flight Test Delay in Peacekeeper Programme*, GAO/NSIAD-89-105 (Washington, DC: USGAO, 9 March 1989), p. 3.

83. GAO, *Status of Intercontinental Ballistic Missile Programme*, p. 16; Wayne Biddle, 'First MXs to be Deployed Before Fully Tested', *IHT* (8 March 1985); 'Phase I of MX Testing a Brillant Success', *Air Force Magazine* (August 1984), p. 24.

84. GAO, *Status of Intercontinental Ballistic Missile Programme*, p. 15.

85. Bruce Smith, 'Weld Failure Cited in Third MX Test Flight', *AW&ST* (23 January 1984), pp. 20–1; 'Phase I of MX Testing a Brillant Success', pp. 23–4; 'Problems Reported with MX Missile', *Radio Free Europe*, transcript (31 January 1984).

86. GAO, *Status of the Intercontinental Ballistic Missile Programme*, pp. 17–18.

87. 'In Silos, First 10 MX Missiles Are Declared Operational', *Washington Post* (24 December 1986); GAO, *ICBM Modernization: Availability Problems*, pp. 2–3, 12–13.

88. Fred Hiatt, 'MXs May be Deployed Before Completion of Testing, Report Says', *IHT* (14 March 1984).

89. GAO, *ICBM Modernization: Availability Problems*, pp. 2, 12.

90. GAO, *ICBM Modernization: Availability Problems*, p. 13.

91. GAO, *ICBM Modernization: Availability Problems*, pp. 1–2, 4, 15–6.

92. Barbara Amouyal, 'Rice Proposes A-12 Sacrifice for B-2', *Defense News* (9 April 1990), p. 4.

93. Mark Thomson, 'Stealth: It Can Fly but It Can't Hide, Navy Says', *Norfolk Virginian-Pilot* (18 May 1990), p. 1.

94. Glenn W. Goodman, Jr, 'USAF's Case for the B-2 Opens Pandora's Box for the Navy', *AFJI* (September 1991), p. 5.

95. Bruce van Voorst, 'Stealth Takes Wing', *Time* (31 July 1989).

96. Fred Kaplan, 'B-2 Bomber Fails Test of Radar Evasion', *Boston Globe* (22 May 1991), p. 3; Joe Brenan, 'Air Force Secretary Says Bush Still Faithful to B-2', *Omaha-World Herald* (21 June 1991), p. 13.

97. Eric Schmitt, 'Bush is Reported Ready to Cut Back on Planes', *NYT* (25 October 1991), pp. 1, 3, 4; John Broder and Ralph Vartabedian, 'Bush Seen as Cooling on Fleet of 75 B-2s', *Los Angeles Times* (26 October 1991), p. 2.

98. Melissa Healy, 'The Plug is Pulled on the B-2 Bomber', *IHT* (9 January 1992).

99. Wayne Biddle, 'US Stealth Bomber is a Flying Wing', *IHT* (12 August 1985).

100. John Morrocco, 'Weinberger Stamps Approval on White House Two-Bomber Strategy', *Defense News* (12 May 1986), p. 7; Hugh Lucas, 'The Pentagon Releases ATB Cost Details', *JDW* (14 June 1986); GAO Report to the Chairman of the HASC, *Strategic Bombers: B-2 Programme Status and Current Issues*, GAO/NSIAD-90-120 (22 February 1990), p. 1.

101. GAO, *Strategic Bombers: B-2 Programme Status and Current Issues*, p. 2.

102. Michael Dornheim, 'Air Force Cites 1984 B-2 Redesign As Major Reason for Schedule Lag', *AW&ST* (7 November 1988), p. 20.

103. Defensive avionics refers to electronic hardware and computer software used to defend a plane from atack. Offensive avionics refers to the electronic hardware and computer software used to guide a plane and its weapons onto their targets. CBO, *The B-1B Bomber and Options for Enhancements* (Washington, DC: USCBO, August 1988), pp. 12, 19.

104. According to Michael Brown the low altitude penetration requirement was added to the programme in 1984 and this led to the redesign of that year. In its first unclassified major report on the B-2, the GAO noted that this requirement had in fact been added in early 1981. A quick read of one of the two articles Brown draws upon seems to confirm his account of events. However, upon closer inspection, it becomes clear that General Welch refers to two redesigns in the article: an initial redesign when the low altitude capability requirement was first established, which he merely alludes to, and the 1984 redesign which is the focus of the General's comments. Brown, 1992, p. 297; Dornheim, 'Air Force Cites 1984 B-2 Redesign'; GAO, *Strategic Bombers: B-2 Programme Status and Current Issues*, p. 13.

105. Dornheim, 'Air Force Cites 1984 Redesign'.

106. CBO, *The B-1B Bomber and Options for Enhancement*, pp. 19–22; see also Brown, 1992, pp. 287.

107. GAO Report to the Chairman of the HASC, *B-2 Programme: Trends in Manufacturing*, GAO/NSIAD-91-211 (Washington, DC: USGAO, 30 July 1991); GAO, *Strategic Bombers: B-2 Programme Status and Current Issues*, p. 13.

108. GAO, *Strategic Bombers: B-2 Programme Status and Current Issues*, p. 13.

109. The first B-2 needed 100,000 hours of additional manufacturing work. GAO Testimony before the HASC, *The B-2 Programme: Procurement Decisions Should Be Based on Demonstrated Performance*. GAO/T-NSIAD-91-45 (Washington, DC: 17 July 1991), p. 4.

110. GAO, *B-2 Programme: Trends in Manufacturing*.

111. GAO, *Strategic Bombers: B-2 Programme Status and Current Issues*, p. 17.

112. GAO, *The B-2 Programme*, pp. 3–5.

113. GAO, *B-2 Programme: Trends in Manufacturing*, p. 11; GAO Unclassified Summary to Congressional Committees, *B-2 Bomber: Early Radar Signature Tests*, GAO/NSIAD-91-188 (Washington, DC: USGAO, 15 April 1991), p. 6.

114. GAO Unclassified Summary to Congressional Committees, *B-2 Bomber: Initial Flight Tests*, GAO/NSIAD-90-284 (Washington, DC: 4 September 1990).

115. GAO, *B-2 Bomber: Early Radar Signature Tests*, p. 5.

116. GAO, *The B-2 Programme*, p. 6.

117. 'Controversy Looms Over Jagged-Back Edge of Air Force's Stealth Bomber', *Inside the Pentagon*, p. 1.

118. 'Controversy Looms'.

119. Bill Richards, 'Boeing Knew B-2 Detectable By Secret Radar, Expert Says', *Seattle Post-Intelligencer* (3 October 1991), p. 1.

120. GAO, *B-2 Bomber: Early Radar Signature Tests*, p. 5.

121. Fred Kaplan, 'B-2 Bomber Fails Tests of Radar Evasion', *Boston Globe* (22 May 1991), p. 5.

122. Dagnija Sterste-Perkins, CRS Issue Brief, *B-2 Strategic Bomber* (Washington, DC: CRS/The Library of Congress, 16 October 1991), pp. 8–9.
123. Patrica Gilmartin, 'Senate Tightens B-2 Restrictions In Wake of Stealth Testing Dispute', *AW&ST* (23 September 1991)
124. Melissa Healy, 'AF: Fixed-Up B-2 Would Rate an 8', *Los Angeles Times* (17 September 1991), p. 1; Richard Stevenson, 'Stealth Bomber's Tests Point to Flaws in Ability to Duck Enemy Radar', *IHT* (13 September 1991).
125. Gilmartin, 'Senate Tightens B-2 Restrictions'; Tony Capaccio, 'Lawmakers Warn: B-2 Snags Are Not "Insignificant" ', *Defense Week* (23 September 1991), p. 1.
126. Maj. General Stephen Croker, Assistant Air Force Secretary for Acquisition, 'Testing the B-2 Stealth Bomber', *Los Angeles Times* (7 December 1991), p. B5.
127. 'Bomb Command Dropped', *Guardian* (19 July 1991).

4 Budgetary Issues

1. Glenn W. Goodman, Jr, 'Bell-Boeing Team Eyes Structural Contractual Changes for V-22 Programme' *AFJI* (January 1992), p. 8; James C. Hyde, 'House Panel Takes Fresh Look At Tac Air, Says Play or Pay on V-22', *AFJI* (June 1992), p. 8.
2. Fred Kaplan, 'Closing Up Sides on the Midgetman', *Boston Globe* (29 March 1987), p. 25.
3. In my Ph.D. thesis I also measured civilian control over defence expenditure by the degree of congressional micromangement of defence expenditure. I found that congressional micromanagement has increased steadily throughout the 1970s to 1990s. Consequently, it did not provide a useful way of measuring fluctuations in the budget climate. See Report to the President by the Secretary of Defence, *White Paper on the Department of Defense and the Congress* (Washingon, DC: DoD, January 1990), pp. 6–11. Furthermore, this trend is more likely due to Congress adopting a more assertive role in defence policy than increasing congressional concern over defence expenditure, especially, as Congress supported increases in defence expenditure in the late 1970s and early 1980s.
4. Office of the Comptroller of the Department of Defense, *National Defence Budget Estimates for Fiscal Year 1993* (Washington, DC: DoD, March 1992) pp. 1–2.
5. Carter's defence programme still allowed for a real increase in defence spending but it fell far short of that intended by Ford: the Ford defence plan required an 8 per cent real increase in defence spending per annum whereas under Carter the increase was only 1.5 per cent per annum (Williams, 1983, pp. 17–18)
6. Kaufman, 1989, p. 55. Indeed, according to Weinberger, Reagan 'found things in considerably worse shape when we got here than what he thought during the campaign'. USIS, 'Defense Secretary Weinberger Interviewed on NBC-TV's 'Meet the Press' (London: 28 March 1983), p. 9. See Chapter 2 for a discussion of the myth of the window of vulnerability.

7. Paul Taylor, '6 Former US Cabinet Secretaries Criticize Pace of Military Buildup', *IHT* (28 March 1983).
8. Alex Brummer, 'Congress Threat to Cut Reagan Defense Plans', *Guardian* (24 January 1983); Brummer, 'Pressure to Remove Weinberger from Defense', *Guardian* (2 February 1983).
9. Smith, 1988, pp. 210–12; Lou Cannon and David Hoffman, 'Clark-Baker Rivalry Apparently Affecting Reagan's National Security Programme', *IHT* (18 April 1983), p. 3; Michael Gordon, 'The Pentagon Under Weinberger May Be Biting Off More Than Even It Can Chew', *National Journal* (4 February 1984), p. 205.
10. Richard E. Cohen and Timothy B. Clark, 'Congress Is Trying to Convince the Voters It Is Really Worried about the Deficit', *National Journal* (21 April 1984), pp. 758–62.
11. Anthony H. Cordesman and Deborah M. Kyle, 'Congress in FY85 – The Real Defense Debate', *AFJI* (March 1984), p. 66.
12. Theodore H. White, 'Weinberger on the Ramparts', *NYT Magazine* (6 February 1983), p. 20.
13. Blechman, 1990, p. 36; Walter Andrews, 'Congress Prepares to Cut Back Defence Despite Televised Reagan Bid For More', *Washington Times* (27 February 1986) p. 5.
14. Senator Sam Nunn, 'The Changed Threat Enviroment of the 1990s' (29 March 1990), pp. 4–5.
15. Interview with senior staff member of the SASC (Washingon, DC: May 1990).
16. Interview (Washingon, DC: May 1990).
17. Interview with Soviet expert in the State Department (Washingon, DC: May 1990).
18. Stephen Daggett and Richard A. Best, Jr, CRS Issue Brief, *Defense Budget for FY 1992: Authorization and Appropriations* (Washingon, DC: CRS/The Library of Congress, 15 August 1991), p. 2.
19. Stockton, 1993, pp. 242–3; Interviews with a senior staff member of the SASC and with Jay Collins of Center for Strategic and International Studies (CSIS) (Washingon, DC: May 1990).
20. Senator Sam Nunn, 'Defense Budget Blanks' (22 March 1990); 'The Changing Threat Environment in the 1990s'; 'DoD Action on Military Personnel Reprogrammings' (29 March 1990); 'A New Military Strategy' (19 April 1990); 'Implementing a New Military Strategy: The Budget Decisions' (20 April 1990).
21. Interview with senior staff member of the SASC (Washingon, DC: May 1990); Nunn, 'The Changed Threat Environment of the 1990s'.
22. Interviews with State Department officials (Washingon, DC: May 1990).
23. Nunn, 'The Changed Threat Environment of the 1990s', p. 1.
24. Stockton, 1993, pp. 243–4; GAO Testimony before the SASC, *Defense Budget and Programme Issues in the Fiscal Year 1991 Budget*, GAO/T-NSIAD-90-18 (Washingon, DC: USGAO, 1 March 1990), p. 3.
25. GAP Testimony before the SASC, *Defense Budget and Programme Issues Facing the 102nd Congress*, GAO/T-NSIAD-91-21 (Washingon, DC: USGAO, 25 April 1991), p. 4.
26. Daggett, *Defense Budget for FY 1992*, p. 3; see also Glenn W. Goodman, Jr, 'Powell Details Base Force Concept', *AFJI* (November 1991), p. 19.

27. Stephen Daggett, CRS Issues Brief, *The FY 1992 Budget Debate: How Much for Defense?* (Washingon, DC: The Library of Congress, 12 August 1991), p. 1.
28. Meyer, 1991/92. According to Hedrick Smith, 'it was the crumbling of the coup from within [that was crucial]: the critical divisions and defections within the military command, and even the KGB' (1991, p. 634).
29. Dick Cheney, Secretary of Defence, *Annual Report to the President and the Congress* (Washington, DC: USGPO, February 1992), p. 22.
30. Hyde, 'House Panel Takes a Fresh Look', p. 8.
31. Interview with senior staff member of SASC (Washingon, DC: May 1990).
32. GAO Testimony, *Defense Budget and Programme Issues in the FY 91 Budget*, pp. 2–3.
33. The BEA is title XIII of the 1990 Omnibus Reconciliation Act.
34. Daggett, *The FY 1992 Budget Debate*, pp. 2–3.
35. Daggett, *The FY 1992 Budget Debate*, p. 2.
36. GAO Report to the Congress, *Defense Budget Increases: How Well Are They Planned and Spent?*, GAO/PLRD-82-62 (Washington, DC: USGAO, 13 April 1982).
37. Gansler, 1989, p. 976–7; Odeen, 1985, p. 376. For criticisms of the PPBS and its failure to achieve these objectives see Odeen, 1985, p. 376–7; Komer, 1985, p. 220; Art, 1990, p. 61; GAO Report to the Congress, *Defense Budget Increases: How Well Are They Planned and Spent?*, GAO/PLRD-82-62 (Washingon, DC: 13 April 1983), p. 56.
38. Brown, *Annual Report, FY82*, p. 295.
39. Harold Brown, Secretary of Defence, *Annual Report to the Congress, Fiscal Year 1981* (Washington, DC: USGPO, 29 January), p. 282, Harold Brown, Secretary of Defence, *Annual Report to the Congress, Fiscal Year 1982* (Washingon, DC: USGPO, 19 January 1981), pp. 302–3.
40. Brown, *Annual Report, FY82*, p. 297
41. William Perry, USD(R&E), *The FY 1979 Department of Defence Programme for Research, Development and Acquisition* (Washingon, DC: DOD, 1 February 1978), p. 1.11, quote p. 1.9 (emphasis added).
42. Perry, *FY79 Programme*; William Perry, USD(R&E), *The FY 1980 Department of Defence Programme for Research, Development and Acquisition* (Washingon, DC: DOD, 1 February 1979).
43. The DRB was chaired by the Deputy Secretary of Defence and its membership included the USD(P), USD(R&E), ASD(PA&E), the DoD Comptroller and the ASD for Manpower, Reserve Affairs and Logistics. The CJCS was also on the board but only as an *ex officio* member. Brown, *Annual Report, FY81*, pp. 283–4.
44. Brown, *Annual Report, FY82*, p. 298.
45. Puritano, 1985, p. 363; Weinberger, *Annual Report, FY83*, p. 133. This review led to the number of DSARC milestones being reduced from four to two. Weinberger, *Annual Report, FY83*, p. 134.
46. Weinberger, *Annual Report, FY83*, p. 142.
47. 'Reagan Backs Shifts in Military Structure', *IHT* (3 April 1986); 'Sweeping Pentagon Reforms Approved', *Guardian* (4 April 1986).
48. George Wilson, 'Defense Reorganization Enacted', *Washington Post* (18 September 1986), p. 15; Bernard Trainor, 'Defense Reorganization: New Bill Centralizes Authority at the Joint Chiefs', *NYT* (19 September 1986), p. B5.

49. Michael Ganley, 'Senate Armed Services Resolves Most Issues in DoD Reorganization Bill', *AFJI* (March 1986), p. 18.

50. Gerald Seib, 'Overhaul America's Military Chain of Command', *Wall Street Journal* (15 August 1984); Bill Keller, 'Panal Advocates Changing Structure of US Military', *IHT* (23 January 1985), p. 1; Bill Keller, 'Goldwater, Nunn Call US Military System Wasteful', *IHT* (7 October 1985), pp. 1, 6; 'Changes Draw Protests From Pentagon Brass', *Congressional Quarterly* (8 March 1986), p. 573; Pat Towell, 'Senate Backs Major Changes In Organization of Pentagon', *Congressional Quarterly* (10 May 1986), p. 1031; 'Reagan Backs Shifts in Military Structure', *IHT* (3 April 1986).

51. GAO Report to the Chairman of the IS of the HASC, *Acquisition Reform: Military Department's Response to the Reorganization Act*, GAO/NSIAD-89-70 (Washingon, DC: USGAO, 1 June 1989), p. 2; GAO Fact Sheet for Senator William V. Roth, *Defense Management: Status of Recommendations by Blue Ribbon Commission on Defense Management*, GAO/NSIAD-89-19FS (Washington, DC: USGAO, 4 November 1988), pp. 11–24, 29–59.

52. GAO, *Defense Management: Status of Recommendations by Blue Ribbon Commission*, pp. 26–7; GAO Report to the Chairman of the IS of the HSAC, *Defense Reorganization: Roles of Joint Military Organizations in Resource Allocations*, GAO/NSIAD-90-76 (Washington, DC: USGAO, 21 June 1990).

53. Congress established the position of USD(A) in the 1986 Military Reform Act, located this position in the OSD under the 1986 Defense Reorganisation Act, and defined the duties, responsibilities and authority of the USD(A) in the 1987 Defence Authorization Act. GAO, *Acquisition Reform: DOD's Efforts to Streamline*, p. 12.

54. There was some disagreement between the Senate and House over the degree of influence to be given to the new acquisition czar in the defense authorisation bill. The Senate favoured a less intrusive role, mandating the USD(A) to 'supervise' services' purchases, the House insisted that the new official should 'direct' weapons acquisition. 'Pentagon Gets a New Procurement Czar', p. 2679.

55. GAO Report to the Chairman of the IS of the HASC, *Acquisition Reform: Military Department's Responses to the Reorganization Act*, GAO/NSIAD-89-70 (Washington, DC: USGAO, 1 June 1989), pp. 16–7, 30–1, 51; Hugh Lucas, 'US Naval Command in Effort to Reduce Bureaucracy', *JDW* (27 April 1985).

56. David Lockwood, CRS Issue Brief, *Defense Acquisition: Major Structural Reform Proposals* (Washingon, DC: The Library of Congress, 11 July 1986), p. 2; Lucas, 'US Naval Command Scrapped.'

57. GAO, *Acquisition Reform: DOD's Efforts to Streamline*, p. 11.

58. GAO, *Acquisition Reform: DOD's Efforts to Streamline*, pp. 4–5, 22–3, 30–1, 43.

59. GAO, *Acquisition Reform: DOD Efforts to Streamline*, p. 15.

60. David E. Lockwood, CRS Issue Brief, *Under Secretary of Defence for Acquisition: Role and Responsibilites* (Washington, DC: CRS/The Library of Congress, 12 October 1988), p. 5.

61. GAO, *Acquisition Reform: DOD's Efforts to Streamline*, p. 15.

62. David E. Lockwood, CRS Issue Brief, *Defense Procurement Reform* (Washingon, DC: CRS/The Library of Congress, 2 March 1990), p. 5.
63. GAO, *Acquisition Reform: DOD's Efforts to Strealine*, p. 14. As it happens, *The Economist* had predicted that Godwin would 'flounder in his new job' given that he had 'no knowledge of the Pentagon bureaucratic jungle'. 'Defence: Reining in Service Rivalries', *The Economist* (29 November 1986).
64. Lockwood, *Defense Procurement Reform*, p. 5.
65. Lockwood, *Under Secretary of Defence for Acquisition*, p. 7.
66. Molly Moore, 'B-2 Bomber Cancellation Is Urged', *Washington Post* (19 May 1989), p. 1.
67. DoD, *Implementation of the Secretary of Defense's Defence Management Report to the President*, Progress Report Detail (Washingon, DC: DOD, May, 1992), pp. 1, 6–8.
68. GAO, *Acquisition Reform: Authority Delegated Under the Secretary of Defence for Acquisition*, pp. 1–2.
69. Pat Towell, 'Cheney Threatens to Pull Plug On Navy's Troubled A-12', *Congressional Quarterly* (22 December 1990).
70. Unless specified otherwise, *all* dollar figures in the next four (case study) sections are in TY $.
71. 'Navy Says It Turned Jet Prices Around', *IHT* (6 November 1985).
72. GAO Report to Chairman of the HASC, *Navy A-12: Cost and Requirements*, GAO/NSIAD-91-98 (Washingon, DC: USGAO, 31 December 1990), p. 18.
73. GAO, *Navy A-12: Cost and Requriements*, pp. 5, 8–10.
74. Towell, 'Cheney Threatens to Pull Plug on Navy's Troubled A-12', p. 4023.
75. GAO Report to Chairman of the House Government Operations Committee, *Naval Aviation: Status of Navy A-12 Contract and Material at Termination* (Washington, DC: USGAO, 24 July 1991) pp. 1, 7, 31.
76. Pat Towell, 'Cheney Pulls Plug on A-12, Looks for Substitute', *Congressional Quarterly* (12 January 1991), p. 84.
77. GAO Testimony before the IS of the HASC, *A-12 Default Termination Issues*, GAO/T-NSIAD-91-14 (Washington, DC: USGAO, 9 April 1991); GAO Testimony before the Legislation and National Security Subcommittee (LNS) of the HGOC, *Information on the A-12 Default Termination*, GAO/T-NSIAD-91-15 (Washington, DC: USGAO, 11 April 1991); GAO Testimony before the IS of the HASC, *Deferment Actions Associated With the Navy A-12 Aircraft*, GAO/T-NSIAD-91-51 (Washington, DC: USGAO, 5 July 1991).
78. Amy Wilentz and Bruce van Voorst, 'No More Time for Sergeant York', *Time* (9 September 1985), p. 34.
79. GAO Report to the Chairman of the SASC, *DoD Programme Acquisition Programmes: Status of Selected Systems*, GAO/NSIASD-87-128 (Washingon, DC: 2 April 1987), p. 13.
80. GAO Report to the Chairmen of the Defense Appropriations Subcommittees, *Major Acquisition Programmes: Selected Aspects of the Army's Forward Area Air Defence System*, GAO/NSIAD-90-191 (Washington, DC: 25 June 1990), pp. 2, 5; Bruce van Voorst, 'Son of the Sergeant York', *Time* (11 August 1986), p. 23; see also Marvin Leibstone, 'FAADS: Item One', *Military-Technology* (October 1986), pp. 20–9.
81. CBO Study, *Army Air Defence for Forward Areas: Strategies and Costs* (Washingon, DC: USCBO, June 1986), pp. 10–7.

82. Tactical Warfare Subcommittee (TWS) of the SASC, *Hearings on the Oversight on the Division Air Defence Gun System (DIVAD)*, 98th Congress, 2nd session (1984), pp. 22–3.

83. TWS, *Oversight on the DIVAD*, p. 15.

84. TWS, *Oversight on the DIVAD*, p. 60.

85. Bill Keller, 'Demise of the Sgt. York Gun: Model Weapons Turns Dud', *NYT* (2 December 1985), p. 3-F.

86. TWS, *Oversight on the DIVAD*, p. 8; see also p. 30.

87. Statement by Lt. General Louis C. Wagner, Army Deputy Chief of Staff for Research, Development and Acquisition, before the TWS, *Oversight on the DIVAD*, p. 43; 'The Army Defends its DIVAD Acquisition', *Chicago Tribune* (29 Septmber 1984).

88. Statement of Col. Charles C. Adsit, DIVAD Programme Manager, before the PMNSS of the HASC, *Hearings on Military Posture and HR 6495*, pt.2, 96th Congress, 2nd session (1980), p. 804.

89. TWS, *Oversight on the DIVAD*, pp. 33–4.

90. GAO Report to the Chairman of the Senate Governmental Affairs Committee, *Sergeant York*, GAO/NSIAD-86-89 (Washingon, DC: 30 May 1986), p. 1.

91. TWS, *Oversight on the DIVAD*, p. 72.

92. Wilentz and van Voorst, 'No More Time for Sergeant York', p. 34; 'DIVAD Shot Down'; Fred Kaplan, 'Why Weinberger Abandoned the York', *Boston Globe* (8 September 1985), p. 1

93. Wilentz and van Voorst, 'No More Time for Sergeant York', p. 34.

94. Millard Barger, 'Congress Ices DIVAD, Pending Tests: Program's Defenders Firing Blanks?', *AFJI* (November 1984), p. 33.

95. GAO Report to the Congress, *The MX Weapon System: A Programme With Cost and Schedule Uncertainties*, GAO/PSAD-80-29 (Washington, DC: USGAO, 29 February 1980), pp. 19–20.

96. GAO Report to the Congress, *The MX Weapon System: Issues and Challenges*, GAO/MASAD-81-1 (Washington, DC: 17 February 1981), pp. 4–5.

97. Smith, 1988, pp. 738–59; Hampson, 1989, p. 145–9; Elizabeth Drew, 'A Political Journal', *New Yorker* (20 June 1983), pp. 39–75; Les Aspin, 'The MX Bargain', *Bulletin of Atomic Scientists* (November 1983), pp. 52–4.

98. David C. Morrison, 'Missile Gridlock', *National Journal* (7 June 1986), pp. 1366–70.

99. GAO Report to the Chairman of the HASC, *Strategic Bombers: Estimated Costs to Deploy the B-1B*, GAO/NSIAD-88-12 (Washington, DC: 7 October 1987), pp. 1–2.

100. GAO Report to the Chairman of the HASC, *Navy Strategic Forces: Trident II Proceeding Toward Deployment*, GAO/NSIAD-89-40 (21 November 1988), p. 2.

101. GAO, *Navy Strategic Forces*, p. 2; Scott Shuger, 'The Stealth Bomber Story You Haven't Heard', *The Washington Monthly* (2 January 1991), p. 1.

102. Lindsay, 1991, p. 71; GAO, *Navy Strategic Forces*; GAO Report to the Chairman of the SASC, *Defense Acquisition: Fleet Ballistic Missile Programme Offers Lessons for Successful Programmes*, GAO/NSIAD-90-160 (Washington, DC: 6 September 1990).

103. Morrison, 'Missile Gridlock'; 'Lawmakers Clash on Missile', *NYT* (30 December 1986), p. B20; Peter Adams, 'Congressional Support Wanes for Midgetman', *Defense News* (16 March 1987), p. 1; 'Welch, Perle Agree on MX Priority Over SICBM', *Aerospace Daily* (17 March 1987), p. 397; 'Pentagon-Congress Clash Over MX and Midgetman', *JDW* (29 March 1987).

104. GAO, *Status of the Intercomtinental Ballistic Missile Programme*, pp. 7, 21.

105. R. Jeffrey Smith, 'Cheney Advises Bush to Approve Mobile MX Missile System', *IHT* (20 April 1989).

106. GAO, *The MX Weapon System: A Programme With Cost and Schedule Uncertainties*, pp. 21–2.

107. GAO, *The MX Weapon System: Issues and Challenges*, pp. 6–7.

108. GAO, *Status of the Intercontinental Ballistic Missile Programme*, p. 15.

109. GAO Report to the Congress, *ICBM Modernization: Status, Survivable Basing Issues, and Need to Reestablish a National Consensus*, GAO/NSIAD-86-200 (Washington, DC: 19 September 1986), p. 32.

110. GAO Report to the Chairman of the HASC, *Strategic Bombers: B-2 Programme Status and Current Issues*, GAO/NSIAD-90-120 (Washington, DC: USGAO, 22 Fenruary 1990), pp. 11, 13.

111. David C. Morrison, 'It Costs WHAT?!', *National Journal* (5 August 1989), p. 2012.

112. Wayne Biddle, 'US Stealth Bomber Is a Flying Wing, Goldwater Says', *IHT* (12 August 1985).

113. John Morrocco, 'Weinberger Stamps Approval on White House Two-Bomber Strategy', *Defense News* (12 May 1986), p. 7; Hugh Lucas, 'The Pentagon Releases ATB Cost Details', *JDW* (14 June 1986).

114. George C. Wilson, 'Stealth Called Nuclear Deterrent', *Washington Post* (17 May 1988), p. 10.

115. Morrison, 'It Costs WHAT?!'.

116. GAO Report to congressional Committees, *Weapons Acquisition: Improving DoD's Weapons Systems Acquisition Reporting*, GAO/NSIAD-90-20 (Washington, DC: USGAO, 14 November 1989), p. 1.

117. CBO Special Study, *A Review of the Department of Defence December 31, 1981 Selected Acquisition Report* (Washington, DC: USCBO, May 1982), chap. 3; CBO Special Study, *A Review of the Department of Defence December 31, 1982 Selected Acquisition Report* (Washington, DC: USCBO, August 1983), chap. 3; CBO Special Study, *A Review of the Department of Defence December 31, 1983 Selected Acquisition Report* (Washington, DC: USCBO, July 1984), chap. 3.

118. GAO Report to the Congress, *DoD Needs to Provide More Credible Weapon Systems Cost Estimates to the Congress*, GAO/NSIAD-84-70 (Washington, DC: USGAO, 24 May 1984), p. iv.

119. GAO, *DoD Needs to Provide More Credible Weapon Systems Cost Estimates to the Congress*; GAO, *Weapons Acquisition: Improving DoD's Weapons Systems Acquisition Reporting*.

120. Alice C. Maroni, CRS Issue Brief, *Special Access Programmes and the Defence Budget: Understanding the 'Black Budget'* (Washington, DC: CRS/The Library of Congress, 24 October 1989), p. 10.

121. Maroni, *Special Access Programmes and the Defence Budget*, pp. 8–9.

122. Shuger, 'The Stealth Bomber Story You Haven't Heard', pp. 18–19.
123. Morrison, 'It Costs WHAT?!'.
124. Morrison, 'It Costs WHAT?!'.
125. GAO Report to congressional Committees, *Strategic Weapons: Long-Term Costs Are Not Reported to Congress*, GAO/NSIAD-90–226 (Washingon, DC: USGAO, 10 August 1990), p. 3.
126. Patricia A. Gilmartin, 'Full B-2 Cost Put at $155 Billion As Congressional Opposition Mounts', *AW&ST* (4 February 1990). The decrease in the Trident II estimates from the DoD figure of $155 billion was probably due to the programme being scaled down somewhat.
127. GAO, *Strategic Bombers: B-2 Programme Status and Current Issues*, p. 5; Fred Kaplan, 'Cheney Stealth Cuts: Potent of Legislative Turbulence', *Boston Globe* (30 April 1990), p. 3.
128. GAO, *Strategic Weapons: Long-Term Costs Are Not Reported to Congress*, pp. 32–3.
129. Les AuCoin, 'The B-2 Bomber: Not to Be', *AFJI* (September 1990), pp. 80–2.
130. Lt. General William E. Thurman, 'USAF Defends Stealth Programs', *International Defence Review* (May 1988), pp. 517–18.
131. Mark Thompson, 'B-2 Price Questioned by Aspin', *Philadelphia Inquirer* (9 May 1989).
132. Dagnija Sterste-Perkins, CRS Issue Brief, *B-2 Strategic Bomber* (Washingon, DC: CRS/The Library of Congress, October 1991), pp. 4–5.
133. Donald J. Atwood, 'Stealth "Sticker Shock" Is Obscuring the Long View', *IHT* (28 July 1989); Rice, 1990, pp. 122–4.
134. Bill Sweetman, 'B-2 Costs: When a $ is not a $', *JDW* (23 September 1989), p. 619.
135. Ralph Vartabedian, 'Bomber Costs Soar: Rand Study May Prompt Pentagon to Restructure Stealth Project', *Los Angeles Times* (July 8 1987), p. 1.
136. GAO, *Strategic Bombers: B-2 Programme Status and Current Issues*. pp. 11–12; Brown, 1990, p. 144.
137. Thompson, 'B-2 price Questioned by Aspin'; Les Aspin, 'The Biggest Weapon System Decision in History', *AFJI* (September 1990), p. 76.
138. Aspin, 'The Biggest Weapon Decision in History'.
139. Tony Capaccio, 'Confusion Reigns Over New B-2 Cost Estimates', *Defense Week* (16 March 1992), p. 1.
140. Bruce van Voorst, 'The Stealth Takes Wing', *Time* (31 July 1989), p. 45.
141. Wilson, 'Stealth Called Nuclear Deterrent'.
142. Aspin, 'The Biggest Weapon System Decision in History'.
143. GAO Fact Sheet for the Chairman of the HASC, *B-2 Bomber: Contract Structure and Selected Provisions*, GAO/NSIAD-90-230FS (Washington, DC: USGAO, 17 August 1990), p. 1.
144. Barbara Amouyal, 'Senate Legislation Requests "Speedy, Merciful" Death of B-2 Bomber', *Defense News* (29 January 1990), p. 44; Pamela Fessler, 'Cheney's Spending Blueprint Faces Welter of Changes', *Congressional Quarterly* (3 February 1990), p. 337; Benjamin F. Schemmer, 'Senate May be Unable to Salvage B-2 After House Nixes It Twice with GOP Help', *AFJI* (July 1991), p. 6.
145. Pat Towell, 'Targeting Strategic Arms Programs', *Congressional Quarterly* (10 February 1990), p. 398.

146. Bill McAllister, 'Stealth Mission: All-Out Hype', *IHT* (8 May 1991).
147. Schemmer, 'Senate May Be Unable to Salvage B-2'; James C. Hyde, 'SASC Wants Commision to Decide on Women Combat Pilots; OKs B-2, SDI', *AFJI* (December 1991), p. 8.
148. Sterste-Perkins, *B-2 Strategic Bomber*, p. 11; James C. Hyde and Glenn W. Goodman, Jr, 'Congress Fully Funds Nearly 70% of DoD's Top Programs', *AFJI* (December 1991), p. 8.
149. Pat Towell, 'Aspin Urges Shifting $7 Billion from Pentagon to Cities', *Congressional Quarterly* (16 May 1992), p. 1361; 'Inside Congress', *Congressional Quarterly* (5 September 1992), p. 2628.
150. 'Aspin May Tie B-2 Funding to USAF Commitment to Conventional Use of Bomber', *Inside the Air Force* (5 July 1991), p. 3.
151. Michael Glennon, 'House Armed Services Committee: Committee for the Defense', *Journal of Defence and Diplomacy* (May 1984), p. 27; David C. Morrison, 'Sharing Command', *National Journal* (13 June 1992), p. 1398.
152. That said, there is at least one example of a programme which benefited by having these qualities. The Navy were able to persuade Secretary of Defence Charles Wilson in 1956 to allow it to develop the Polaris SLBM by claiming that this would prove cheaper than proceeding with the Jupiter Intermediate Range Ballistic Missile which the service was developing jointly with the Air Force. This is not an example of a weapon programme designed to reduce defense expenditure because the Navy knew that the Polaris would end up costing more than Wilson was led to believe (Spinardi, 1994, pp. 30–1).

5 Weapons Without a Cause

1. Wayne Biddle, 'Pentagon Is Investigating 45 Contractors', *IHT* (25 April 1985).
2. $2.7 billion was spent on the A-12 before it was cancelled and $1.8 billion and $45 billion were spent respectively on DIVAD and the B-2 before they were prematurely terminated. GAO Report to the Chairman of the HCGO, *Naval Aviation: Status of Navy A-12 Contract and Material at Termination*, GAO/NSIAD-91-261 (Washington, DC: 24 July 1991), p. 1; 'The Divad Gun: Shot Down', *The Economist* (31 August 1985); Glenn W. Goodman, Jr, and James C. Hyde, 'DoD's FY93 Budget Born in Turmoil, Sent Incomplete to Skeptical Congress', *AFJI* (March 1992), p. 12.
3. I found 23 press reports on these scandals alone between March and early May 1985 (Farrell, 1994, p. 273, fn.4)
4. 'US Reveals Probe of the 10 Biggest Weapons Suppliers', *IHT* (20 June 1985); Nancy Dunne, 'Top 10 Defense Groups Face Prices Probes', *Financial Times* (21 June 1985).
5. Biddle, 'Pentagon Is Investigating 45 Contractors'.
6. Michael Ganley, 'Is Congress Clearing the Air or Mudding the Water?', *AFJI* (August 1985), p. 42.
7. Terry Dodsworth, 'Defense Groups Charged Pentagon $110m Unfairly', *Financial Times* (30 April 1985).

8. 'General Dynamics, NASA Head Indicted in Fraud', *IHT* (3 December 1985); Paul Taylor, 'Pentagon Bars General Dynamics From Fresh Work', *Financial Times* (4 December 1985).

9. Correspondance (7 June 1994), p. 2.

10. Adam and Kosiak, 1993, p. 36; Benjamin F. Schemmer, 'Huge Weapons Cuts Yield Small Saving as US Procurement Funds Shrivel 30%', *AFJI* (June 1991), pp. 18–21; Glenn W. Goodman, Jr, and James C. Hyde, 'DoDs FY93 Budget Born in Turmoil, Sent Incomplete to Skeptical Congress', *AFJI* (March 1992), pp. 8–18.

11. Mark Tran, 'US Defense Contractors Squeezed', *Guardian* (28 September 1994), p. 14.

12. DoD, *Implementation of the Secretary of Defense's Defence Management Report (DMR) to the President*, Progress Report Detail (Washington, DC: DoD, May 1992), p. 8; Dick Cheney, Secretary of Defence, *Annual Report to the President and the Congress, 1992* (Washington, DC: USGPO, February, 1992), pp. 30–1; *Congressional Quarterly Almanac*, 101st Congress, 2nd session, 1990 (Washington, DC: Congressional Quarterly Inc., 1990), p. 682.

Bibliography of Secondary Sources

BOOKS AND MONOGRAPHS

Allard, C. Kenneth. 1990. *Command, Control and the Common Defense* (New Haven and London: Yale University Press).

Allison, Graham T. 1971. *Essence of Decision* (Boston: Little, Brown).

Ambrose, Stephen E. and James A. Barber (eds). 1972. *The Military and American Society: Essays and Readings* (NY: The Free Press).

Arkin, William and Peter Pringle. 1983. *SIOP: Nuclear War from the Inside* (London: Sphere).

Art, Robert, Vincent Davis and Samuel P. Huntington (eds). 1985. *Reorganizing America's Defense* (McLean, VA: Peagamon-Brassey's).

Avant, Deborah D. 1994. *Political Institutions and Military Change: Lessons from Peripheral Wars* (Ithaca, NY: Cornell University Press).

Ball, Desmond and Jeffrey Richelson (eds). 1986. *Strategic Nuclear Targeting* (Ithaca, NY: Cornell University Press).

Betts, Richard K. 1987. *Nuclear Blackmail and Nuclear Balance* (Washington, DC: Brookings Institution).

Blackwell, James A. and Barry M. Blechman (eds). 1990. *Making Defense Reform Work* (Washington, DC, NY and London: Brassey's).

Blair, Bruce G. 1993. *The Logic of Accidental Nuclear War* (Washingon, DC: Brookings Institution).

Blechman, Barry. 1990. *The Politics of National Security: Congress and US Defense Policy* (Oxford: Oxford University Press).

Bobbit, Philip, Lawrence Freedman and Gregory F. Treverton (eds). 1989. *US Nuclear Strategy* (London: Macmillan).

Brown, Michael E. 1992. *Flying Blind: the Politics of the US Strategic Bomber Program* (Ithaca, NY: Cornell University Press).

Brzosha, Michael and Peter Lock (eds). 1992. *Restructuring of Arms Production in Western Europe* (NY: Oxford University Press-Stockholm International Peace Research Institute).

Builder, Carl H. 1989. *The Masks of War: American Military Styles in Strategy and Analysis* (Baltimore: Johns Hopkins University Press).

Bundy, McGeorge. 1988. *Danger and Survival: Choices About the Bomb in the First Fifty Years* (NY: Random House).

Buzan, Barry. 1987. *An Introduction to Strategic Studies: Military Technology and Strategic Studies* (London: Macmillan-International Institute for Strategic Studies).

Campell, Colin S. J. and Bert A. Rockman (eds). 1981. *The Bush Presidency: First Appraisals* (Chatham, NJ: Chatham House).

Cannon, Lou. 1991. *President Reagan: the Role of a Lifetime* (NY: Simon and Schuster).

Carter, Jimmy. 1982. *Keeping Faith: Memoirs of A President* (London: Collins).

Clarke, Asa, Peter W. Chiarelli, Jeffrey S. McKitrick and James W. Reed (eds). 1984. *The Defense Reform Debate: Issues and Analysis* (Baltimore: Johns Hopkins University Press).

Clarke, Duncan L. 1989. *American Defense and Foreign Policy Institutions: Towards a Sound Foundation* (NY: Harper and Row).

Daniel, Donald C. 1993. *Beyond the 600 Ship Navy*, Adelphi Paper 261 (London: International Institute for Strategic Studies).

Demchak, Chris C. 1991. *Military Organizations, Complex Machines: Modernization in the US Armed Services* (Ithaca, NY: Cornell University Press).

Dews, Edmund and Michael Rich. 1986. *Improving the Military Acqusition Process: Lessons from RAND Research*, RAND-Project Air Force Report, R-3373-AF/RC (Santa Monica: RAND).

—— 1987. *Thoughts on Reforming the Military Acquisition Process*, RAND-Project Air Force Paper, P-7352 (Santa Monica, CA: RAND).

Dunn, David H. 1995. 'The Politics of Threat: The Issue of ICBM Vulnerability in the Carter and Reagan Administrations' (Ph.D. thesis, University of London).

Evangelista, Matthew. 1988. *Innovation and the Arms Race: How the United States and the Soviet Union Develop New Military Technologies* (Ithaca, NY: Cornell University Press).

Fallows, James. 1981. *National Defense* (NY: Random House).

Farrell, Theo. 1994. 'Weapons Without A Cause: The Politics of Weapons Acquisition in the United States' (Ph.D. thesis, University of Bristol).

Fishel, Jeff. 1985. *Presidents and Promises* (Washington, DC: Congressional Quarterly).

Gansler, Jacques S. 1989. *Affording Defense* (Cambridge, MA: MIT Press).

Garthoff, Raymond L. 1985. *Detente and Confrontation: American-Soviet Relations from Nixon to Reagan* (Washington DC: Brookings Institution, 1985)

—— 1990. *Deterrence and the Revolution in Soviet Military Doctrine* (Washington, DC: Brookings Institution).

—— 1994. *The Great Transition: American-Soviet Relations and the End of the Cold War* (Washington, DC: Brookings Institution).

Glaser, Charles L. 1990. *Analyzing Strategic Nuclear Policy* (Princeton: Princeton University Press)

Gray, Colin S. 1986. *Nuclear Strategy and National Style* (Lanham, MD and London: Hamilton Press, Abt Books).

Halperin, Morton H. 1974. *Bureaucratic Politics and Foreign Policy* (Washington, DC: Brookings Institution).

Hampson, Fen. 1989. *Unguided Missiles: How America Buys Its Weapons* (New York: W. W. Norton).

Heisbourg, Francois (ed.). 1989. *The Changing Strategic Landscape* (London: Macmillan-International Institute for Strategic Studies).

Hendrickson, David C. 1988. *Reforming Defense: The State of American Civil-Military Relations* (Baltimore: Johns Hopkins Univeristy Press).

Hilsman, Roger. 1987. *The Politics of Policy Making in Defense and Foreign Affairs: Conceptual Models and Bureaucratic Politics* (Englewood Cliffs, NJ: Prentice-Hall).

Holland, Lauren H. and Robert A. Hoover. 1985. *The MX Decision: A New Direction in US Weapons Procurement Policy?* (Bouldor, CO: Westview).

Hosmer, Stephen T. and Glenn A. Kent. 1987. *The Military and Political Pontential of Conventionally Armed Heavy Bombers*, RAND-Project Air Force Report, R-3508-AF (Santa Monica, CA: RAND).

Huntington, Samuel P. 1961. *The Common Defense: Strategic Programs in National Politics* (NY: Cornell University Press).

Ikenberry, G. John (ed.). 1989. *American Foreign Policy: Theoretocal Essays* (Boston: Scott, Foresman).

International Institute for Strategic Studies. 1994. *The Military Balance, 1994–95* (London: IISS-Brassey's).

Isaacson, Walter. 1992. *Kissinger* (Boston: Faber and Faber).

Jervis, Robert. 1976. *Perception and Misperception in International Politics* (Princeton: Princeton University Press).

—— 1989. *The Meaning of the Nuclear Revolution: Statecraft and the Prospects of Armageddon* (Ithaca, NY: Cornell University Press).

Kaldor, Mary. 1981. *The Baroque Arsenal* (London: Abacus).

Kaplan, Fred. 1983. *The Wizards of Armageddon* (NY: Simon and Schuster).

Kaufmann, William W. 1992. *Assessing the Base Force: How Much is Too Much?* (Washington, DC: Brookings Institution).

King, Gary, Robert O Keohane and Sidney Verba. 1994. *Designing Social Inquiry: Scientific Inference in Qualitative Research* (Princeton: Princeton University Press).

Kotz, Nick. 1988. *Wild Blue Yonder: Money, Politics and the B-1 Bomber* (Princeton: Princeton University Press).

Kull, Steven. 1988. *Minds at War: Nuclear Reality and the Inner Conflicts of Defense Policymakers* (NY: Basic Books).

Lehman, John F. 1988. *Command of the Seas: Building the 600 Ship Navy* (NY: Charles Scribner's Sons).

Lindsay, James M. 1991. *Congress and Nuclear Weapons* (Baltimore: John Hopkins University Press).

MccGwire, Michael. 1991. *Perestroika and Soviet National Security* (Washington, DC: Brookings Institution).

MacKenzie, Donald. 1990. *Inventing Accuracy: A Historical Sociology of Nuclear Missile Guidance* (Cambridge, MA: MIT Press).

McNamara, Robert. 1968. *The Essence of Security: Reflections in Office* (London: Hodder and Stoughton).

McNaugher, Thomas. 1989. *New Weapons Old Politics: America's Military Procurement Muddle* (Washington, DC: Brookings Institution)

Mayer, Kenneth R. 1991. *The Political Economy of Defense Contracting* (New Haven: Yale University Press).

Nathan, James A. and James K. Oliver. 1987. *Foreign Policy Making and the American Political System* (Boston: Little, Brown).

Neustadt, Richard E. 1980. *Presidential Power: the Politics of Leadership from FDR to Carter* (NY: John Wiley and Sons).

Nolan, Janne E. 1989. *Guardians of the Arsenal: The Politics of Nuclear Strategy* (NY: Basic Books).

Posen, Barry R. 1991. *Inadvertent Escalation: Conventional War and Nuclear Risks* (Ithaca, NY: Cornell University Press).

Pringle, Peter and William Avkin. 1983. *SIOP: Nuclear War from the Inside* (London: Sphere).

Ragsdale, Lyn. 1993. *Presidential Politics* (Boston: Houghton Mifflin).

Ripley, Randall B. and James M. Lindsay (eds). 1993. *Congress Resurgent: Foreign and Defense Policy on Capitol Hill* (Ann Arbor: University of Michigan Press).

Rose, Richard. 1976. *Managing Presidential Objectives* (London: Macmillian).

—— 1991. *The Postmodern President: George Bush Meets the World* (Chatham, NJ: Chatham House).

Rosen, Stephen Peter. 1991. *Winning the Next War: Innovation and the Modern Military* (Ithaca, NY: Cornell University Press).

Sagan, Scott. 1989. *Moving Targets: Nuclear Strategy and National Security* (Princeton: Princeton University Press).

—— 1993. *The Limits of Safety: Organizations, Accidents and Nuclear Weapons* (Princeton: Princeton University Press).

Sarkesian, Sam C. (ed). 1979. *Defense Policy and the Presidency: Carter's First Years* (Boulder, CO: Westview).

Scheer, Robert. 1982. *With Enough Shovels: Reagan, Bush and Nuclear War* (London: Secker and Warburg).

Schelling, Thomas. 1980. *The Strategy of Conflict* (Cambridge: Harvard University Press).

Scoville, Henry. 1981. *MX: Prescription for Disaster* (Cambridge, MA: MIT Press).

Shultz, George P. 1993. *Turmoil and Triumph: My Years As Secretary of State* (NY: Charles Scribner's Sons).

Smith, Hedrick. 1988. *The Power Game: How Washington Works* (Glasgow: Fontana-Collins).

—— 1990. *The New Russians* (London: Vintage).

Spinardi, Graham. 1988. 'The Development of US Fleet Ballistic Missile Technology: Polaris to Trident' (Ph.D. thesis, University of Edinburgh).

—— 1994. *From Polaris to Trident: the Development of US Fleet Ballistic Missile Technology* (NY: Cambridge University Press).

Stein, Robert M. 1992a. *Patriot ATBM Experience in the Gulf War* (Raytheon pamphlet).

Stockman, David A. 1986. *The Triumph of Politics* (London: Bodley Head).

Talbott, Strobe. 1985. *Deadly Gambits* (London: Picador).

Trachtenberg, Marc. 1991. *History and Strategy* (Princeton, NJ: Princeton University Press).

Weinberger, Casper. 1990. *Fighting For Peace* (NY:Warner Bros).

Wildavsky, Aaron (ed). 1975. *Perspectives on the Presidency* (Boston: Little, Brown).

Woodward, Bob. 1991. *The Commanders* (London: Simon and Schuster).

Yarmolinsky, Adam. 1971. *The Military Establishment: Its Impact on American Society* (NY: Harper and Row).

Zuckerman, Solly. 1982. *Nuclear Illusions and Reality* (London: Collins).

ARTICLES AND PAPERS

Adams, Gordon and Steven M. Kosiak. 1993. 'The United States: Trends in Defense Procurement and Research and Development Programmes', in Herbet

Wulf (ed.), *Arms Industry Limited* (NY: Oxford University Press-Stockholm International Peace Research Institute), pp.29–49.

Allison, Graham T. 1989 (1969). 'Conceptual Models and the Cuban Missile Crisis', in Ikenberry (ed.), *American Foreign Policy*, pp.332–77.

Allison, Graham T. and Frederic A Morris. 1976. 'Armaments and Arms Control: Exploring the Determinants of Military Weapons', in Franklin Long and George Rathjens (eds) *Arms, Defense Policy and Arms Control* (NY: W. W. Norton), pp.99–129.

Allison, Graham T. and Morton H. Halperin. 1989 (1972). 'Bureacratic Politics: A Paradigm and Some Policy Implications', in Ikenberry (ed.), *American Foreign Policy*, pp.378–408.

Altfield, Michael F. 1985. 'The MX Debate: Evaluating the Arguments', *Defense Analysis* (December), pp.255–68.

Arkin, William. 1985. 'The Drift Towards First Strike', *Bulletin of the Atomic Scientists* (January) pp.5–6.

Arkin, William M., Thomas B Cochran. and Milton M. Hoeing. 1984. 'Resource Paper on the US Nuclear Arsenal', *Bulletin of the Atomic Scientists* (August–September), pp.3–15.

Art, Robert J. 1985. 'Congress and the Defense Budget: Enhancing Policy Oversight', in Art *et al* (eds), *Reorganizing America's Defense*, 404–27.

—— 1989 (1973). 'Bureaucratic Politics and American Foreign Policy: A Critique', in Ikenberry (ed.), *American Foreign Policy*, pp.433–59.

—— 1990. 'From Real Wars to Budget Wars: The Pentagon and Biennial Budgeting', in Blackwell and Blechman, *Making Defense Reform Work*, pp.25–69.

—— 1991. 'A Defensible Defense: America's Grand Strategy After the Cold War', *International Security*, 15/4, pp.5–53.

Ball, Desmond. 1982–3. 'U.S. Strategic Forces: How Would They Be Used?', *International Security*, 7/3, pp.31–60.

—— 1986a. 'Toward a Critique of Strategic Nuclear Targeting', in Ball and Richelson (eds), *Strategic Nuclear Targeting*, pp.15–32.

—— 1986b. 'The Development of the SIOP, 1960–83', in Ball and Richelson (eds), *Strategic Nuclear Targeting*, pp.57–83.

—— and Robert C. Toth. 1990. 'Revising the SIOP: Taking War-Fighting to Dangerous Extremes', *International Security*, 14/4, pp.65–92.

Bartels, Larry M. 1991. 'Constituency Opinion and Congressional Policy Making: The Reagan Defense Buildup', *American Political Science Review*, 85/2, pp.457–74.

Bendor, Jonathan and Thomas H. Hammond. 1992. 'Rethinking Allison's Models, *American Political Science Review*, 86/2, pp.301–22.

Brooks, Linton F. 1986. 'Naval Power and National Security: The Case for the Maritime Strategy', *International Security*, 11/2, pp.58–88.

Brown, Michael E. 1989. 'The US Manned Bomber and Strategic Deterrence in the 1990s', *International Security*, 14/2, pp.5–46.

—— 1990. 'The Case Against the B-2', *International Security*, 15/1, pp.129–153.

Brzoska, Michael and Peter Lock. 1992. 'Introduction' in Brzosha and Lock (eds), *Restructuring of Arms Production in Western Europe*, pp.3–16.

Carnesale, Albert and Charles Glaser. 1982. 'ICBM Vulnerability: The Cures Are Worse Than the Disease', *International Security*, 7/1, pp.70–85.

Chayes, Antonia Handler. 1987. 'Managing the Politics of Mobility', *International Security*, 12/2, pp.154–62.

Cimbala, Stephen J. 1988. 'Strategic Vulnerability: A Conceptual Reassessment', *Armed Forces and Society*, 14/2, pp. 191–213.

Clarke, Asa. 1984. 'Interservice Rivalry and Military Reform', in Clarke *et al* (eds), *The Defense Reform Debate*, pp.250–71.

Codevilla, Angelo. 1984. 'Understanding Ballistic Missile Defense', *Journal of Contemporary Strategic Studies* (Winter), pp.19–35.

Collender, Stanley E. 1992. 'The Budget Deficit', in Gillian Peele, Christopher J. Bailey and Bruce Cain (eds), *Developments in American Politics* (Basingstoke: Macmillan), pp.280–93.

Coniglio, Sergio. 1990. 'The ATF Contenders: A First Appraisal', *Military Technology*, 14/12, pp.14–21.

Cote, Owen. 1991. 'The Trident and the Triad: collecting the D-5 Dividend', *International Security*, 16/2, pp.117–45.

Cronin, Thomas E. 1975 [1970]. 'Everybody Believes in Democracy Until He Gets to the White House: An Examinations of White House-Departmental Relations', in Wildavsky (ed.), *Perspectives on the Presidency*.

Davis, Vincent. 1979. 'The President and the National Security Apparatus', in Sam C. Sarkesian (ed.), *Defense Policy and the Presidency: The Carter Years* (Boulder, CO: Westview), pp.53–110.

Deering, Christopher J. 1993. 'Decision Making in the Armed Services Committees', in Ripley and Lindsay (eds), *Congress Resurgent*, pp.155–82.

Dibb, Paul. 1989. 'Is Soviet Military Strategy Changing?', in Heisbourg (ed.), *The Changing Strategic Landscape*, pp.18–30.

Donnelly, Christopher N. 1983. 'Soviet Operational Concepts in the 1980s', in Report of the European Security Study, *Strengthening Coventional Deterrence in Europe: Proposals For the 1980s* (London: Macmillan Press).

Dougherty, Russell E. 1987. 'The Value of ICBM Modernization', *International Security*, 12/2, pp.161–72.

Duncan, Jeffrey S. 1985. 'The Tomahawk Nuclear Cruise Missile: Arguments For and Against', *Oceanus*, 28/2, pp.55–9.

Easterbrook, Gregg. 1982. 'Divad', *Atlantic Monthly* (October), pp.102–19.

Eden, Lynn. 1992. 'Learning and Forgetting: The Development of Organizational Knowledge about US Nuclear Weapons Effects', paper presented at the American Political Science Association (APSA) annual meeting (Chicago, September).

Farrell, Theo. 1993. 'Weapons Without A Cause: Buying Stealth Bombers the American Way', *Arms Control*, 14/2, pp.116–50.

—— 1995. 'Waste in Weapons Acquisition: How the Americans Do it All Wrong', *Contemporary Security Policy*, 16/2, pp.192–218.

Friedman, Norman. 1985. 'US Maritime Strategy', *International Defense Review* (July), pp.1071–5.

—— 1987. 'The Maritime Strategy and the Design of the Fleet', *Comparative Strategy*, 6/4, pp.415–35.

Gaddis, John Lewis. 1987. 'Expanding the Data Base: Historians, Political Scientists, and the Enrichment of Security Studies', *International Security*, 12/1, pp.3–21.

Garwin, Richard L. 1983. Will Strategic Submarines Be Vulnerable?, *International Security*, 8/2, pp.52-67.

George, Alexander L. 1979. 'Case Studies and Theory Development: The Method of Structured, Focused Comparison', in Paul Gordon Lauren (ed.) *Diplomacy: New Approaches in History, Theory and Policy* (NY: Free Press), pp.43–68.

Glaser, Charles. 1992. 'Nuclear Planning Without an Adversary: U.S. Planning for the Post-Soviet Era, *International Security*, 16/4, pp.34–78.

Gray, Colin S. and Jeffrey G. Barlow. 1985. 'Inexcusable Restraint: The Decline of American Military Power in the 1970s', *International Security*, 10/2, pp.27–69.

Hanne, William G. 1983. 'Airland Battle: Doctrine Not Dogma', *International Defense Review* (August), pp.1035–40.

Hartley, Thomas and Bruce Russet. 1992. 'Public Opinion and the Common Defense: Who Governs Military Spending in the United States', *American Political Science Review*, 86/4, pp.905–15.

Herring, Eric. 1991. 'The Decline of Nuclear Diplomacy', in Ken Booth (ed.), *New Thinking About Strategy and International Security* (London: Harper-Collins), pp.90–107.

—— 1992. 'Double Standards and the Myth of the Third World Nuclear Fanatic', paper presented at the APSA annual meeting (Chicago, September).

Herspring, Dale R. 1989a. 'The Soviet Military and Change', *Survival*, 31/4, pp.321–38.

—— 1989b. 'The Soviet High Command Looks ar Gorbachev', in Heisbourg (ed.), *The Changing Strategic Landscape*, pp.31–45.

Holloway, James L. 1985. 'The US Navy – A Functional Appraisal', *Oceanus* (July), pp.3–11.

Jacobs, T. L. 1985. 'Maneuver at Sea', *US Naval Institute Proceedings* (December), pp.60–4.

Jacobson, Gary C. 1993. 'Deficit-Cutting Politics and Congressional Elections', *Political Science Quarterly*, 108/3, pp.375–401.

Kaldor, Mary. 1986. 'The Weapons Succession Process', *World Politics*, 38/4, pp.577–95.

Kaufmann, William W. 1989. 'A Defense Agenda for Fiscal Years 1990–1994', in John Steinbruner (ed.), *Restructuring American Foreign Policy* (Washington, DC: Brookings Institution), pp.48–93.

Komer, Robert S. 1982. 'Maritime Strategy vs. Coalition Defense', *Foreign Affairs*, 60/5 pp.1124–44.

—— 1985a. 'Strategymaking in the Pentagon', in Art *et al.* (eds), *Reorganizing America's Defense*, pp.207–29.

—— 1985b. 'What "Decade of Neglect"?', *International Security*, 10/2, pp.70–83.

Korb, Lawrence J. 1992. 'Real Defense Cuts – And the Real Defense Issues', *Arms Control Today* (May), pp.5–9.

Kossiakoff, Alexander. 1980. 'Conception of New Defense Systems and the Role of Government R&D Centers', in Franklin Long and Judith Reppy (eds), *The Genesis of New Weapons* (NY: Pergamon Press), pp.61–85.

Krasner, Stephen D. 1989 (1971). 'Are Bureaucracies Important? (Or Allison Wonderland)', in Ikenberry (ed.), *American Foreign Policy*, pp.419–33.

Kurth, James R. 1989 (1971). 'A Widening Gyre: The Logic of American Weapons Procurement', in Ikenberry (ed.), *American Foreign Policy*, pp.14–37.

Lautenschlager, Karl. 1983. 'Technology and the Evolution of Naval Warfare', *International Security*, 8/2, pp.3–51.

Lebow, Richard N. 1984. 'Windows of Opportunity: Do States Jump Through Them', *International Security*, 9/1, pp.147–86.

LeLoup, Lance T. 1993. 'The Fiscal Straitjacket: Budgetary Constraints on Congressional Foreign and Defense Policy-Making' in Ripley and Lindsay (eds), *Congress Resurgent*, pp.37–66.

Lemann, Nicholas. 1984. 'The Peacetime War', *Atlantic* (October), pp.71–94.

Lepingwell, John W. K. 1989. 'Soviet Strategic Air-Defense and the Stealth Challenge', *International Security*, 14/1, pp.64–100.

Levitt, Barbara and James G. March. 1988. 'Organizational Learning', *Annual Review of Sociology*, 14, pp.319–40.

Lind, William S. 1988. 'The Maritime Strategy: Bad Strategy', *US Naval Institute Proceedings* (February), pp.54–61.

Lindenfelser, James. 1990. 'Establishing Military Requirements', in Blackwell and Blechman (eds), *Making Defense Reform Work*, pp.237–55.

Lindsay, James M. 1990. 'Congressional Oversight of the Department of Defense: Reconsidering the Conventional Wisdom', *Armed Forces and Society*, 17/1, pp.7–33.

Lynn, Laurence E. and Richard I. Smith. 1982. 'Can the Secretary of Defense Make a Difference?', *International Security*, 7/1, pp.45–69.

Mason, R. A. 1991. 'The Air War in the Gulf', *Survival*, 33/3, pp.211–29.

Mearsheimer, John J. 1986. 'A Strategic Misstep: The Maritime Strategy and Deterrence in Europe', *International Security*, 11/2, pp.3–57.

Meyer, Stephen M. 1988. 'The Sources and Prospects of Gorbachev's New Political Thinking on Security', *Internataionl Security*, 13/2, pp.124–63.

—— 1991/92. 'How the Threat (and the Coup) Collapsed: The Politicization of the Soviet Military', *International Security*, 16/3, pp.5–38.

Miller, Steven E. 1984. 'Politics over Promise: Domestic Impediments to Arms Control', *International Security*, 8/4, pp.67–90.

—— 1992. 'Western Diplomacy and the Soviet Nuclear Legacy', *Survival*, 34/3, pp.3–37.

Morrison, David C. 1991. 'Deep-Sixing the A-12', *Government Executive* (March), pp.30–3.

Nitze, Paul H. 1976. 'Assuring Strategic Stability in an Era of Detente', *Foreign Affairs*, 54/2, pp.207–32.

—— 1976–7. 'Deterring Our Deterrent', *Foreign Policy*, no.25, pp.195–210.

Nixon, Richard M. 1989 (1970). 'US Foreign Policy for the 1970s', reproduced in Bobbit, *et al.* (eds), *US Nuclear Strategy* p.477.

Odeen, Philip. 1985. 'A Critique of the PPBS System', in Art *et al.*, *Reorganizing America's Defense*, pp.207–29.

Parrott, Bruce. 1988. 'Soviet National Security Under Gorbachev', *Problems of Communism*, 37/6, pp.1–36.

Peterson, Pete E. and Mark Rom. 1988. 'Lower Taxes, More Spending, and Budget Deficits', in Charles O. Jones (ed.), *The Reagan Legacy* (Chatham, NJ: Chatham House). pp.213–40.

Polsby, Nelson W. 1994. Executive Branch Interests Differ From President's, Need His Protection', *Public Affairs Report*, 35/2 (Institute of Governmental Studies), pp.4–5.

Posen, Barry R. 1982. 'Inadvertent Nuclear War? Escalation and NATO's Northern Flank', *International Security*, 7/2, pp.28–54.

Postal, Theodore A. 1991–2. 'Lessons of the Gulf War Experience With Patriot', *International Security*, 16/3, pp.119–71.

—— 1992. 'Correspondance: Patriot Experience in the Gulf War', *International Security*, 17/1, pp.225–40.

Puritano, Vincent. 1985. 'Resource Allocation in the Pentagon', in Art *et al.*, *Reorganizing America's Defense*, pp.359–74.

Quandt, William B. 1986. 'The Electoral Cycle and the Conduct of Foreign Policy', *Political Science Quarterly*, 101/5, pp.825–37.

Reppy, Judith. 1992. 'Responses of the US Arms Industry', in Brzosha and Lock (eds), *Restructuring of Arms Production in Western Europe*, pp.59–68.

Rice, Condoleezza. 1989. 'Is Gorbachev Chaning the Rules of Defense Decision-Making', *Journal of International Affairs*, 42/2, pp.377–97.

Rice, Donald. 1990. 'The Manned Bomber and Strategic Deterrence', *International Security*, 15/1, pp.100–28.

Richelson, Jeffrey. 1986. 'The Dilemmas of Counterpower Targeting', in Ball and Richelson (eds), *Strategic Nuclear Targeting*, pp.159–70.

Rochlin, Gene I. and Chris C. Demchak. 1991. 'The Gulf War: Technological and Organizational Implications', *Survival*, 33/3, pp.260–73.

Rockman, Bert A. 1987. 'Mobilising Political Support for US National Security', *Armed Forces and Society*, 14/1, pp.17–41.

Romjue, John L. 1984. 'The Evolution of the AirLand Battle Concept', *Air University Review* (May–June), pp.5–15.

Rosen, Stephen Peter. 1988. 'New Ways of War: Understanding Military Innovation', *International Security*, 13/1, pp.134–68.

Rosenberg, David Alan. 1981/82. ' "A Smoking Radiating Ruin at the End of Two Hours": Documents on American Plans for Nuclear War with the Soviet Union, 1954–55', *International Security*, 6/2, pp.3–17.

—— 1983. 'The Origins of Overkill: Nuclear Weapons and American Strategy, 1945–60', *International Security*, 7/4, pp.3–71.

Russet, Bruce. 1990–1. 'Doves, Hawks and US Public Opinion', *Political Science Quarterly*, 105/4, pp.515–38.

Sagan, Scott D. 1994. 'The Perils of Proliferation: Organization Theory, Deterrence Theory, and the Spread of Nuclear Weapons', *International Security*, 18/4, pp.66–107.

Sestanovich, Stephen. 1988. 'Gorbachev's Foreign Policy: A Diplomacy of Decline', *Problems of Communism*, 37/1, pp.1–15.

Schilling, Warner R. 1981. 'US Strategic Nuclear Concepts in the 1970s', *International Security*, 6/1, pp.48–79.

Shuger, Scott. 1991. 'The Stealth Bomber Story You Haven't Heard, *Washington Monthly* (January), pp.14–21.

Sinnreich, Richard H. 1984. 'Strategic Implications of Doctrinal Change: A Case Analysis', in Keith Dunn and William Staudenmaier (eds), *Military Strategy in Transition* (Boulder, CO: Westview).

Slocombe, Walter. 1981. 'The Countervailing Strategy', *International Security*, 5/4, pp.18–27.

—— 1985. 'Why We Need Counterforce at Sea', *Arms Control Today* (September), pp.10–12.

—— 1990. 'Organization of the Office of the Secretary of Defense', in Blackwell and Blechman (eds), *Making Defense Reform Work*, pp.87–104.

Sloss, Leon and Marc Dean Millot. 1984. 'US Nuclear Strategy in Evolution', *Strategic Review* (Winter), pp.19–28.

Snyder, Jack. 1984–5. 'Richness, Rigor and Relevance in the Study of Soviet Foreign Policy', *International Security*, 9/3, pp.89–108.

—— 1988. 'Science and Sovietology: Bridging the Methods Gap in Soviet Foreign Policy Studies', *World Politics*, 40/2, pp.169–93.

Sperlich, Peter W. 1975 [1969]. 'Bargaining and Overload: An Essay on *Presidential Power*', in Wildavsky, *Perspectives on the Presidency.*

Spinardi, Graham. 1990. 'Why the U.S. Navy Went for Hard-Target Counterforce in Trident II (And Why It Didn't Get There Sooner)', *International Security*, 15/2, pp.147–90.

Stein, Robert M. 1992b. 'Correspondence: Patriot Experience in the Gulf War', *International Security*, 17/1, pp.199–224.

Stockton, Paul N. 1991. 'The New Game on the Hill: The Politics of Arms Control and Strategic Force Modernization', *International Security*, 16/2, pp.146–70.

—— 1993. 'Congress and Defense Policy-Making For the Post-Cold War Era', in Ripley and Lindsay (eds), *Congress Resurgent*, pp.235–60.

Sullivan, Terry. 1990. 'Bargaining With the President: A Simple Game and New Evidence', *American Political Science Review*, 84/4, pp.1167–93.

Toomay, John C. 1987. 'Strategic Forces Rationale – A Lost Discipline?', *International Security*, 12/2, pp.193–202.

Turner, Stansfield. 1982–3. 'Comment and Correspondance: Maritime Strategies', *Foreign Affairs*, 61/2, pp.456–7.

Turner, Stansfield and Thibault, George. 1982. 'Preparing for the Unexpected: The Need for a New Military Strategy', *Foreign Affairs*, 61/1, pp.122–35.

Warner, Edward L. 1989. 'New Thinking and Old Realities in Soviet Defense Policy', *Survival*, 31/1, pp.13–31.

Warwick, Graham. 1986. 'ATF: Balance Tips the Scales', *Flight International* (December), pp.28–30.

Wass de Czege, Huba. 1984. 'Army Doctrinal Reform', in Clark *et al.* (eds), *The Defense Reform Debate*, pp.101–20.

Welch, David A. 1992. 'The Organizational Process and Bureaucratic Politics Paradigm: Retrospect and Prospect', *International Security*, 17/2, pp.112–46.

Wells, Samuel F. 1983. 'A Question of Priorities: A Comparison of the Carter and Reagan Defense Programs', *Orbis* (Fall), pp.641–66.

Wettig, Gerhard. 1988. 'New Thinking on Security', *Problems Of Communism*, 37/2, pp.1–14.

White, Joseph. 1993. 'Decision Making in the Appropriations Subcommittees on Defense and Foreign Operations' in Ripley and Lindsay (eds), *Congress Resurgent*, pp.183–206.

Williams, John Allen. 1983. 'Defense Policy: The Carter–Reagan Record', *Washington Quarterly*, 6/4, pp.77–110.

Williams, Phil. 1987. 'The President and Foreign Policy', in Malcolm Shaw (ed.), *Roosevelt to Reagan* (London: C. Hurst and Co.).

Wilson, Pete. 1985. 'The President's Foundering Strategic Modernization Plan', *Strategic Review* (Summer), pp.9–13.

Wit, Joel S. 1982. 'American SLBM: Counterforce Options amd Strategic Implications', *Survival*, 24/2, pp.163–73.

Yankelovich, Daniel and Richard Smoke. 1988. 'America's New thinking', *Foreign Affairs*, 67/1, pp.1–17.

Yuseph, Alan R. 1990. 'The Acquisition Process', in Blackwell and Blechman (eds) *Making Defense Reform Work*, pp.215–35.

Zakheim, Dov S. and Jeffrey M. Ranney. 1993. 'Matching Defense Strategies to Resources: Challenges for the Clinton Administration', *International Security*, 18/1, pp.51–78.

Index

224